MW00340243

Have Bow, Will Travel

Also by E. Donnall Thomas, Jr.

HAVE BOW, WILL TRAVEL

Around the World Adventure with Longbow and Recurve

by E. Donnall Thomas, Jr.

Foreword by David Petersen

Raven's Eye Press
Durango, Colorado

Raven's Eye Press
Durango, Colorado
www.ravenseyepress.com

Copyright © 2010 E. Donnall Thomas, Jr.

All rights reserved. This book, or parts thereof, may not be re-
produced in any form without permission from the author.

Thomas, Jr., E. Donnall.
   Have Bow, Will Travel: Around the World Adventure with
Longbow and Recurve/E. Donnall Thomas, Jr.
   p. cm.

1. Hunting
2. Travel
3. Adventure
4. Wildlife
I. Title

ISBN 978-0-9816584-6-9

Cover & interior design by Lindsay J. Nyquist, elle jay design
All photography by Don & Lori Thomas

Printed in the United States of America
1 3 5 7 9 10 8 6 4 2

Contents

Dedication

In memory of Bill Baker, Larry Schweitzer,

and the Bentler family.

While life goes on for the friends they left behind,

it will never be the same without them.

Acknowledgements

WHILE ALL MATERIAL has been completely re-worked for inclusion in this book, parts of many chapters have previously appeared in print as follows:

- *Traditional Bowhunter Magazine*—Chapters 1, 2, 3, 4, 6, 8, 11, 15, 16, 19, 22, 23, 24, 25, 26, 27, 28, 31, 32, 34.
- *Bowhunter Magazine*—3, 14, 17, 20, 23, 29.
- *Gray's Sporting Journal*—7, 10, 18, 30, 33.
- *Outdoor Life*—9.
- *Successful Hunting*—10.
- *Alaska Magazine*—13.

Parts of Chapter 2 also appeared in the anthology *The Giant Book of Hunting Stories*, and parts of Chapter 5 in *Redfish, Bluefish, Ladyfish, Snook*, both published by Skyhorse Press.

In all cases, the author appreciates the opportunity to re-work the material for inclusion in this volume.

[x]

The Genuine Article

THE AUTHOR OF THIS DELIGHTFUL BOOK, E. Donnall Thomas, Jr., M.D., is unique in the world of outdoor journalism, several times over.

To begin, very few writers—in any literary genre, much less the sub-genre of hook-and-bullet writing—share the sparkling clear style and natural storytelling ability embodied by Don Thomas.

Even fewer have the ongoing, constantly refreshed base in boots-on-the-ground hunting and angling experience that Thomas writes from. Unlike the majority of professional outdoor scriveners, Don needn't attempt to creatively recycle a limited number of hunts and fishing adventures by constantly respinning the same old yarns within a fresh basket of fluff, since he is *out there doing it*, hunting and fishing and adventuring and experiencing and learning, almost constantly.

And who else among professional outdoor scriveners but Don Thomas has enjoyed such strong and tenacous success, as both sportsman and sporting writer, across such a wide spectrum of outdoor activities including traditional bowhunting, upland bird hunting, waterfowling, and saltwater fly fishing?

But most impressive of all to me, as one who has written professionally for more than 30 years, is Thomas's literary productivity.

Moreover, there's never a hint of quality being sacrificed to quantity.

In short, the author of this book you now hold is the increasingly rare *genuine article* among outdoor writers. When he's not outside doing it, he's at his Montana home writing about it.

And reading about it, as Don Thomas is a voracious researcher and student, always eager to learn new information—natural history and historical biography are among his favorite intellectual curiosities—to further enrich his outdoor stories.

I am openly in awe, if not downright jealous, of each and all these Thomas qualities, and more.

Even so, when our mutual publisher at Raven's Eye Press suggested that I'd be "a good one" to write a foreword to *Have Bow, Will Travel*, I initially blinked and shied away, thinking just the opposite. After all, while I've spread out a bit in recent years, I am decidedly *not* a globe-trotting sportsmen. So initially, I declined, noting that I'd have gladly written a foreword for Don's prior book, *How Sportsmen Saved the World*. "Conservation. Now *there's* a topic I know something about," I told the publisher.

"Just read a few chapters I'll send you," the publisher (Ken Wright, himself an active outdoorsman) encouraged. "If you still don't feel a personal connection, we'll drop it."

So I did read. And almost immediately I did feel a personal connection. And so here I am, and happy for the opportunity. The meat of the matter, as the author implies but doesn't detail in his introduction, is that this collection of far-flung traditional bowhunting adventures is different, deeper and more subtle in underlying message, with a common thread of humility and wisdom connecting all. In short, *Have Bow, Will Travel* takes hunting, and us, to another level.

Beyond those generous hints I'll leave it up to readers to find the trail for themselves—faint but hardly hidden—and follow it to wherever it may lead them.

—David Petersen
San Juan Mountains, Colorado

Preface

AS A LIFELONG OUTDOORSMAN, I have grown progressively more concerned about the state of modern big game hunting and the writing—not to mention television and other media—that describes it. As a model of the first person hunting story, I have always looked to the work of Col. James Corbett. Although he wrote about hunting man-eating tigers and leopards in India, Corbett always kept his own courage and accomplishments in the background while he gave center stage to the wildness of the jungle where he hunted, the bravery of the native people in the Indian highlands, and above all the great cats themselves.

Nowadays, however, such considerations all too often seem forgotten as the writer or videographer rushes to promote products, sponsors, and himself. Even the conduct of the hunt seems to have grown irrelevant in the quest for the more and bigger "trophies" that have become the de facto measure of success in the field. These developments leave me saddened and offended on so many levels that I can't do the subject justice in this short space.

However, these concerns do explain the choice of material that follows. I have enjoyed my share of success with the bow, and the reader will indeed encounter some dead animals on the way to this collection's finish. But many chapters contain no killing at all. As I look back over my decades in the field, many of these episodes remain personal favorites for a variety of reasons: the challenging nature of the hunt, the wildness of the terrain, the fascinating people I met along the way. These factors explain their inclusion in this volume, which was never intended to be a record of personal accomplishment. Readers enamored of the conventional modern video style ("16 Actual Bow-Kills!!") should seek gratification elsewhere.

—Don Thomas
Lewistown, MT

Section I

AFRICA

AFRICA

CONSIDERING the relatively small number of outdoorsmen who have braved the distances, time, and expense required to travel there, Africa has generated a remarkable body of hunting literature. Some of it--Roark, White, and Hemingway at his occasional best come to mind--deserves to be called classic. Other books--Roosevelt's *African Game Trails*, say--offer a worthy and intriguing historical view of wild country gone forever. A few contemporary works—Tom McIntyre's *Dreaming the Lion*, Robert Jones's *African Twilight*--get it right, but most, unfortunately, succumb to a swaggering tone that leaves me thankful I've never had to share a camp with the author. Little has been written from the bowhunter's perspective (exceptions: Hill, Swinehart and Bill Negley's remarkable *Archer in Africa*). Most has been written by outsiders rather than locals, which ought to teach us a lesson. There is something about Africa and its wildlife that practically compels its visitors to share their experiences with others.

There is also something about Africa that practically compels its visitors to go back, and I stand guilty on both counts. Ever since my first visit to Zimbabwe I've returned at every opportunity, so often I really can't tell how many times without deliberate calculation. (I suppose I could just measure the hole in my bank account and come up with a rough idea.) And I couldn't resist writing about it either (*The Double Helix*, plus scores of magazine articles). But Africa represents such a quintessential destination for the traveling bowhunter that I couldn't resist beginning this volume with a little bit more.

From our distant, naïve perspective, there's a tendency to view the

African bowhunting experience as homogenous, with not much difference among destinations there except for price and a few entries on the list of available game species. Nothing could be farther from the truth. Africa is a huge continent, offering a wide variety of terrain, climate, flora, and fauna. Some venues are relatively tame while others represent adventure travel in every sense of the term. Granted, most visitors will begin and end with the former, but others will respond to the urge to venture across new boundaries and explore even when that means working harder for opportunities to shoot. Since adventure has always mattered more to me than tally, we'll share a few of those experiences in the chapters that follow.

I've enjoyed my share of conventionally defined success over the course of trips to multiple African locations, and many of those hunts were both challenging and memorable. However, I've chosen to ignore most of the killing in the chapters that follow, perhaps in subconscious rebellion against the safari genre I protested against earlier. But there's more to it than that. Hunting from blinds, as most visiting bowhunters do nowadays, turns out to be a bit too easy. Granted, I've done it and enjoyed the experience at the time. But back in the early days, nobody knew anything, to cite the old Hollywood dictum, and we were directly involved in every stage of the hunt, learning about Africa and its wildlife right along with our hosts, as they learned about bowhunting. Nowadays, that's all more or less a matter of routine, and as bowhunting from blinds has grown easier, I've found it progressively less interesting.

That's why I've hunted by stalking on my last four trips to Africa, save for visits to a blind armed with nothing but a camera. Stalking African plains game with a bow may be the most challenging form of hunting on earth, and it certainly involves far more hunting than killing. But that's what I've chosen to write about here for the most part, since people, places, and wildlife should always matter just as much to the traveling hunter as the horns on the wall when the hunting is done. And in the case of Africa, there is no limit to what deserves to be seen, heard, and experienced.

CHAPTER ONE

The Company of Friends Namibia

SOFT SHADOWS had finally started to reappear upon the hot, red sand after an assault by the midday African sun. Comfortably attuned to the rhythms of the veldt, I closed my eyes and listened to turtledoves calling softly from the acacias and the distant yap of a jackal. Then another sound rose above the birds' chorus and the sigh of the breeze, a faint evenly-cadenced tapping that might have come from castanets at the beginning of a flamenco number in a smoky cabaret. Finally: the eland.

The mystery of the clicking noise Africa's largest antelope make as they walk has a counterpart closer to home. Back when I lived in Alaska, I listened to numerous arguments about the source of the sound caribou produce when they trot across the tundra. While some Alaskans ascribed this characteristic click to the caribous' hoofs, most felt it came from the tendons in their feet. While I didn't have any definitive answers at the time, as a physician I suspected that any tendon making that much noise would likely rupture in short order. Then, on my last hunt in northern Namibia with Allan Cilliers two years earlier, I made an observation that settled the issue once and for all. While photographing eland from a pit blind, I watched an old bull approach straight toward me with his feet at my eye level. As his front hooves sank into the soft sand, they spread apart, and when he lifted them the lobes snapped back together, producing a sharp click. Given the structure of a caribou's hoof, I'm convinced the mechanism that produces this sound is the same for both species. Who says observations made in exotic locales are meaningless to North American hunters?

On that trip, I hadn't really been interested in tackling an eland with my bow. Because of their size – a big bull will outweigh a moose – eland always impressed me as an animal best worked up to slowly. But this time around, an eland was really the only plains game animal I'd come to Africa to hunt, and after several day of glassing bulls and marveling at their odd combination of size and grace, I felt ready to draw down and release an arrow.

With the fingers of my right hand tight against the bowstring, I settled back and tried to determine the direction of the animals' measured approach with my ears. As I waited, I considered all the strange events that had preceded the climax of my ninth African bowhunt.

After spending two weeks exploring potential bowhunting opportunities in Zambia, Lori, our old friend Dick LeBlond, and I flew to Windhoek, rented a vehicle, and set off to explore Namibia's remote Skeleton Coast on our own. After several more days of adventure that included everything from surviving a burglary to fly-fishing for sharks, we finally drove north to Grootfontein for the last leg of the trip, a rendezvous with Allan and the group of friends from home who would form our bowhunting family for the rest of the month: John and Lisa Roseland and Ed Evans from our home town in Montana and Mike Bentler and his wife Sandy from Iowa. Like an ethnically diverse platoon in a vintage war movie, our group arrived with widely differing backgrounds and interests. Although Dick had lived in Africa for a year while teaching medicine in Uganda, he'd never enjoyed an opportunity to hunt there. An intensely analytical individual, I knew he'd eventually arrive at a specific focus for his efforts with the bow. As a first timer in Africa, Mike looked ready for anything. Ed had hunted Zimbabwe with me before, but had never seen desert antelope like springbok, hartebeest, and gemsbok, and he planned to concentrate on these species.

In many ways, introducing Rosey and Lisa to Africa represented the personal high point of the trip. The previous year, Ed, mutual friend Larry Schweitzer and I talked about how much fun it would be to see the two of them enjoy an opportunity to hunt Africa and simply decided to make it happen. But after we went to work on the arrangements, Larry experienced a sudden bout of chest pain while cougar hunting. To make a tragic story short, he didn't survive the emergency bypass surgery. But Mike generously stepped in to help keep the idea alive, and when we finally met at Allan's camp, we all sensed that matters had turned out exactly as Larry would have wished.

And to think that all I really wanted out of the trip for myself was an eland…

Gemsbok represented a high priority for everyone other than Lori and me, and no wonder. Majestic, strikingly marked animals, they practically define the habitat along the Namibian edge of the Kalahari. I'd had plenty of experience with gemsbok, enough to appreciate their toughness and the deceptively forward position of their vitals, lessons I took pains to share with everyone else before they ventured into the field. My recommendation was simple: gemsbok should only be taken quartering away, to allow the broadhead to slide forward behind the massive forequarter and into both lungs. Three days into the hunt, everyone who wanted a gemsbok had one, but surprisingly long recoveries had made believers of several highly experienced American bowhunters who finally realized that African game really is different.

All of which I kept in mind as I listened to the eland herd's steady approach. I'd geared up to a set of #85 limbs just prior to our departure to be prepared for the possibility of buffalo in Zambia, an opportunity that never arose. I considered using my heavy set up on eland because of their size, but I knew I wasn't as accurate as I was with my #72 pound limbs, and decided to stick with my lighter tackle on the theory that accuracy trumps foot-pounds of energy under all but the most exceptional circumstances. After extensive discussion with Allan, I felt that a well-placed arrow from this bow would achieve penetration sufficient to kill an eland bull.

But the eland's bulk did influence my thinking about shot placement. Like gemsbok, eland carry their vitals fairly far forward, inviting a quartering away shot. But on any animal, the steeper the angle of penetration, the more "dead" hide and bone the arrow will have to traverse to reach pay dirt. Furthermore, the more acute the angle between broadhead and rib, the greater the chance of deflection, especially from a rib the size of an eland's. After considering all these factors, I decided to wait for a shot that was perfectly broadside, and to use the accuracy my lighter limbs afforded to tuck the arrow immediately behind the shoulder.

Suddenly, the time arrived to translate all my reasoning into action. As the clicking in the brush reached a crescendo, the first tawny form slid into view. Eland cows sport horns that are often longer than bulls', although not as massive. Selecting a good animal requires some study, especially in the presence of a large herd. As the little clearing began to fill with eland, I identified two bulls among the several dozen cows and calves. Neither looked exceptional, but both were representative of the species. After weeks of fly rods and cameras, I felt ready to release an arrow and began to concentrate on anatomy rather than headgear.

The first bull passed my position well within range but without offering a suitable shot angle. The second arrived shielded by two cows, and for a moment I thought I'd have to let him pass as well. But suddenly the sea of tan parted, and as the bull paused broadside I picked a hair fractionally behind the shoulder crease and midway up the chest, and watched with immense satisfaction as my reliable old recurve buried the arrow to the nock at precisely that spot.

The explosion of animals and a sudden cloud of dust made it difficult to sight-track the bull at first, but I finally identified him lurching along behind the rest of the herd as they disappeared into the scrub.

Although I couldn't have been happier with the arrow's placement or penetration, I settled back to give the track the time even a solid hit deserves. When Allan arrived an hour before dark, I assured him the animal should be lying dead a hundred yards back in the brush.

But, as I'd been busy reminding everyone all week, African game really is different. By the time we'd sorted the bull's track out of the mess of spoor the herd had left behind and followed it for a quarter mile through the thorns, I knew I had a problem. And when we spotted the bull standing in a patch of scrub half an hour later, my spirits began to sink. I truly felt I'd made a perfect shot, and I expect perfect shots to produce perfect results. I couldn't tell which bothered me more, the possibility of losing the animal or my utter bewilderment over the fact that he was still alive.

In Africa, the constant presence of jackals and other scavengers makes it risky to leave any wounded animal out overnight, and in the course of my experience there I'd seen whole kudu reduced to skeletons in a matter of hours. But I sensed that pushing the animal in failing light would be a mistake and we backed off, leaving me to face one of the longest sleepless nights in memory.

Fortunately, this frustrating story had a happy ending. The following morning, after some determined effort by Nisi, one of Allan's amazing Bushman trackers, and Mickey, the camp Jack Russell terrier, we caught up with the wounded bull once again. I eventually slipped in and sent a second arrow just behind the last rib with the animal quartering sharply away. My concerns about penetration at this angle proved groundless. The arrow disappeared completely from sight and the bull tottered and fell without taking another step. An autopsy revealed that my first arrow had penetrated the chest cavity completely, but despite an entry wound right in the shoulder crease, the broadhead had passed a fraction of an inch behind and beneath the near lung.

And suddenly I felt myself listening to the echo of the advice I'd dispensed so freely earlier in the week. *African animals are different...*

By the end of the week, all members of our party had made

exemplary progress in the pursuit of their own goals. Ed had his gemsbok and Lori her springbok, the animals each of them had come to Namibia to pursue. Mike and Rosey had taken a cross section of plains game to make any first time African hunter proud: gemsbok, kudu, springbok, zebra, duiker, and wart hog. As anticipated, Dick had found a project to pursue. After spotting an exceptional kudu mid-week, he had hunted that bull exclusively, and when he killed it we all joined in reminding him that the successful pursuit of one special animal may be the most satisfying accomplishment in bowhunting.

But despite the satisfaction of my bull's spiral horns and the delicious quality of the eland steaks on the table, I just couldn't get that prolonged recovery out of my mind. Technically, it was fairly easy to define the problem. Like gemsbok, eland lungs sit high and forward. Had my arrow passed an inch differently in either direction the bull would have been down at once. A quartering away angle would have solved the problem easily, but my concerns about penetration biased me against that shot, unnecessarily as matters turned out. At least I'll know how to do it right next time.

The fine points of shot placement on an animal many hunters will never even see may not seem a matter of general interest, but I think this story illustrates points applicable to us all. First, any time you tackle a new quarry, you should learn everything you can about it, whether it's a turkey or a moose. The best way to accomplish this goal is to listen to bowhunters who have had experience with the species. In this regard, I accept my share of responsibility for events. Allan told me that he thought a slight quartering away shot would be optimal, but I let other concerns overrule his recommendation.

And this illustrates a point that bears directly on everything bowhunters do in the field. I was guilty of what analysts call a system failure, an improper processing of data that led to an erroneous conclusion. Successful bowhunting requires the integration of many complex skills, most of which are best acquired through experience. The downside of this process is that we sometimes depend on our experience too readily, a logical flaw that paradoxically tends to have the

[10]

greatest impact on those who have done the most hunting. I *knew* the shot I made would have put any game animal in North America down for the count immediately, and because I'd experienced that result so many times I essentially refused to believe it wouldn't happen again under different circumstances. The result was a cautionary lesson that applies to all bowhunters whether they're after whitetails or elephants.

On our last night in camp, we all agreed we'd just participated in one of our most enjoyable hunts ever, because of the quality of the company even more than conventional measures of bowhunting success. Then we paused for a moment to remember Larry, who had contributed so much to making the trip possible in the first place even though he was no longer there to share the good times. We sprinkled a box of his ashes over the campfire, and as the smoke drifted off toward the great wilderness of Bushmanland to the east, Rosey launched a ceremonial last arrow into the star-studded night sky. Finally, we wandered off to our tents, secure in the knowledge that while hunters may come and go, the hunt will always continue.

Little did we know that within a few short seasons not one but two of us seated around the campfire that night would be gone as well.

The late Mike Bentler with a fine gemsbok.

Lori with the Bushman trackers who helped her become the first woman to kill a big game animal with a bow in Namibia.

CHAPTER TWO

Among the San
Namibia

AS A CULTURE, we have forgotten the art of sitting still. Bowhunting and wildlife photography have given me lots of practice and I do it better than most, but I still have my limitations. As I watched Ghao settle into the dirt at the base of the shepherd's tree, I realized I was watching a master in action. He didn't fidget. His eyes didn't drift shut. He simply sat, elegant and motionless, waiting for the next phase of the stalk to begin as if he had all the time in the world, which I suppose he did.

We had kept pace with the wildebeest for over two hours while the sun burned the last of the overnight winter chill from the sand beneath our feet. The herd was grazing slowly into the wind, and the big bull we were after refused to detach himself from his company long enough to let us try to slip in for a shot. Left to his own devices, I'm sure Ghao would have headed off into the bush to look for a more promising track, but I wanted a wildebeest. So there we sat.

As the dark, strange-looking animals frisked about the dry pan, the sounds of the veldt filled my ears: the buzz of insects, the three-note dirge of the doves roosted in the acacias, a springbok ram's distant snort. Yielding to the spell of the place, I soon found myself watching and listening with an infinite supply of patience. As we waited

[13]

for the animals to make their next move, I found myself reflecting idly upon our remarkable circumstances: a visiting American bowhunter and a representative of the world's oldest surviving hunting culture, improbably joined against the long odds and difficult geometry of capricious winds and wary eyes. And I realized that during all my travels around the world, I'd never run into anyone quite as intriguing as Ghao and his fellow Bushmen.

An ethnically and linguistically unique people, the Bushmen-- or San--were southern Africa's original inhabitants, ranging in nomadic fashion from modern Zimbabwe and Zambia all the way to the Cape. No one knows just how long the San have been around, but their abundant rock paintings date back at least 5000 years. Early in the last millenium, the area experienced an influx of pastoral, Bantu-speaking tribes from the north. Agriculturalists and cattle-tenders, the new arrivals' social structure conflicted sharply with the Bushmen's hunter-gatherer lifestyle. Furthermore, the northern tribesmen introduced a new concept to the region, one that the San had fortuitously managed to avoid: organized warfare.

The results were inevitable. Relentlessly displaced from their original homelands, the San slowly retreated to the inhospitable Kalahari, where their finely honed survival skills and an incredibly harsh environment provided them with a natural means of insulation from their enemies. While the arrival of European colonists four centuries ago certainly increased their isolation, the San had given up much of their original territory long before Europeans arrived on the scene to add to their woes. And the San endured only by the most demanding means imaginable: by learning to thrive in harsh terrain in which no other humans could survive.

Short, finely featured, and almond-colored in complexion, the San appear physically distinct from other indigenous African peoples. Punctuated by baffling clicks, their unique speech has intrigued linguists for years. Their democratic social customs also distinguish them from other inhabitants of the region. In San culture, for example, women enjoy full participation in the decision-making process, a rarity

[14]

in Africa. But as a bowhunter, I have to admit that these unique physical and cultural traits pale before my appreciation of their hunting and tracking abilities. Simply stated, they are the best, and every time I've hunted with them I've come away from the experience awed by their apparently superhuman abilities.

Reserved without being diffident, the Bushmen are quick to laugh and provide unfailingly good company in the field. The only flash of animosity I ever saw from them came one morning when we stumbled across a horned adder while trailing a gemsbok. The Bushmen quickly armed themselves with sticks and beat the nasty looking little snake to a pulp. My old friend Allan Cilliers translated the flurry of discussion that followed for our benefit: *We might walk this path again tomorrow.*

Please note that one does not simply arrive in Africa and go hunting with the Bushmen. Today, most Bushmen live in Botswana and Namibia. Many have lost contact with their traditions through inevitable cultural assimilation. Those who have not often live in geographic isolation compounded by formidable language barriers. My own opportunities to hunt with the San have come through Allan, an accomplished and widely renowned Namibian PH who enjoys a unique relationship with the Bushmen based on years of experience with their culture. Despite his own accomplishments and abilities, Allan clearly holds the Bushmen in the highest esteem, and it's equally obvious that the sense of respect extends both ways. In Allan's camp, the Bushmen are more hunting partners than employees. Even the simplest walk through the bush with Allan quickly turns into a fascinating lecture on the local flora and fauna and how the Bushmen utilize them in their daily life. Furthermore, Allan's huge, game-rich hunting concession borders immediately on Bushmanland, a huge trackless area where the San still enjoy their traditional way of life in as unspoiled a manner as possible.

While architects and engineers have debated the relationship between form and function for years, the design of Bushman archery tackle begins on an even more basic level: they have to make do with the raw materials at hand.

[15]

Bushman bows are simple affairs. Whittled from a variety of woods, especially the brandybush (*Grewia flava*), they are usually only 30 – 35 inches long and draw no more than 20 pounds. Oil derived from the sour plum (*Ximenia caffra*) keeps the wood from cracking in the dry desert heat. Strings come from a variety of material including hide and sinew, but most are made from plant fiber harvested from a tough succulent known as mother-in-law's tongue (*Sanseviera aethiopia*), which the Bushmen roll into cord upon their thighs. The Kalahari San fashion lovely cylindrical quivers from the root bark of the umbrella thorn (*Acacia luerdertzii*). Farther to the south, bark from the aptly named *kokerboom* (quiver tree) serves the same purpose.

As often seems the case in indigenous hunting societies, bow design ultimately reflects the availability of suitable arrow materials, and the traditional Bushman hunting arrow clearly represents the most sophisticated and imaginative element of their hunting tackle. Shafts are made from sections of a variety of stiff grasses similar to our own river cane. These grasses are not widely distributed, and on our last trip into hunting camp Allan thoughtfully stopped by the side of the road as we passed a known thicket of the stuff and harvested a supply for his hunters.

Between joints, the cane is quite straight and true, but single segments are too short to make an effective arrow. The Bushmen solve this problem by whittling a male-male ferrule from giraffe bone with which they link two segments of cane together, resulting in an arrow approximately 20 inches long. Shafts are unfletched and completed with a simple self-nock. Tips traditionally came from carved bone, but nowadays most are made from scavenged steel (wrecked cars are a favorite source) laboriously filed into delicate triangular heads. Steel points represent one of only three ready concessions to modern society I observed on the part of the San, the other two being the surplus Namibian military jackets the Bushmen wear against the cool Kalahari winters and, inevitably I suppose, tobacco.

By itself, this simple, lightweight equipment obviously lacks the punch needed to bring down gemsbok and other large antelope.

Bushmen hunters overcome these limitations by poisoning the tips of their arrows. Under certain conditions, they use a variety of plant-derived toxins for this purpose, but most arrows are embellished with a potent poison derived from several species of flea beetle grubs, especially *Diamphidia simplex*. Bushmen carefully harvest the larvae from known locations at certain times of year and store them. Eight or ten grubs are needed to treat one arrow. Based on descriptions of the poison's effects, I surmise that it affects the autonomic nervous system, leading to loss of coordination, stupor, and eventual collapse as it absorbs into the blood stream. The poison takes from hours to days to work depending on the nature of the hit and the size of the animal and does not affect the edibility of the meat.

All this makes Bushman arrow design appear especially ingenious. Hunters only apply the toxin to the distal segment of the shaft, not the tip itself, so the arrows remain relatively safe to handle. Furthermore, embedded arrows usually fracture at the ferrule, leaving the toxic segment in the quarry. Arrow making remains a highly esteemed art in Bushman culture. Hunters frequently pass arrows back and forth as tokens of gratitude and respect, and in the elaborate formula Bushmen use to divide meat among the band after a kill the maker of the lethal arrow receives first share no matter who actually fired the killing shot. (Attention American arrowsmiths: does that sound like a good deal or what?)

Hunting with Ghao, I was surprised to note that when we came to open areas I often spotted game at a distance before he did even when I wasn't using my binoculars. At first I thought he might have something wrong with his eyes, but I quickly realized that when he needed to he could spot game far away in the brush quite well. I finally realized that he just didn't care about spotting animals hundreds of yards away. Seeing game told him nothing he didn't already know based on the sign underfoot.

The Bushmen seemed fairly indifferent to terrain features when planning stalks and were often quite willing to advance upon sharp-eyed animals in plain sight. They get away with this because of their spooky ability to anticipate the quarry's head movements. Ghao always seemed to know just when to freeze and when to start moving again. They only stalk early in the morning and late in the afternoon, when long shadows cover the ground, and they stick to the shadows meticulously as they move. They regard stalking at midday and during low light as a complete waste of time.

In traditional Bushman culture, hunting is very much a group effort, largely because of the need to have lots of help at hand upon the successful conclusion of a hunt, to avoid meat loss to spoilage or scavengers. When I hunted with two or more of Allan's trackers, I noticed that they conversed in animated fashion on the trail, especially when the track demonstrated some unique or confusing feature. In this regard, their unique language seemed especially adaptive as their flurries of clicks usually disappeared on the desert breeze with little trace of the human voice. Allan confirms that he has often observed the Bushmen holding one of these discussions within earshot of wary game without spooking the animal.

The Bushmen use two gaits to close within bow range. The first is a stooped-over duck walk they can sustain at brisk speed almost indefinitely. The second they call the "leopard crawl": down on all fours, with long feline strides that result in almost no change in profile from the quarry's perspective. Watch the family cat stalk a robin on the lawn for an appreciation of what this method entails. Of course, the short, light Bushman bows prove ideally suited to this kind of stealthy maneuvering, and I found it difficult to keep up while leopard crawling with my recurve.

Once within bow range, the Bushmen shoot with a quick, plucking style: a short draw, free-floating anchor and thumb release. Shot placement as we know it matters very little to them. The idea is simply to get the tip of an arrow (or two) into the animal anywhere and let the poison go to work. Several times when we stalked together, Ghao obviously expected me to take a shot at what I considered an unacceptable angle and rolled his eyes in frustration when I declined (frustration, I admit, that quickly turned to boyish laughter as we set

[18]

out in search of the next set of tracks). I tried my best to explain my reservations in pantomime, but I'm not sure I ever made much of an impression.

As finely adapted as their equipment and hunting methods may be, the Bushmen truly distinguish themselves tracking game, wounded or otherwise. Over the course of multiple trips to Africa, I've hunted with a number of trackers whose skill level ranged from no better than my own to very good indeed. But none could begin to approach the remarkable level of ability I observed when hunting with Ghao, Tsisaba, and the rest of Allan's incredible crew.

The soil in Allan's hunting area consists mostly of soft, sugary sand. Granted, that kind of footing can hold lots of tracks, but individual hoof prints rapidly lose their definition. Furthermore, game densities are so high that every square foot of ground contains tracks left by multiple animals. Nonetheless, the Bushmen could easily follow the trail of an individual animal through this riot of sign at a dead run. They could also tell exactly how far away the animal was, it's condition, the precise nature of any wounds, and what it was likely to do next... even when tracking at night by moonlight supplemented occasionally by matches at particularly confusing points along the trail.

One day during our last visit with Allan, Lori shot a kudu bull. The shot placement sounded perfect, but she was shooting from a pit blind and Lori doesn't stand that far off the ground in the first place. The steep upward track of the arrow resulted in a one lung hit... and an opportunity for the Bushmen to do what they do best.

As we listened to Lori's description of the shot, one of the younger trackers started immediately for the edge of the brush where Lori had last sight-tracked the bull. Ghao called him back sharply and delivered what sounded like a stern lecture. As Allan explained, Ghao was chiding him for ignoring the first part of the track even though we all knew where it led. Ghao explained that it was always important to take the track from the very beginning, to learn as much about the animal as possible. In fact, by the time we reached the acacias Ghao knew the age and size of the kudu, exactly what Lori's arrow had done, and what the likely outcome of the pursuit would be… estimates that all proved remarkably accurate by the time we successfully recovered the bull.

I'll spare readers most of the long, hot miles through the thorns. The only tracking hitch came in a flurry of sand some two miles into the chase. As the trackers sat down to smoke and consider the situation, Allan explained Ghao's interpretation of events. Lori's bull had run into the middle of a large herd of kudu and the sight of the arrow's bright fletchings protruding from its chest had scattered the animals in all directions. Half an hour later, Ghao had sorted out the mess and we were back on track again.

After five hours and an estimated eight miles, Ghao stopped trotting and began to creep forward like a cat, fully aware that we were about to make contact with the wounded kudu. Several hundred yards farther ahead, he suddenly pointed to a dense patch of thorns from which two spiral horns protruded, and it was time for a strategy discussion. Allan's rifle offered an effective if unattractive option. Ghao explained that based on the spoor he felt the kudu was distracted and that Lori should be able to slip in for a killing shot, and after some last minute discussion I watched her leopard crawl into the brush.

After one of the longest hours of my life, Ghao suddenly leapt to his feet in excitement. Moments later, the bull charged past trailing another one of Lori's brightly fletched arrows from its previously healthy side. When the kudu piled up a hundred yards away, Lori enjoyed the distinction of becoming the first modern woman archer to kill a big game animal in Namibia… with a little help from her friends.

Back in the dry riverbed, the wildebeest have finally started to stir. Rising slowly from his lair at the base of the shade tree, Ghao tests the wind. Using hand signals and crude diagrams scrawled in the dirt, we offer one another thoughts on our next approach, each shaking off a suggestion or two from the other like pitchers who want to throw curves when their catchers are calling for fastballs. Finally we reach a tentative agreement of sorts and begin to ooze forward through the brush.

And suddenly I realize just what a remarkable life experience bowhunting can be. Here we stand, two men of approximately the same age separated by nearly impossible gulfs in culture, language, and background, setting off together on one of the most seminal and difficult tasks our species can face. But a simple realization tempers my high spirits: I will never be able to emulate Ghao's remarkable talents here on the veldt. While he was learning how to stalk and track, I was studying biochemistry and English literature, noble efforts in their own right that suddenly feel strangely devoid of meaning.

A century ago, our culture tried to destroy Ghao's with rifles, roads, and fences. Today, we threaten the same end through the process of assimilation: radios, money, Coca-Cola, and all the empty promises of easy living. How will the story of the San conclude? Perhaps it's foolish to be optimistic. But in the meanwhile, I'll do my best to keep to the shadows and start every track from the beginning, just as I'll remain grateful for the opportunity to appreciate the potential skills that lie dormant inside us all.

Postscript: Some ten years after Ghao and I spent our morning with the wildebeest, Lori and I were enjoying a glass of wine before dinner at a ranch house in the middle of South Africa's Karoo. The property had been in our host's family for generations. I'd been telling stories about my experiences with the Bushmen in Namibia when he carefully handed me a piece of paper with a remorseful look on his face and said, "Don, this is something you MUST see."

The document was a hunting license from the pre-Boer War era, and it contained a list of the game to which it entitled the bearer. *One eland*, the list began. *Two kudu, two gemsbok…* And there at the very end was the line that nearly brought me to my knees: *one Bushman.*

The gods must be crazy indeed.

The caracal team.

CHAPTER THREE

Blue Bulls & Brown Kitties
South Africa

LUSH, GREEN FOLIAGE – rare in southern Africa during the dry safari season – covered the draws and ridges sweeping downhill toward the Kariega River. Off in the distance, the blue waters of the Indian Ocean gleamed beneath the rising sun. We were exploring new territory in South Africa's Eastern Cape, and on our first morning in camp I couldn't remember seeing a more spectacular vista during any of my dozen previous trips to the Dark Continent.

But scenery wasn't the only thing on my mind. Professional hunter Adrian Purdon and I had already spotted a blue wildebeest in an excellent position for a stalk. In contrast to the scrawny acacias that dominate the landscape in much of Southern Africa's hunting terrain, thick clumps of brush offered an inviting series of steps between my position and the unsuspecting bull. Furthermore, while wildebeest are generally herd animals with lots of eyes and ears around to complicate approaches to bow range, this old bull was grazing by himself. With a gentle breeze starting to push uphill in my face, it was hard to imagine a more favorable situation. Trying my best to brush off the effects of jet lag and a largely sleepless night, I quickly checked my recurve and the edge on my broadheads and eased downhill into the brush.

I had a lot invested in this stalk. Among the dozens of African game species I'd hunted over the years, the wildebeest had become my official Curse Species. Although hardly the rarest or wariest of African plains game, you couldn't prove anything easy about them by me. Even in areas known to hold plenty of them, they often seemed to disappear just as I arrived. When I targeted them on stalks, winds switched erratically, other animals interrupted unexpectedly, and Africa never seemed to run out of ways to make hours of patient belly-crawling unravel. Hunting from blinds, the wildebeest always seemed to water where I wasn't, leaving hunting partners who didn't care about them shooing them away while I waited patiently in vain. And at the time I set off down that hill the only African animal I'd ever wounded but failed to recover had been a blue wildebeest in Zimbabwe whose tough shoulder blade had turned a good looking arrow away from its vitals as if by magic.

I want that animal, I told myself as I settled into the hyper-alert rhythm of the stalk. *And this time, I'm going to get him.*

Years ago, I noticed that most experienced bowhunters seem to have one or two species that drive them to distraction. Ironically, some of those individuals are among the best bowhunters I know. There's no rational reason why one variety of game should give them so much trouble when they've done well with all the rest. Assuming by default that supernatural powers must be involved, I term these animals Curse Species.

Here in Montana, I know a local bowhunter who had killed a dozen bull elk before he ever brought home his first whitetail. Despite their reputation for wariness whitetails are actually one of the easiest animals we hunt, especially if you're not fussy about horns. He wasn't being selective, he lives in an area crawling with deer, and he hunted them hard. He just couldn't kill one.

Down south, I have another friend who's one of the best turkey callers I know. But for over a decade, he couldn't kill a wild turkey with his bow. The new and inventive routes to failure he created each spring became a standing joke among our circle of friends. The good news: his curse eventually lifted, and the Rio Grande gobbler he finally killed completed his Grand Slam.

When I lived in Alaska, another hunting partner had enjoyed a remarkable string of success on such challenging species as sheep and goats without ever being able to connect on a caribou. As we began a long September float trip for caribou and moose, I told him that since I'd killed plenty of the former he could have first crack at any caribou we encountered. A week later, we were piloting two separate rafts down a raging river swollen with floodwaters when we rounded a bend and found ourselves in the middle of hundreds of caribou. I pulled over to a flooded sandbar, where a dozen big bulls promptly surrounded me in the willows at point blank range. Because of the current conditions, my partner couldn't reach shore until he was a half-mile downstream, from which point it was impossible for him to secure his raft and hike back through the floodwaters to the animals. His caribou curse survived that trip; in fact, he has yet to kill one.

Here in North America, my personal Curse Species proved to be another Alaska native that's supposed to be relatively easy to kill: the Sitka blacktail deer. Adverse conditions undid my first several deer hunting trips to Kodiak. Sometimes crunchy snow underfoot made stalking impossible while on other trips severe storms kept us so busy trying to stay alive that we scarcely had time to hunt. When I finally overcame those obstacles, I forgot how to shoot my bow. On one boat-based trip, I ran out of arrows and had to borrow extras from a friend. I've never claimed to be a great archer, but I've never experienced a shooting meltdown like that either. While I've killed a number of blacktail bucks for camp meat since that miserable performance, the big ones have continued to elude me. Given the Sitka blacktail's reputation as a relatively easy quarry and the amount of time I've spent hunting them, I can imagine no explanation other than black magic.

You don't see much about Curse Species in print. Outdoor writers themselves are responsible for the illusion that they never miss. It's certainly easier to write a story about a big buck you killed than about one that you didn't. But I'm not too proud to learn from my mistakes – or to acknowledge them in public.

I've fared well in Africa over the years, although I frankly attribute my high ratio of animals collected to animals shot at to conservative shot selection and luck more than skill. While wildebeest are very tough animals that can take a hit with the best of them, they're still generally regarded as easier quarry than a number of plains game species I've taken without difficulty. So why couldn't I kill one?

Simple: they're my African Curse Species.

Back on the ridge above the Kariega, I made steady progress downhill toward the bull. Although he was grazing in open grass, a dense, unfamiliar species of shrub provided excellent cover as I angled ahead of the feeding animal, trying to reach a position between where he was and where he wanted to be. When his head disappeared behind a clump of brush, I eased to the other side, planning to let him feed right into me.

He'd been less than 15 yards from the bush when I lost sight of him, but he'd moved off as he fed and when I finally spotted him again he stood just under 30 yards away. That's marginal range for me on wary African game, but he was quartering away at an inviting angle with his eyes hidden by the grass. After reviewing his anatomy (I'd already promised myself that I'd made my last shoulder shot on a wildebeest), I picked a spot at the back of his rib cage and slowly came to full draw.

This was the point at which most bowhunting stories end with a well-placed arrow, but it was not to be. As my right hand reached its anchor point, a red warning light flashed deep inside my brain. I'd just completed two straight days of intercontinental travel. I felt sleepy and disoriented. There had been no time for practice shots after assembling my takedown recurve in the dark that morning. The shot didn't feel right and I didn't take it.

I still thought I might have an opportunity to get close enough to the bull for the slam dunk I wanted, but when he disappeared behind the next bush and I eased forward again, I spooked an impala ewe and that was that. After watching the wildebeest snort and canter away, I returned to my original position, picked out a tuft of grass where the bull had stood and center-punched it with my blunt. I *knew* I could make that shot and I was right... I guess.

But that wasn't good enough. When we regrouped back on the ridge, Adrian naturally asked me why I had let down instead of shooting and I did my best to tell him. He was relatively new to bowhunting, and I'm not sure my explanation sank in at first, but by the time we'd spent a few more days hunting together he understood that I'd rather pass up a tempting opportunity than risk wounding an animal.

I had several more exciting wildebeest stalks with Adrian but never released an arrow. And as it turns out, there were no wildebeest at the next three places Lori and I visited on that exploratory trip, so the curse of the blue wildebeest remains intact. I've thought a lot about the opportunity I declined, but I have no real regrets.

For my curse has given me something more valuable than any set of horns: an excuse to go back to Africa.

But there is more to the Eastern Cape than wildebeest. While talk of African cats usually evokes images of the feline 40% of the Big Five, the Dark Continent is home to a number of smaller cat species, none more intriguing than the caracal, or African lynx. Widely distributed and despised by ranchers and game managers because of their ability to take down hoofed animals the size of impala, springbok, and domestic sheep, caracal are plentiful in most southern African bowhunting destinations. However, thanks to their secretive, nocturnal habits you'll almost never see one unless you make a specific effort. And with over 20 years of experience hunting cougars with my own hounds, I was eager to see African houndsmen and their dogs in action.

Which is why I jumped at the chance when Adrian raised the subject almost as an aside. Before dawn the next morning, we were standing on a ridge top listening to a chorus of hounds work out a track in the dense, rugged terrain below us. Thandekile, the local Xhosa dog handler, obviously knew his charges well and he kept nearly two dozen hounds of every possible description moving along in concert through the thorns. His young son carried an ancient shotgun in case the dogs encountered a leopard, and I felt relieved when I personally confirmed that the weapon wasn't loaded. Finally the dogs were barking treed across the canyon, and we set off in a wild scramble that reminded me of the final sprint to the tree on a cougar hunt, but with less snow and a lot more thorns.

After a dozen trips to Africa, this was my first glimpse of a caracal. The sound of the dogs seemed to recede like a dream as I nocked an arrow and studied the tawny, tuft-eared figure overhead. Back home, this is the point when we always carefully tie our hounds up to trees in order to prevent encounters between dogs and wounded lions, but Thandekile would have none of that. Consequently, after the shot all of us – Adrian, Lori, Thandekile, his son, and myself – tumbled headlong downward through the thorns and rocks to race the dogs to my dead caracal. We made it before the dogs had a chance to tear the dead cat to pieces... barely.

The caracal provided a memorable interlude from the demands of stalking wary African plains game, but it was hard to ignore the conclusion that something was missing. I've always held that cougar hunting at home is all about the dogs, and we'll revisit that subject in a later chapter. But since these dogs weren't mine, it wasn't really my hunt. I'm glad I've hunted caracal once, but have never felt the urge to do so again... unless, of course, I could somehow smuggle my own Walkers and blueticks aboard a flight to Africa.

CHAPTER FOUR

Beyond Waterholes
South Africa

LENGTHENING SHADOWS marked the arrival of the witching hour along the Eastern Cape's Kariega River. A 30-yard swath of fresh, tender grass carpeted the banks between the waterline and the thorn brush where we'd seen bushbuck emerge every night to feed: dark chestnut on emerald green, reminding me oddly of bears on the tide flats back in Alaska. PH Graeme Hjuls had hiked back to pick up the vehicle where we'd started the long afternoon hunt while Lori and I planned to sit quietly on a point that allowed us to see up and down the bank in both directions until a ram appeared in a position that invited a stalk.

Although not as familiar or majestic as the closely related kudu, the bushbuck is one of my favorite African quarries. Barely the size of whitetail does, the harlequin markings on their dark coats give them a striking appearance and their sharp, spiral horns can make them one of Africa's most dangerous antelope when cornered or wounded. The same secretive habits that make them a tough quarry for riflemen paradoxically make them well suited to pursuit with the bow, since bushbuck will often hold still and rely on their camouflage rather than sprinting away at the first sign of danger. I acquired my taste for bushbuck hunting along Zimbabwe's Save River where I'd killed a fine ram years before. With Zimbabwe consumed by chaos, I'd been eager to explore new places to hunt bushbuck, and we knew we'd struck gold in the lush, broken terrain of South Africa's Eastern Cape. All that remained was to connect the dots.

"Bushbuck!" Lori hissed urgently as I kicked aside the thorns at the edge of the brush to create a comfortable place to sit. Assuming she'd spotted an animal far off down the bank, I went about my business only to be stopped short by a piercing look from my wife. Pivoting slowly, I finally appreciated the source of her excitement: a ram that had just emerged from the cover less than 40 yards away.

Close may count in horseshoes and nuclear wars, but in bowhunting it's nothing but a good start. Sinking slowly to my knees, I began to consider how I might convert this golden opportunity into a dead bushbuck. As promising as the situation seemed, the smart money still had to be on the ram. Understanding why illustrates important points about stalking African plains game, as difficult a challenge as I've faced on any continent.

An important point at the outset: African plains game is so sharp that hunting it with a bow is challenging under any circumstances. The premise here is not that there is anything wrong with hunting from blinds. But no matter where you're hunting, raising the bar by continuing to limit your means of take in the field offers ever-increasing levels of satisfaction and challenge.

Bowhunters accustomed to stalking game in our mountain West or Alaska often ask how much tougher it can really be in Africa. The simple answer: plenty, even though you may have to experience it yourself to believe it. Consider the problem from a biological perspective. Because of terrain, habitat, and climate, southern Africa supports game densities far greater than anywhere in North America, and that means high predator densities as well. It's not just a matter of an occasional lion or leopard. African ungulates face daily threats from adversaries as diverse as pythons, painted hunting dogs, caracal, raptors, and Bushmen. The dumb ones were culled millennia ago, leaving us to hunt animals blessed with survivor genetics. These animals possess senses superior to their sharpest North American counterparts and operate at a state of Red Alert that never seems to slacken. I can honestly say that the easiest species to stalk in Africa are more difficult to approach than the hardest here at home.

Africa offers plenty of compensation, however. The same high carrying capacities that produce smart game through selective pressure also provide abundant opportunities for bowhunters to learn from their mistakes and give the quarry chances to make mistakes of its own. An Alaskan hunt for sheep or moose often involves days spent just looking for an animal to stalk, even in prime habitat. In comparable African cover, it's rare to spend a morning on foot without multiple encounters with animals of various species, increasing both the level of excitement and the odds of eventual success.

There are practical as well as romantic reasons why any bowhunter considering an African adventure should be prepared to do some stalking. Suppose you set out for a 10-day hunt from waterhole blinds only to arrive in the middle of a rainstorm? Of course that's not supposed to happen during southern Africa's dry winter hunting season... but don't bet the farm. On my first trip to Zimbabwe we arrived during torrential rains that ended several years of drought, and on my last trip to South Africa rain chased us from Port Elizabeth to Kimberley over the course of a month. We even had snow fall on us in the middle of the Karoo. Decades of experience hunting antelope in Montana have taught me that if there's free water standing anywhere, hunting waterholes is a complete waste of time. The same holds true in Africa, but if you go prepared to do some stalking you'll be able to salvage a memorable hunt in any weather conditions.

Furthermore, variety is the spice of life in Africa as nowhere else and a number of important game species seldom frequent waterholes. Small antelope like steenbok and duiker can survive on the moisture content of their forage while high country species like klipspringer, rheebok, and mountain reedbuck subsist on dewfall at higher elevations. I have never seen a bush pig at a waterhole. If you want to tackle any of these intriguing animals, you'll have to get out and hunt them.

Years ago while scouting on the Montana prairie during the off-season, a rancher friend and I were looking over a herd of antelope in a green winter wheat field. Aware of my enthusiasm for stalking pronghorns, he surveyed this apparently hopeless lie and asked how I ever got close enough to kill one with a bow.

"First of all," I replied, "I don't waste time stalking antelope in winter wheat fields."

The point is that some terrain simply isn't well suited to stalking with a bow, and southern Africa has its share. Dry thorn veldt habitat in many popular destinations supports abundant game, but stalking there is usually difficult. The acacia species that dominate the landscape don't offer solid eclipses, and because of their inverted triangle branch structure game can often see your feet move even when you feel hidden. Factor in crunchy footing on dry, rocky ground and it's easy to see why approaching wary game on foot in such terrain is so difficult.

But Africa is a huge place offering ample variety of habitat as well as wildlife, and some locations are far better suited to stalking than others. For years, my favorite African hunting locale lay along the Save River in southern Zimbabwe. Thick riverine forest offered great cover, the game density was high enough to keep encounters coming non-stop, and elephants created convenient walking paths through the brush (as well as providing some memorable close range encounters of their own). Unfortunately, the adverse political situation has now made hunting Zimbabwe problematic.

An exploratory trip to the Republic of South Africa revealed some exciting alternatives in the Eastern Cape. The countryside near the Indian Ocean was the site of the area's first permanent European settlement. Because of this lengthy history and the productivity of the local farmland, properties tend to be smaller and less remote than they are farther north. However, the terrain is extremely well suited to stalking, with plenty of good cover and contour and enough elevation to allow effective glassing at a distance, a rarity on flat thorn veldt.

Even in locations with more open habitat, you can almost always find some areas reasonably suited to stalking. Riverbeds and creek bottoms may be bone dry during the African winter, but the vegetation there will often be dense enough to provide some good cover.

Your choice of PH may be as important as your choice of terrain. Dropping hunters off at blinds in the morning and picking them up again in the afternoon makes for a pretty easy day, and some PH's prefer to keep life simple. On the other hand, I know others who get just as excited about high-intensity, walk-and-stalk hunting as I do. Express your interests early in the safari's planning stages. Remember that most African professional hunters still have limited experience with bows. You may have lots to learn about African game, but the educational process is likely to be a two-way street.

I recently decided to spend a day stalking mountain reedbuck on top of a rugged mesa in the Northern Cape. Our host Julian sent me off accompanied by a sharp-eyed tracker named Noppie, whose initially non-existent English improved considerably as I chatted him up during the ride out to the mountain in the dark. Of course he had never seen a recurve bow before, and as we finally set off uphill through the rocks he asked me: "How far?"

"Twenty-five meters," I replied, without trying to explain that I'd prefer even less.

"Twenty-five meters," he mused. "No problem." Given the rocky but otherwise open terrain and the reedbuck's superb eyes, this I had to see.

An hour later, we'd watched a great ram bed down in some jumbled boulders across a draw and set out on a long, tortuous stalk. As we neared the area where we'd last seen the reedbuck, Noppie eased around a bush ahead of me and then urgently pantomimed instructions to nock an arrow. My own memory of the landmarks suggested that we were still some distance from the quarry, but when I hesitated Noppie excitedly whispered "Twenty-five meters!" and urged me forward. Peering through the last of the scrub, I spotted the reedbuck...bedded down a good 90 yards away.

"Shoot, Don, shoot!" Noppie urged in a perfect parody of the classic line to Howard Hill. But I'm not Howard, and as the ram bounced away over the horizon I couldn't do anything but laugh.

"How far is it to that rock down there, Noppie?" I asked as a pointed to a boulder a hundred yards away on the hillside.

"Twenty-five meters!" he answered cheerfully. Suspicions confirmed.

Over the years I've hunted over two-dozen species of African game. While all are challenging with traditional archery tackle, some invite stalking more than others.

As a general rule, open country grazers are difficult because of the terrain they inhabit, their universally great eyes, and their tendency to travel in herds. You'll do better stalking species that prefer thicker cover and travel alone.

As those familiar with javelina and feral hogs well know, pigs are always a great place to start. Southern Africa offers two: the warthog and the bush pig. While both have weak eyes compared to antelope species, that verdict is relative and I've certainly had warthogs spot me at considerable distances. While bush pigs are largely nocturnal, they are active at first and last light when they can be located by sound and stalked successfully as they feed. As with all pig hunting, wind is the paramount concern.

While the continent is home to over a dozen duiker species, only the gray duiker occurs commonly throughout southern Africa. Although these small, graceful antelope always appear alert and have very keen senses, they occasionally make the kind of mistakes that can allow bowhunters to kill them while stalking. In fact, stalking duiker and the even smaller steenbok early and late in the day is one of my favorite ways to hunt in Africa.

As noted earlier, the bushbuck is perhaps the most inviting quarry of all because of its habits, habitat preferences, and drop-dead gorgeous appeal. Since they inhabit thick cover, you won't find them at many bowhunting destinations. I've always said I would go back to Africa anytime just to stalk bushbuck, and South Africa's Eastern Cape turns out to be an ideal place to do so.

The most abundant game at many destinations in southern Africa, impala contradict most of the rules outlined earlier for selecting species to stalk: they avoid the thickest cover, remain incredibly alert at all times, and usually travel in herds with lots of extra eyes. However, their numbers also provide lots of opportunities and it can be done; the key is patience. Impala remind me of our own pronghorn, with tremendous distant vision but limited ability as problem solvers and pattern recognizers. Years ago in Zimbabwe, my hunting partner proved that if you were willing to spend an entire morning with a group of impala, one will eventually make a mistake and wander into bow range. Just don't waste time trying unless you're willing to commit long hours to the task.

While you can take a break from a blind and set off for some casual stalking with little specific preparation, a few additional items of equipment will make the process more productive and enjoyable.

In Africa, thorns and sharp rocks can make crawling miserable. I always wear a leather glove on my bow hand to provide some protection, and padding sewn into pockets over the knees of your hunting pants makes moving (or holding still for long periods) far more comfortable.

Binoculars are very useful for picking game out of thick brush even at close range. A chest harness will make them easier to manage when you're moving on hands and knees.

Graeme Hjuls asked me to bring him over some Bear's Paw-style stalking slippers during our last visit. While I've had a pair kicking around my closet for years, I never used them much at home. Stalking with Graeme while he was wearing them made me a believer. A lot of African terrain contains extremely noisy footing, but thorns make going barefoot risky. I have now made these padded slipovers a routine entry on my equipment list for stalking under dry conditions both at home and in Africa.

I don't think choice of camo pattern matters much, but I've

[35]

learned to avoid leafy or mesh-type material, which Africa's ubiquitous thorns love to snag. There's a good reason why they're called wait-a-bit thorns. Choose clothing less likely to catch.

Bowhunting Africa serves as a good reminder of how many little tricks and techniques we've developed for getting close to game here at home. There such possibilities remain largely unexplored, which you can consider either an obstacle to success or an opportunity for innovation. I've obviously taken the latter approach.

Consider the issue of calling game, a technique we've polished here at home for species ranging from turkeys to moose. Bowhunting is still so new in most of Africa that the thought has scarcely occurred to anyone, and in some jurisdictions it's actually illegal for reasons that escape me even after listening to several explanations. But in western Africa, Pygmies routinely call various duiker species into bow range, and I know American bowhunters who have done so themselves. I'm still experimenting with calls for species like duiker and reedbuck in southern Africa. All I can report at this time is that I feel confident it can be done.

Meanwhile, Graeme recently showed hunting partner Dick LeBlond and me how to "call" warthogs by twisting grass out of the ground and smacking our lips... noises I've often heard feeding warthogs make from considerable distances. I admit that I was skeptical at first, but the same day we received our first demonstration Dick proved that it worked... not just on warthogs but on bushbuck as well. Moral: away from waterholes, African bowhunting techniques are still in their infancy. What a time to be there.

Meanwhile, back at the river... Soft breeze at his back, the bushbuck began to feed slowly toward us. I needed better cover, and every time he lowered his head to browse I oozed forward until I reached a low bush that I thought might allow me to draw undetected. Lori was the problem, through no fault of her own. The ram had caught her out on the exposed bank with nowhere to go, leaving her nothing to do but flatten out and try her best to look like nothing... no easy task with a thick mane of blonde hair atop her head.

At 25 yards the ram paused nearly broadside with his head lowered and I almost took the shot, but *nearly* didn't feel quite good enough. On point as he continued forward, I realized that my arrow was rattling on the riser as I experienced my first genuine case of buck fever in years. The ram finally came around the corner of the bush less than ten yards away. I thought I'd timed my draw perfectly and perhaps I did, but by the time my right hand reached my face the bushbuck had zeroed in on Lori. I couldn't stop my release, but the animal had swapped ends by the time the arrow arrived to register a clean miss. The ram's explosive alarm bark shattered the calm and then it was over, as if we'd awakened from a dream.

"I could see you shaking the whole time he was walking down the bank," Lori observed. "I haven't seen you that excited about a shot in years!"

"This is exciting business," I replied, and that's the truth. Waterhole blinds have their place on bowhunting safaris, but for sheer intensity there's nothing like matching wits *mano a mano* with the sharpest game in the world.

And even though a lot of stalks will unravel in the end, you'll come home a better hunter.

Don with a bushpig taken by stalking in Zimbabwe.

[37]

Better times—the school at the Humani Ranch in the old days.

CHAPTER FIVE

Paradise Lost
Zimbabwe

THE SMOKE FROM THE FIRES dotting the veldt hung like a gauze curtain over the sky. Even mid-morning the sun glowed ineffectively through the haze, a fuzzy orange ball suspended by magic above a horizon undulating through simmering waves of heat. These were the green hills of Africa, but the smoke, the torpor, and the promise of worse to come infused northern Zimbabwe's rolling terrain with a sense of vulnerability I'd never experienced there before.

All of which made the river look especially inviting as it tumbled down out of the highlands on its way to the Zambezi a hundred miles to the north. I'd expected something dirty and sluggish, full of jungle menace, but the clear water laughed and beckoned as it danced along through the rocks. By the time Lori and I watched our old friend Will Schultz bounce away in the Land Rover and picked our way down a game trail to the bank, I'd already decided the stream was the best thing to happen to us in days. Forget our grim expectation of crocodiles and bugs. Lower the water temperature ten degrees and do something about the bucket-sized piles of elephant dung piled up along the waterline and it could have been a high country trout stream back home in Montana.

On unfamiliar water nothing gladdens the heart like the sight of fish, and as I climbed along the worn boulders and stared down into the first pool, there they lay, a dozen green shapes holding lazily just beneath the surface. We had come in search of tigerfish, southern Africa's signature fresh water fly rod quarry, but these were plainly something else: bream, as locals collectively refer to a dozen-odd species of tilapia and their relatives. Bream don't arouse the faraway looks common to Africa veterans telling tigerfish stories, but they allegedly can be caught on flies and some of the specimens lying in the pool looked as if they weighed three or four pounds. Besides, we were growing weary of warthog stew, and bream enjoy an excellent reputation on the table. As intent on sizzling fillets as sizzling lines, we quickly rigged our gear and went to work.

My first selection – a small, yellow popping bug – earned nothing but a yawn from the bream, as did several small streamers. I realized I needed something more delicate, and would have paid a hundred dollars for a Hare's Ear nymph. But we had come equipped for tigers and my flies looked suspiciously large in comparison to the fish we were trying to catch. Finally, I dug up a corroded Crazy Charlie left over from some forgotten bonefish expedition. Reasoning that bream lying in deeper water might be more aggressive than their sunbathing cohorts, I double-hauled my way across the pool to a deep slot of current against the opposite bank, and when the line straightened, all hell broke loose.

Tigers can run and jump with the best, but the most memorable aspect of a tigerfish encounter is always the strike. The moment of contact between angler and quarry usually feels like something you're doing to the fish, but not in the case of tigers, which always seem to be trying to do something to you. Even though this one didn't weigh more than a few pounds, it flashed and bucked and tore around the pool as if it were several sizes too big for the water before it finally came to rest in the shallows at my feet.

Nothing can adequately prepare an angler for that first good look at *Hydrocyon lineatus*. I've never seen a photograph that truly does the species justice. The camera can catch the powerful, bullet-shaped

[40]

profile and the gleaming, heavily barred flanks, but the intense orange hue of the fins and tail always eludes the lens. Then there's the business end of the fish. Think barracuda; the teeth are that impressive. While tigers do not behave aggressively toward humans in the water, they need to be handled with care and Will bears an ugly scar on his leg to prove it.

We never did solve the mystery of the diffident bream, but I landed and released another small tiger before the heat drove us off the water and back into the shade. As we waited for our ride, an African man carrying a cane pole appeared on the wooden bridge that spanned the river, trailed by a young boy carrying several bream on a stick. I meant to walk up the bank and ask how they'd caught the fish, but it was just too hot to move. When the man caught sight of us, we smiled and waved, and he and the boy smiled and waved back. In an instant, the truth occurred to me. Everyone in Zimbabwe needed to take time out and go fishing.

The civil war that led to Zimbabwe's independence in 1980 was as nasty as that kind of thing ever gets. But the young nation quickly began to defy the expectations of its own recent history, thanks to its functional infrastructure and robust agricultural economy. While South Africa wrestled with apartheid, Mozambique and Angola nurtured sputtering armed conflicts, and Congo stubbornly remained Congo, Zimbabwe seemed determined to show its neighbors how to enter the post-colonial world successfully. That was the country I'd fallen in love with ten years earlier. I formed warm friendships there with Zimbabweans both black and white, and the memory of the hills, valleys and teeming wildlife drew me back like a siren's call year after year.

But this trip felt immediately and shockingly different, and not just because of our departure in the wake of the September 11 catastrophe. The Mugabe government's relentless descent into demagoguery and violence had brought the country to the brink of anarchy. Once the breadbasket of southern Africa, Zimbabwe's agricultural production had fallen by 50% in five years while the Zim dollar spiraled away into inflationary hyper-space. The National Health Service was down to fewer than 20 physicians and 80 nurses to treat a population of over twelve million. And the once fertile, productive farmlands north of Harare had acquired the sullen ambience of an undeclared war zone.

Make of the politics what you will; as a simple outdoor story, this really isn't the forum for that debate. But the first casualty of civil turmoil in Africa has always been its wildlife, a principle nowhere more tragic than on Zimbabwe's high veldt. Once, no other part of southern Africa offered such intriguing bio-diversity or comparable abundance of freely ranging wildlife outside the inevitably sanitized venue of national parks and fenced preserves. But no longer, not since fire became the medium of choice for disgruntled government sympathizers.

For in hot, dry country that depends upon agricultural production for economic stability, a book of matches can turn anyone into an efficient terrorist. Granted, fire is a normal part of the seasonal African cycle of rejuvenation, but lightning never made the landscape look the way we found it that year. And the populace had turned as surly as the smoke-filled sky overhead. I remember when everyone used to smile at everyone else in rural Zimbabwe, when motorists always stopped for hitchhikers and people shared what they had to share. No longer.

What a perfect time for a bowhunting trip.

As we dropped over the lip of the great escarpment that marks the southern border of the Zambezi valley, only the smoke remained to remind us of the turmoil we'd left behind. The country there is too wild to fight over, which suited us – and teeming herds of elephant and buffalo – just fine. But as we wound our way down out of the highlands toward the river and Will's houseboat, the temperature and humidity began to climb. By the time we reached Kariba I needed a cold Castle as badly as I've ever needed a beer in my life.

In 1960, Queen Elizabeth threw a ceremonial switch on the

newly completed dam spanning the Zambezi between what was then Southern and Northern Rhodesia, initiating a new era of electrical power in southern Africa. This ambitious project came with an ecological price tag; dams always do. But it also created a huge impoundment surrounded by a complex shoreline that provides ideal habitat for fish and wildlife. Fueled by a rich forage base of minnow-sized kapenta, the lake's tigerfish population ranks among Africa's most robust.

As does its population of another high-end predator, the Nile crocodile. Back in his wild and crazy days B.C. (Before Cindy, his wife of then three years), Will and his rugby mates used to dive Kariba waters regularly to spearfish for bream. Now Will lamented that he had no one to dive with anymore, not after crocodiles hit three of his friends in separate incidents. Miraculously, all escaped without crippling injuries, no small testimonial to the hardy African survival instinct. But in contrast to other diving friends who went right back into the ocean after adverse encounters with sharks, none of the three ever swam Zambezi waters again. Will just couldn't understand it, but somehow I could.

It didn't take us long to dub his houseboat the *African Queen*. As we slid down the shoreline to the reliable throb of its twin diesels, Lori spotted crocs off the bow with her binoculars while I watched a kapenta fishing rig head off toward the sunset to begin its long night's work. Dried in the sun and packaged for distribution, these tiny fish provide the region with an unlikely source of high quality protein.

Sunrise the following morning found us casting steamers toward a sunken drop-off while a belligerent hippo grunted and blew in the reed bed behind us. Not *too* belligerent, I hoped; the skiff wasn't that big and I didn't think it was that fast either. Despite the dry October weather, the lake level remained relatively high, reflecting ample reserves from the last rainy season. While I had naively envisioned fishing for Kariba tigers like northern pike, Will informed us they would be near the bottom, a point he promptly proved by hooking a powerful ten-pound fish on bait. Stubbornly devoted to my fly rod, I switched to a sinking-tip line and kept firing away.

The first strike didn't feel anything like the electrical jolt I

[43]

remembered from the little stream two days earlier, and no wonder. After a minute of head-shaking near the bottom, the fish I horsed up from the depths proved to be a barbel. There's something about catfish that inevitably makes me think about frying pans, and it quickly wound up in the cooler next to the beer. But I did catch it on a fly.

I've listened to a number of anglers tell me that tigers are a lot harder to catch with flies than conventional tackle. I'm used to that kind of skepticism, and as a fly rod diehard I've enjoyed disproving such statements with regard to species as diverse as walleyes and halibut. But as Will hooked several nice tigers on bait while Lori and I drew blanks, my confidence began to erode. Clearly, we still had a lot to learn about Kariba tigerfish.

Casting an 8-weight fly rod may not sound like aerobic exercise, but when the temperature and humidity both reach triple digits life itself can become exhausting. I seldom cry uncle in the presence of uncaught fish, but by ten o'clock the tropical sun had brought me to my knees. As we ran the skiff back toward the bay where the *Queen* lay at anchor, we spotted a herd of elephants feeding on the bluff overlooking the lake and powered the boat across a thick weed bed to make a stalk with the telephoto. The elephants had disappeared by the time we climbed the bank – not always a bad outcome in the case of wild elephants – and we returned to find the skiff hopelessly mired in the grass. We'd seen so many crocs along the shoreline that even Will wasn't enthusiastic about going overboard, so we had to extricate ourselves by lassoing a series of snags and towing our way laboriously to open water by hand. When we finally reached our mother ship, I was too worn out to do anything but collapse in the shade.

By the time the sun began to lower in the western sky, we had Lori's reel rigged with a fast-sinking shooting head I'd thrown in my gear bag as an afterthought. We were drifting slowly past a hauled-out croc when the first fish struck somewhere in the depths below. Lori always whoops when a good fish hits her fly – one of several reasons she's so much fun to fish with – and by the time the sound of her voice spooked the crocodile back into the water the tiger had gone airborne, silhouetted against the crimson reflection of the sunset. Ten minutes later I proved it hadn't been an accident by drawing a second strike on the same rig, and then it was time to race the darkness toward home base.

If only the rest of Africa's problems could be solved so easily.

Back in the high veldt three days later, I sat atop a termite mound in the welcome shade of a towering fig tree and watched Lori edge cautiously across a broad expanse of dry grass toward a fine reedbuck ram. We were hunting a farm adjoining Will's family property. On an earlier visit, I'd noted tremendous numbers of reedbuck and oribi ranging freely about the property and Lori and I had returned with the specific intention of trying to stalk both species with our bows. Approaching wary African plains game in open terrain is always a tremendous challenge however, and between the two of us we'd already attempted a dozen stalks that morning without releasing an arrow.

But this time Lori looked as if she was about to pull it off. Distances always prove deceptive when you're watching a stalk through binoculars, but as I monitored her progress while she inched through the grass, I finally realized that she really had closed within less than twenty yards of the ram. I felt my own heart in my throat as she nocked an arrow and rose slowly to one knee, but at the last instant the spell of secrecy shattered and the reedbuck bounded off unscathed. Lori's spirits still seemed high when she finally rejoined us at the truck, but Juoa, our Shona tracker, who had never participated in a bowhunt before, wasn't so sure. "Miss Lori," he intoned solemnly as she rejoined us, "I think this is a job for Jesus." And I had to admit that divine intervention would have been most welcome.

On the way back to camp that afternoon, we stopped at another neighbor's place where we'd heard rumors of a fresh leopard kill. Although the owner and his wife welcomed us warmly, the mood inside the farmhouse felt subdued. The story didn't take long to unfold. With his place recently scheduled for "resettlement" by urban government supporters, the farmer had just met with his work force to tell them he could no longer provide them with employment. Many of the workers' families had lived and worked on that farm in relative prosperity for generations. He provided directions to the site of the reported kill, but my heart wasn't in it and I actually felt relieved when our search proved fruitless. Not even the sight of a magnificent sable bull at last light could convince me to take advantage of our host's invitation to stay as long as we liked and hunt whatever we wished.

The following morning, we stood outside camp watching angry tongues of flame claw their way skyward just across the valley. "The neighbor found some illegal snares last week and pulled them," Will explained. "These days, this is what you get in return." Although Will felt confident that the fire would sweep away downhill to the east, I didn't like the wind direction, and his suggestion that it would be nice to do something for the wildlife was all it took. Our original hunting plans forgotten, we piled into the vehicle and set off toward hell.

I wasn't sure we could do much with nothing but a few pangas and shovels, but Will remembered an old firebreak that ran down our side of the valley and we bailed out there to take a stand. Fighting wildfire is a dirty job on any continent, but the dazed kudu scampering past us through the smoke quickly convinced us of our mission's worth. With a little help from the wind we held the line, and by evening we stood watching the fire burn itself out in a steep canyon below camp. This fire, this time… at least we'd saved something, and for now that was all we could hope to accomplish.

To the extent that our own news media have paid any attention to the plight of Zimbabwe's farmers, reporters have tended to fall back on worn assumptions left over from coverage of the old apartheid days… never mind the fact that those sad events took place in another country. I wish a few of them had been with me on our last night in Zim that year.

We spent the evening with Will's sister Sue and her family at their modest farmhouse. As an officer in the crack Selous Scouts, her husband carried a price on his head at the end of the war of independence, and their family temporarily moved to Canada where they still maintained citizenship and passports. Of all the farmers we met on our journey, none would have had an easier time leaving the country and its troubles behind. But there were two problems, and they both scampered freely across my lap as we sat in the living room and talked: Crista and Abraham, age four and six, abandoned foundlings Sue had taken into her home and raised as her own, both black and one HIV positive. Because there were no official adoption papers, departure for Canada would have meant leaving them behind to a grim fate in a local orphanage and Sue refused to do so even if the decision meant keeping herself and the rest of her family in harm's way. So much for the dismissal of white Zimbabwean farmers as uncaring racists.

We of the outdoor press stand guilty of similar offenses, if only as a matter of neglect. In the course of our travels, we too often report accurately enough on what interests us at the expense of the human substrate that lies beneath the immediate story. In our own way, we're creating travel posters while we apply the willing suspension of disbelief to the dark side of every paradise we visit. Sometimes you have to search out the truth beneath the veneer, but occasionally it kicks you in the butt as it did in Zimbabwe that year. And I know I owe my friends there an honest job of reporting.

Since our departure, Will's family farm has been officially occupied by Mugabe supporters and his aging parents have been robbed at gunpoint. Sue and her family have made their way to an uncertain future in South Africa, Crista and Abraham included. Will's second sister, Moira, a lovely lady who hosted us at her ranch on several occasions, was shot and killed by an unknown assailant as she drove down the road one evening; her husband was seriously wounded in the attack. Abandoned fields lie untended beneath the sun while Zimbabwe's populace faces the prospect of massive food shortages. And the kudu and sable that once roamed freely through the hills face decimation by fire and snares.

But I've learned never to underestimate the African capacity for perseverance. The victims of this upheaval are as tough as they are fair. Those who can survive attacks from crocodiles should be able to survive, period. And I remain confident they'll find a way.

This essay, which contains a limited amount of hunting and hardly any killing at all (you forgot all about that barbel, didn't you?) may seem a strange entry in a collection of hunting stories, especially since Africa provides the venue for some of the most body-strewn accounts in the history of the outdoor sporting genre. In fact, it suggests a theme that recurs in the text that follows. I was lucky; I enjoyed the opportunity to see Zimbabwe and enjoy its hunting at the best of times, just as I did in Siberia, Melville Island, and a host of other locations around the world. For a variety of reasons those opportunities are gone now, at least in the way my hunting partners and I once experienced them.

At the time I participated in all of those exploratory trips, there were countless reasons not to go: my medical practice was too busy, the destination was unsafe, I couldn't afford it. In retrospect, I can only be grateful for my lack of common sense. As each of those opportunities fell by the wayside, I received calls from friends around the country expressing regret that they hadn't gone with me when I invited them the year before.

They were right; they should have gone. And therein lies a lesson for us all.

Section II

THE SOUTH PACIFIC

THE SOUTH PACIFIC

SINCE the earliest years of its exploration, the middle reaches of our greatest ocean have exerted a nearly magical attraction upon visitors from colder climates, and little wonder. Once the snow has started to fly at home, the mere thought of warm seas, swaying palms, and pristine beaches--of a setting in which clothes remain an optional social convention rather than a matter of immediate necessity--produces a nearly irresistible urge to travel, whether by running off to sea in older times or maxing out the credit card in our own. From Gaugin to Hollywood, artists have portrayed the tropical Pacific in terms that suggest a real life version of paradise, and in the section that follows we'll visit locations that justify nearly every bit of that hyperbole.

But no corner of the world enjoys a history entirely free of our own species' rough edges. Captain James Cook, the great navigator, died violently at the hands of native Hawaiians. New Zealand's indigenous Maori offered the British Empire the stiffest resistance it encountered anywhere during the age of colonial expansion. And of course Australia served for years as a continental-sized penal colony, earning a reputation for cruelty so horrible that "transportation" became regarded as a one-way ticket to hell. Reasons to avoid these places today? Hardly. But one travels better if one looks beyond the travel posters for history's lessons.

From the traveling bowhunter's perspective, all these isolated island ecosystems share an important feature in common: a nearly complete lack of native game animals. In Hawaii and New Zealand, the only indigenous mammals are bats and seals, while Australia is home to a rich variety of marsupials--biological oddities that thrive almost nowhere else--but no large placental mammals at all. Interesting stuff if you're a biologist, but slim pickings for bowhunters.

For better or worse, or own species changed all that beginning with the introduction of Asiatic swine throughout the Pacific by Polynesian seafarers over a thousand years ago. Early European explorers brought pigs of their own to the islands, as well as feral goats. Over time, homesick settlers and colonial sportsmen introduced a wealth of game species from all over the world: European mouflon sheep and Asiatic axis deer to Hawaii, European red deer to Australia and New Zealand, Indonesian rusa stags to New Caledonia, and more. Theodore Roosevelt even sent North American moose to the South Island of New Zealand, where unconfirmed rumors of moose sign persist to this day, and Australia supports the largest population of wild camels in the world. Of course some of these attempts to help nature fill the vacuum she allegedly abhors ended in failure, but many of the new arrivals thrived in lush new habitat largely free of predators.

Visiting bowhunters will find local game management policies different from what we're accustomed to here at home, to say the least. Since none of these game species really belongs and many have inflicted severe ecological damage upon fragile indigenous flora and fauna, few receive anything like the organized protection and management accorded their counterparts in North America. Nonetheless, free-ranging populations of most of these intriguing animals are doing quite well--too well, according to some observers--and well-behaved hunters remain generally welcome to control their numbers: a tough job, as they say, but someone has to do it.

The title of this section includes a bit of geographic inaccuracy, since Hawaii lies north of the equator and therefore technically outside the bounds of the South Pacific even though most of us think of it otherwise. However, I wished to distinguish the following material from accounts of my experiences much farther north along the Pacific coast, including eastern Russia, as described in my earlier *Longbows In the Far North*, and Alaska, which we'll revisit in a later section of this book.

The image of Pacific islands conveyed by travel literature suggests physically easy hunting, and in cases that's true. But visiting bowhunters planning to tackle Hawaiian high country and parts of New Zealand's South Island ought to be ready to face some of the most challenging terrain of their lives. Moral: don't believe everything you see or read... except here, of course.

And because all of the hunting in this area takes place by honest and not infrequently dangerous stalking, I never felt any reticence about letting arrows fly during the hunts whose descriptions follow. Readers disappointed by the lack of conventional "action" in the previous section, take heart.

So buckle your seat belt, prepare for some flight time across a lot of open sea, and get ready to enjoy a world of hunting you may not have imagined before.

(R to L) Brad Kane, Lori, and the late Bill Baker with a boar from the Basalt Wall.

CHAPTER SIX

Spotted Deer and Basalt Warriors Australia

PERCHED HIGH on seam of black volcanic rock, master Australian bowyer Glenn Newell and I watched Lori and Bill Baker slip cautiously toward a foraging sounder of pigs. Because of our elevated position and the height of the swamp grass below, Glenn and I could actually see the animals more clearly than they could, and appreciated Lori's problem. Her body language established that she could see game, but she was having trouble identifying the big boar we'd glassed at first light.

"She's pretty calm," Glenn whispered as we watched her let a young boar forage past barely five paces to one side. "A lot of guys I know would be backing out of there by now."

"Ignorance is bliss," I pointed out, for Lori didn't seem to be taking the pigs' tusks quite as seriously as I thought she should. At first I'd been a bit skeptical myself about all the charging-boar stories we'd heard, but at the weekend target shoot we'd just attended in nearby Townsville many of the experienced Aussie bowhunters we met bore scars on their legs from encounters with angry hogs.

Just then, the big guy himself waddled out of the grass. As Lori's bow arm began to rise, something alerted him to her presence and he pivoted in her direction and fixed her with an ugly stare. I've always said that any bear that does anything other than turn and run at the first sign of danger is potential trouble, and I imagine the same is true of pigs. I certainly didn't relish the idea of sewing up my own wife's legs back in camp, but we all knew there wasn't anything to do about the confrontation but wait it out.

This adventure began with an invitation to speak at the 25th annual Kev Whiting Memorial Shoot in Townsville, on Australia's Queensland coast, an event that also served as a kick-off event for the new Traditional Bowhunters Club of Australia. And quite a gathering it had been. While I've attended my share of such functions, I can't remember one that involved more good times, camaraderie, and downright enthusiasm for the bow. For three days, we fired arrows and traded stories with one of the most interesting and hospitable groups of bowhunters I've ever met. When the affair broke up, Lori and I left convinced that the Australian bowhunting community has become one of the most dynamic and rapidly growing in the world.

And we learned a bit about Aussie bowhunting history in the process. Kev Whiting, an accomplished and highly respected individual who died before his time, was an Australian equivalent of Saxton Pope, Art Young, and Fred Bear rolled into one. The story of his impassioned effort to persuade the Australian public of the bow's legitimacy as a hunting tool reminded me of the battles our predecessors here at home waged 50 years earlier. We enjoyed the opportunity to visit with his widow Marian and son Steve at the shoot, and when Steve gave me one of his father's old arrows I knew I was holding a true piece of history in my hand.

And I learned a lot about wildlife Down Under as well. Australia didn't start out with a lot of game, since virtually all its indigenous mammals are marsupials of little interest to hunters. Pigs entered the continent courtesy of Asiatic seafarers sometime in the distant past. When British settlers arrived they introduced new swine stocks, which rapidly established tenacious feral populations, not without considerable effect on native wildlife. During the 1800's Australian Acclimatization

Societies also introduced a number of Eurasian deer species, of which six survive with self-sustaining, free-ranging populations: red deer, hog deer, chital (or axis deer), fallow deer, rusa deer and sambar. While all these introduced animals are legal game year around, I don't think I'll offend our hosts by describing the country's approach to managing them as rather directionless. In fact, while I was the first to admit that Americans don't always do everything right (despite our occasional assumptions to the contrary), we all agreed that our game management policies might serve as a useful blueprint Down Under.

But even the most enthusiastic gatherings eventually leave me eager for the silence of wild places, an impulse our hosts had anticipated. At the conclusion of the shoot, we set off with Glenn, Bill, and mutual friend Brad Kane for the vast Toomba Station, which includes a long segment of Queensland's famous Great Basalt Wall. Bill befriended Ernest and Robyn Bastlewaite, the managers of this huge working cattle ranch, years earlier, and they graciously allowed Bill and his friends the run of the place with their bows. The contrast between the bustle of the shoot and the splendid wilderness isolation we found waiting for us could not have been more dramatic.

The Basalt Wall forms part of one of the world's longest continuous lava flows, and the pure aquifer that accompanies the volcanic rock to the surface produces a unique ecosystem of fertile, clear water swamps and marshes that my imagination can only compare to our own Everglades a hundred years ago. The Fletcher River, which drains the area, is the longest true spring creek in the world. (By coincidence, the second longest lies just a mile from our rural Montana home.) Herds of free ranging axis deer thrive there, and the Wall's boars enjoy a wide reputation for their size, tusks, and ill temper. Hence the name Bill coined for them years ago: Basalt Warriors.

I didn't really mean to leave Lori stranded in dire straits like the heroine of an old silent movie serial, lashed to the tracks by the villain while a train approaches. It's just that Australian bowhunting turns out to be such an exotic experience that it's hard to appreciate without a bit of background. And no, I didn't wind up repairing any tusk wounds to her legs with my suture kit back in camp. After a long, anxious face-off, the big boar turned and huffed away without charging or presenting an acceptable shot angle, at which point she did the logical thing, which was to send an arrow into the chest of the second largest boar in the bunch.

As we regrouped to critique the stalk and give the blood trail some time, I spotted a lone boar rooting on the other side of the swamp and set off to investigate. A steady breeze and the pig's determination to keep digging allowed an easy approach to 12 yards, at which point I decided to pass in favor of something bigger. In retrospect that proved an overly principled decision since, as I learned over dinner that night, Ernest and Robyn considered the hogs troublesome pests and would have been delighted for us to shoot them all.

Fortunately, finding something bigger seldom takes long on the Basalt Wall. While the others stayed behind to trail Lori's pig, Bill and I set off for the next swamp. Thirty minutes later, a large black form rose from the grass ahead. While I don't pretend to be a good judge of tusks, the pig was obviously a mature boar -- a "great lump of a pig", as Bill put it – and when he turned quartering away I sent an arrow whistling into the soft spot just behind his last rib.

While I felt confident of the shot, I recommended giving the track a rest, an unnecessary precaution as events proved. When we circled back an hour later, we found the boar dead 50 yards from where I'd shot him. Based on prior discussions with the Aussies, I'd picked my shot correctly as the autopsy proved, for the broadhead had taken out both lungs on its way to the opposite shoulder. While I was familiar with the wild boar's tough fighting shield – the layer of dense cartilage that lies beneath the hide along the forequarters -- from encounters with the species elsewhere, I'd never seen one so dense or extensive, a phenomenon I attribute to the area's high pig density and the amount of fighting boars engage in there. Even with a sharp broadhead and heavy bow, good penetration through that shield would have been difficult, justifying our hosts' endorsement of the quartering-away shot just behind the ribs. My examination of the fallen boar also made me a believer in Bill's insistence on coating broadheads and shafts with Vaseline to improve penetration through hide and gristle, a trick I have since adopted on bears back home.

With a representative Basalt Warrior on the ground, I decided to spend the rest of our stay concentrating on photography and the ever-challenging chital deer.

A day of observation enforced several important points about my quarry, even though I'd already had considerable experience with axis deer in Hawaii. Chital rub and scrape just like whitetails. Creatures of habit, they are easy to pattern, and with abundant trees in the area, hunting from tree stands might well have been an effective tactic. But since I'd killed my last Hawaiian axis deer from a ground blind, I wanted to take my next one by stalking despite the difficulty of approaching within bow range of these highly wary animals.

The following morning, while backing Lori up with the camera as she hunted pigs, I watched a herd of chital feed down a grassy corridor between a creek and a line of basalt with the wind at their backs. All those eyes kept Lori from sneaking into bow range, but we did enjoy a look at a magnificent stag obviously interested in a receptive hind. That was all I needed to convince me to return and still hunt my way down the natural funnel at first light the next day.

After rising in the dark and slogging across a half-mile of swamp, I was pleased to note the same gentle breeze in my face as I began to creep along between the creek and the rock. Suddenly a flicker of motion caught my eye. The new arrivals turned out to be a browsing pair of wallabies. I'd noticed earlier that chital often follow wallabies through the bush much as plains game animals follow baboons in Africa, and with that cue to guide me I settled in behind a clump of brush to await developments. Ten minutes later, spotted deer began to appear and the lead hind soon filed by well within bow range. Convinced the big stag would eventually follow, I held my ground and waited. But he had evidently found a hot date elsewhere, and I wound up letting the whole mob of hinds and young stags pass without taking a shot.

The situation looked so promising that Bill and I returned again the next morning. After hunting my way down most of the corridor without seeing game, I was about to give up when another pair of wallabies appeared. Easing into a clump of brush, I turned down a few twigs to create some shooting lanes and waited. When the first hind popped out of the grass ten minutes later, she fed directly in front of me, stopped six feet away and gave me a long hard stare. I knew the whole outcome of the hunt would depend upon the conclusion she drew. Avoiding eye contact and trying to act as much like a bush as possible, I waited her out, and several long minutes later she continued on her way, passing behind me to my left.

I knew she might hit my scent line, but I couldn't risk turning to monitor her progress. As the rest of the herd filtered into view, I realized the biggest deer of the lot was the young stag at the end of the line, but with our time winding down, I resolved to take him if he presented a shot. With nerves steeled against the growing possibility of an alarm bark behind me, I concentrated on his chest and waited patiently. Ten yards away, he paused and turned his head to scratch his back. At that range, I admit the quartering-on shot looked inviting, but I've been at this too long to succumb to that kind of temptation. Finally, he turned and walked across my best shooting lane while I slowly raised my bow and drew. He stood perfectly broadside by the time my right hand found its place against my cheek, and after reminding myself to pick a spot (literally), I released and sent the broadhead through his heart from a range of eight yards.

When the congratulations were complete back in camp, we all agreed that this deer represented a classic example of horn size not telling the story. I'd seen a number of great axis stags during our brief stay, and after killing two medium sized representatives of the species in Hawaii I felt more than ready to take one of those giants. But somehow, the exquisite pace of the hunt and all those gut-wrenching minutes spent within the inner circle of one of the world's wariest game animals more than compensated for the missing inches of antler. I subsequently killed a large, free-ranging axis buck in Argentina, of all places, but the conduct of the hunt wasn't as nearly as exciting and demanding. So never mind the antlers--my first axis buck from the Molokai alpine and my buck from Toomba are the two that mean the most to me even though they aren't the biggest.

Since that initial visit I've returned to Toomba several times without ever losing my fascination with the place. The combination of abundant boars and challenging axis deer certainly contributes to that fascination, as does the friendship I've developed with Ernst and Robyn. But it's the ecosystem itself that always seals the deal in the end--a unique combination of clear water, birdlife impossible to imagine outside a zoo, complex geology, and limitless opportunities to wander through genuine wilderness. Billy and I often talked about devoting a month to walking the entire length of the Basalt Wall while living off the land, a trek that has likely never been accomplished since Aboriginal times. Now, that's just another dream, for reasons we'll explore in due course.

But nothing can diminish the memory of the morning I blended into a bush, held motionless longer than I ever thought possible, and turned an axis stag into venison... and memories are the one thing in life that no one can ever take away.

CHAPTER SEVEN

Walkabout
Australia

SUNRISE, Mary's River valley, south Queensland. The grating chatter of sulfur-crested cockatoos high in the gum trees yields to a familiar whistle of wings. A flock of Pacific black ducks – a delicately scaled-down version of our own familiar Atlantic flyway staple – rounds the creek-bend downstream and flares overhead, inducing sudden, intense longing for a shotgun. But while waterfowl abound in coastal Australia, no one seems to know quite what to do about them, and our hosts, although dedicated hunters, cannot even confirm any dates for a waterfowl season. Welcome to the real land of Oz, where the wildlife always manages to intrigue and fascinate without ever entirely making sense.

My goal this morning is a bow-range encounter with the red stag we heard roaring in the creek bottom at last light the previous evening. In contrast to the indigenous cockatoos and waterfowl, the deer arrived in Australia the same way the country's European population did: from the old country, by sailing vessel nearly two centuries ago. Thanks to the homesick members of the Australian Acclimatization Societies, the deer came and thrived, whatever their impact on indigenous species the land's new stewards found less worthy. Today, stable populations of free-ranging red deer still inhabit the hills above the Queensland coast, and when the stags roar in April you can close your eyes, listen, and imagine yourself transported to another land half a world away. Australian red deer seldom sport the immense racks sometimes found in New Zealand where deer are artificially managed for trophy quality on some private ranches, but for me at least, the sprawling country and lack of high fences more than compensates.

But despite my fascination with the deer and my genuine desire to slip an arrow through a good stag's ribs, I have to admit my divided attention as I work my way slowly down the bank with the breeze in my face. Most of our Aussie hosts admit they've never actually seen a duck-billed platypus, but we've heard reports that some have been spotted along this very creek. As a life-long amateur naturalist, the thought of an encounter with one of these elusive biologic oddities arouses almost as much excitement as the memory of the stag's roar. Then, as I ease my way over a downed log... contact!

The first impression remains understated to say the least, for the object floating in the pool ahead resembles little more than a waterlogged turd. And for the few observers who actually manage to spot a platypus in the wild, that's as far as matters usually get, for the little guys prove surprisingly wary and usually disappear at the first sign of human intrusion. But, anticipating red deer, I'm operating in stealth mode. Fully camouflaged and motionless, I wait patiently, and moments later most biologists' lead candidate for the title of Strangest Mammal on Earth lies noodling around right at my feet.

While most mammalian species can only count a minor distinguishing feature or two to separate them from the pack, the platypus represents an absolute marvel of dead-end design. The bill looks like an oversized version of the black ducks'. The facial profile lacks external ears. Venomous spurs lie beneath the fur on the hind feet, ready to punish anyone foolish enough to pick one up. And to top off this list of marvels, my furry discovery began life as an egg, as in Denver omelet. Stephen Maturin, the fictional physician/naturalist of Patrick O'Brian's splendid sea-faring novels, spends most of one book absorbed in a study of the platypus. Now I can appreciate his sense of wonder.

And when the stag finally roars a half-mile away down the creek, I find it strangely difficult not to regard his bellow as an interruption.

Thanks to a capricious wind, my encounter with the stag in the creek bottom came to nothing. By midday, I've worked my way uphill through a forest of antler-rubbed eucalyptus not because I think there are any more deer on top of the ridge than at the bottom, but because, as Mallory once observed of a more famous mountain, it is there. Red deer share obvious characteristics with our own familiar wapiti (with which they also share common Eurasian genetics), and I'm relying heavily on my extensive elk hunting experience in my approach to this new quarry. The deer have gone to ground during the heat of the day, and Rule #1 during archery elk season reads: don't bump the animals from the bedding cover. Hence, I'm taking a deliberately unpromising route uphill, at least in terms of encounters with deer.

Which is not to say my hike has proved tedious. Granted, I have not met a koala, which I regret, or a brown snake, which I do not regret at all. In fact, the only reptile spotted has been a relatively benign carpeted python, and on a continent that supports seven of the world's ten most venomous snakes (not to mention saltwater crocodiles, great white sharks, scorpions, and the deadly *Chironex* jellyfish), this meager box score of menace feels positively reassuring. Semi-tropical Queensland's bird life turns out to be nearly as varied and intriguing as Africa's, and my route through the foliage has been virtually free of thorns, a fact I attribute to the area's lack of indigenous ungulate browsers. And then there are the wallabies, in all their various shapes and sizes.

Like most visitors, my preconceptions regarding Australia's unique family *Macropodidae* derived largely from such authoritative sources as childhood readings of *Winnie the Pooh*, from which I concluded that kangaroos and their relatives are all cute, cuddly, and dumb. Cute I'll still grant, at least with regard to the smaller species, but the rest is bunk. The wallabies here seem sharp as whitetail bucks at home, no doubt reflecting predatory pressure from dingoes, tracks of which abound. To make matters worse from a hunter's perspective, as they leap off, spooked wallabies thump the ground with their oversized hind toes much like stotting mule deer, and I've already noticed that everything in the bush pays attention to that sound. By this point in the hunt, the ubiquitous wallabies have already threatened to cross the line between objects of biologic interest and bloody nuisance.

However, my sense of natural curiosity just won't let go yet. Despite the biodiversity the class *Mammalia* has achieved, we've only figured out three ways to produce young from mothers. Placental mammals (including ourselves) dominate every biosphere on earth save one: Australia. Here, the only indigenous placental land mammals are bats. The rest, save for the egg-laying platypus, are marsupials like the wallaby, which are represented almost nowhere else on earth. (Notable local exception: our own southern 'possum.) *Why* is the world's most successful method of birthing totally absent among Australia's large mammals? *Why* are marsupials and egg-bearers found almost exclusively in Australia? These are questions that would have driven my fictional prototype Maturin to distraction, and true to form I want answers almost as badly as I want red deer.

And so, summit achieved at last, I settle into a soft spot in the shade not to glass for game, but to think.

By the time golden afternoon light has started to push the shadows across the hills from the west, I'm no closer to solving this mystery, and when the first stag roars, the transition from observer to hunter feels positively welcome.

Twenty minutes later, I have the deer on my radar: a fine mature stag accompanied by a small harem of hinds. They're working their way slowly down a grassy slope – stag bellowing, hinds feeding with stately disinterest in their would-be mate's attention. Sparse cover makes an approach to bow range look unlikely at first, but if they stay on track, they'll eventually cross a dry creek bed that promises ample room to maneuver.

After dropping back over the edge of the nearest ridge and double-timing downhill and around the corner, I wind up belly-crawling into what should be an excellent position for an ambush, although I'd appreciate a bit more consistency from the wind. When the lead hind passes by within easy range without detecting me, I experience a sudden flush of anticipation. But when the stag finally follows, he chooses a route half again as far away.

I'll ordinarily pass on shots like this especially if there seems to be any chance of closing a few yards, but this time the opportunity looks as good as it's going to get. When the stag grinds to a stop broadside and unsuspecting, I rise to one knee, pick a spot on his chest, draw, and release. Then I watch my cedar arrow sail one harmless inch above his shoulder as the hillside explodes in a clatter of hooves, breaking the spell of stealth under which I've operated for over an hour.

The post-game analysis proves short and sweet. I shoot my bow the same way I shoot a shotgun: by pure instinct, with no conscious estimation of range or trajectory. With long hours of practice, this simple technique works quite well under most circumstances. As I came to full draw, my mental computer flashed a subliminal message to my fire control center: *elk at 30 yards.* But despite all their similarities, red deer are substantially smaller than elk, and my quarry actually stood several paces closer. Simple ballistics took care of the rest.

And the rest, Shakespeare once observed of another well-known screw-up, is silence.

What lessons can I carry down off the hill as I trudge back toward camp, unblooded and mystified still by the alien idea of order surrounding me in the dark? First and foremost, simply this: science and instinct can both come a cropper given sufficient opportunity, and if we rely exclusively on either long enough in the field, each will surely fail us.

But above and beyond this simple measure of comeuppance, my one-day walkabout has allowed me to test the limits of sporting convention and redefine assumptions. In *Sand County Almanac*, Aldo

Leopold offers a splendid portrait of the naturalist as hunter and vice versa, an unstated thesis that has served me well over five decades in the outdoors. In the general rush to return from the field with more and bigger things, we would do well to remind ourselves that hunters are students first, and that the best experiences we enjoy in the woods are primarily the result of curiosity and observation. In conversations with non-hunters, I've often made the point that the best naturalists I know are hunters, and the more one chooses to limit one's methods of take in the field, the more this principle holds true. Our outdoor heritage owes more to the countless Lords who questioned and explored than to Lord Ripon, who simply chose to shoot and tally.

So, in the end, a confession: I don't have a red deer or an answer to all the mysteries wildlife poses in Australia's outback. But I know where to look for both.

CHAPTER EIGHT

Tiwi Bulls: 2003 Australia

WE'D SPENT TEN MINUTES studying the three bulls grazing in the open meadow 60 yards below the ridge, long enough to know that two were youngsters while the third was big enough to deserve an arrow... maybe. Since Australian bowhunter Dan Smith was the designated hitter that first night on northern Australia's remote Melville Island, he began to ease forward through the gum trees while Bill Baker, Brad Kane, and I spread out to help keep an eye on the buffalo. All three of us were glancing around at the trees as we moved, not because we needed more cover but because we wanted to know the location of the nearest escape route in case the hunters became the hunted.

Although he was moving with admirable stealth, Dan had barely taken a dozen steps when something alerted the buffalo to our presence. The two young bulls immediately snorted and trotted off into the scrub, but their big brother proved more belligerent... an adjective that was to occur to me repeatedly during the course of countless close encounters with buffalo to follow. Instead of retreating, he studied our position as if he was trying to decide which one of us had just shot his dog, and then he began to advance up the hill.

Several minutes later, the bull stood facing us some 20 yards from Dan while I mentally gauged my leap into the lower branches of the nearest tree. The frontal shot angle was obviously unacceptable, but to his credit Dan held his ground. At that range, I had no trouble determining that the bull was a representative but by no means exceptional specimen, and I knew that Dan was willing to hold out in hopes of the latter. After a long face-off, the animal turned and I saw Dan's bow arm start to come up, but he hesitated just as the bull evidently decided that he'd seen enough of us. After one last, contemptuous snort, he wheeled and galloped back down the hill in a cloud of dust, leaving us to breathe a collective sigh of relief in the wake of his departure.

"Tell me, Dan," I asked once the tension started to ease. "Did you hold off because he looked too small or because the situation looked too scary?"

"A bit of both, mate!" Dan acknowledged with a laugh.

Welcome to the Tiwi Islands, where the land is wild, the game imposing, and time in the field seldom passes for long without an opportunity to test one's mettle.

From the bowhunter's perspective, none of Australia's non-native ungulates is as imposing as the Asiatic water buffalo.

Originally imported from Timor, buffalo reached tropical Northern Australia in the 1820's. Australian stockmen originally planned to raise them commercially for their meat and hides, but the buffalo proved utterly unmanageable and quickly reverted to their wild state. Today, large populations thrive across Northern Australia's vast outback courtesy of their adaptability, the wildness of the terrain, and the lack of predators other than man. For a gripping account of the early commercial buffalo hunting days, refer to Tom Cole's excellent *Hell West and Crooked*, a first person memoir that offers an excellent portrait of the excitement and demands of life in the Australian bush.

The second largest island in Australia (exceeded in size only by Tasmania), Melville lies in the Arafura Sea an hour's flight north of Darwin, the hub of Australia's "Top End". Along with neighboring Bathurst Island, Melville constitutes the original homeland of the

Tiwi, arguably the most culturally distinct members of Australia's aboriginal people. Wild buffalo range freely on Melville, where they receive virtually no hunting pressure. When Bill Baker told me that he had secured permission to make an exploratory bowhunt on Melville and asked me to come along, I knew I'd just heard an offer I couldn't refuse. This adventure promised everything I love in a hunting trip: remote terrain that has hardly ever seen outsiders, exotic wildlife, and dangerous game. Of course, we recognized the possibility that the trip would turn into an utter bust, but as I've pointed out before, the notion of adventure travel without risk is an oxymoron.

Although I'd hunted Australia before and had a fair amount of experience with dangerous game elsewhere, our hunt was unusual for me in two respects, each defined by a missing piece of equipment.

The first was my own bow. Two months before our scheduled departure for the Islands, I'd headed out to our local bow range with Bill, who was visiting us in Montana at the time. He'd just picked up a new recurve from renowned local bowyer Dick Robertson and was understandably eager to try it out. All went well until I picked up my own bow to follow him on the first target and couldn't make my right arm work. Long story short: an old athletic injury had finally evolved into an acute cervical disc syndrome. By the end of the week, Lori and I had canceled a scheduled trip to Africa and I was headed to the operating room.

We'd spent a lot of time working on a complex African itinerary, and missing our safari was disappointing. In fact, I was ready to get on the airplane and try to make the best of it right arm or no right arm, but Lori put on her nurse's hat and vetoed that idea in short order. But our Tiwi Island adventure, scheduled six weeks later, sounded so exciting that I just couldn't pass it up. There's only one first exploratory trip to virgin country, and I couldn't bear to miss this one. By the time I left for Australia, my spinal surgeon had declared the operation a success, but my right arm was still far too weak to draw a bow capable of driving an arrow through a buffalo. I left anyway, determined to act as scout, tracker, photographer, skinner, and camp fisherman even if I couldn't hunt.

The second missing item was a backup rifle. As a longtime admirer of bowhunting legend Bill Negley, I'd always respected his eventual decision to leave all firearms behind during his final hunts for the African Big Five. While I've hunted all North American dangerous game without backup and spent plenty of time close to elephants and buffalo in Africa with no rifle around, I also recognized that Australian buffalo are huge, unpredictable animals with a deserved reputation for aggressive behavior when wounded. However, one inevitable effect of having a rifle along on a bowhunt is to make dangerous game less dangerous, and after a long discussion in Darwin the night before our departure for base camp in Snake Bay, the four of us made a unanimous decision: when we headed out to our camp in the bush, the .458 would stay behind. While we experienced several situations during the course of the hunt that made us question the wisdom of that decision, in the end we all agreed that we'd learned a whole lot more about buffalo than we would have otherwise.

By the third day of the hunt, Dan had enjoyed multiple close range encounters with buffalo, including several bulls that I frankly would have taken in a heartbeat. But only the hunter himself can decide when an animal meets his personal standards, and as anxious as we all were to see what happened when an arrow struck one of those huge, black bulls, we respected Dan's decision to hold out for one that met his.

By that point, however, I could see Bill's own bow arm start to twitch. Although he was one of Australia's most accomplished and respected bowhunters, he'd never killed a buffalo and not because of lack of effort. Even the most experienced bowhunters often have a curse species as we've seen before, and buffalo were his. He'd logged countless days in the outback chasing buffalo only to be undone by the usual litany of factors that can be a bowhunter's undoing, from treacherous winds to country that didn't contain the animals it was supposed to hold. Now, surrounded by buffalo in a pristine wilderness setting, his own eagerness had grown palpable.

Our original plan had been for Dan to take the first bull and me the second, in the event that my arm recovered sufficiently to let me draw an adequate bow. But with Dan being choosey and my arm still at half-strength, we reached an obvious conclusion over breakfast one morning. We would split our party in two, and Dan would hunt in Brad's capable company while I did my best to help Bill break his curse.

At first light, Bill and I bailed out of the Landcruiser to hunt our way down a long, winding creek to the sea. We'd found buffalo there the morning before as the animals worked their way uphill toward their bedding cover after feeding all night on a large grass flat just above the beach, and Dan had actually passed up a respectable bull there after a careful stalk. With a steady sea breeze in our faces we knew we'd enjoy a favorable wind until mid-morning, and the brush along the creek provided ideal stalking cover.

A half hour later, Bill hit the brakes a few steps ahead of me as the first wave of buffalo appeared right on schedule. With just enough time to take cover in the bushes, we soon had animals in bow range although they all proved to be cows, calves, and young bulls. While cows are substantially smaller than bulls, their horns can be even longer and they are notoriously unpredictable whenever they perceive danger to their young. Needless to say, I kept this fact firmly in mind as the first cow-calf unit wandered past me a dozen steps away, especially since the animals' sudden appearance had caught us farther from the nearest climbing trees than we would have liked.

It took the herd nearly an hour to work its way by. Although some of the animals eventually caught our wind, they managed to trot off uphill without spooking the whole group. "I guess that's it, mate," Bill finally sighed as the last of them disappeared behind us, allowing a welcome opportunity to break radio silence and stretch our knotted muscles.

"But the big bull was lagging behind the main mob yesterday," I reminded him. "Let's wait a bit before we head farther downhill." Just then, a flash of ebony appeared in the foliage ahead, and our binoculars quickly confirmed that this was the animal we were after.

In no apparent hurry, the bull was feeding noisily as he came into view and Bill took full advantage of the cover and the racket to close the gap. At 20 yards, I watched him ease an arrow onto his string, but by pure chance the animal turned to face him. Although still unaware, he no longer offered an acceptable shot angle. Riveted to my field glasses, I watched the unsuspecting buffalo feed his way to a distance from Bill that we later measured at nine paces. At that point, the huge animal glanced up, realized that Bill's camouflaged figure hadn't been there earlier, and began one of the tensest stare-downs I've ever witnessed.

The point blank face-off eventually lasted 30 minutes by my watch. While I give Bill full credit for iron nerves, I couldn't help but notice his occasional sidelong glance in the direction of the nearest trees, none of which looked nearly stout enough to stand up to an angry buffalo. I also realized that if I'd been carrying a rifle I would have had the bead on the animal's neck the whole time, and frankly there were several points during the long confrontation when I missed it. At long last the bull turned, but instead of galloping off, he took a few steps quartering away and that was all Bill needed. Mesmerized, I watched his bow arm come back, and then a sound like a baseball bat hitting a pumpkin rose from the brush, and the bull disappeared into the scrub.

Unable to see the hit or mark the animal's retreat for more than a few yards because of the brush, I eagerly debriefed Bill once the dust had settled.

"It was right there, mate," he assured me. "Tight behind the shoulder angling forward, with plenty of penetration. I'm guessing heart."

Now came crunch time and we both knew it. We debated some options but in the end only one course of action remained. After giving the trail an hour we eased into the cover, taking turns with one of us watching ahead for trouble while the other kept his eyes on the spoor. After a hundred yards of white knuckles, I climbed over a log and there lay the bull, dead in mid-stride by the look of the way his horns had augered into the ground, a broadhead mark in the shoulder crease and, as our subsequent autopsy confirmed, a hole in his heart just as Bill had predicted.

So much for *that* curse.

Two days later, Dan killed a fine old bull with massive horn bases, by happy coincidence the same animal that I'd photographed nearby the night before.

In the interval, interesting events had taken place in and about my neck and right shoulder. Finally, the strength in my biceps and deltoid was beginning to return. Although nowhere near full strength, I found that I could draw Bill's #69 recurve to the center of my chest, and in camp I was consistently hitting empty cans at 20 yards with this unconventional style. On the last day of the hunt I decided I was ready to give it a try, although I made it perfectly clear to my mates that I planned to be conservative and would decline any shot that didn't feel absolutely perfect at the moment of truth.

That afternoon, we struck out for new country: a remote inland lake that Lawrence, our local Aboriginal/Malay companion, said held countless crocodiles within its waters and numerous buffalo about its banks. Since it was too early in the day to hunt, we took a detour past a saltwater creek to fish on the making tide. Barramundi--Australia's premier estuarine game fish--were pouring up the creek. For an hour, we took turns casting and watching for crocodiles while I enjoyed some of the most exciting fly-fishing in memory. Finally, with an Esky (Australian for cooler) full of fresh fish for dinner, we set off in search of a miracle.

After another hour of driving and a short hike through the scrub, we broke out upon a remarkable sight: a broad lake choked with lily pads, teeming with tropical water birds, and surrounded by buffalo. After checking the wind, we eased down the inlet creek--ever mindful of lurking crocs--and wound up 30 yards from the edge of a herd numbering a hundred animals just on the other side. Since the cover across the creek was sparse and no one relished the idea of wading the stream, we appeared to be at a stalemate. But then a cow spotted something and snorted, and our evening grew interesting indeed.

As a handful of cows scattered, the bull behind them began to advance. Several minutes later, he stood facing us in the middle of the stream a dozen yards away. While we'd had several similar encounters with aggressive bulls that week, something about this animal's attitude made me nervous--along with everyone else, I learned later. Nonetheless, I eased an arrow onto the string and resolved to shoot him if he opened up and offered a perfect shot.

While I'm usually crestfallen when a close encounter with game comes to naught, I have to admit that I breathed a sigh of relief when the bull finally turned to gallop off. For just an instant, he presented a quartering angle that I would have taken if I'd been in perfect form and carrying my own 85# bow, but I wasn't. As the bull tore off through the herd, he spooked the whole lot of them and for several minutes we stood and watched the spectacle of buffalo churning wildly across the shallow lake. Somehow, that seemed a perfect way to end a remarkable trip.

"You were going to shoot that bull if he stopped, weren't you mate?" Bill asked once the commotion died down.

"Yeah," I admitted. "I was."

"I was afraid of that," he noted with a laugh. "Don't worry, mate; you'll get him next year when your arm's back in shape."

I certainly hoped so.

But my trip to Australia wasn't over yet, and I still had something to prove even if only to myself. After we left buffalo country, Bill and I paid a quick visit to our friends Ernest and Robyn at Toomba Station. I still couldn't pull my own bow properly since I couldn't raise my arm to shoulder level, but using my unconventional new mid-chest anchor, I did reasonably well with one of Bill's, a gem of a longbow made by our old friend and bowyer Glen Newell, who had stood beside me on our first morning at Toomba as we watched Lori kill the first hog of the trip. After some practice shots, I felt ready to hunt.

That night, I worked my way into a mob of pigs that included two old boars fighting over a sow. With so many keen noses about and a fickle wind, I didn't give the stalk much chance of success. But one of the old Basalt Warriors cut from the pack at just the right time, and when he huffed his way past me, I drew and released. The broadhead cut through his heart before it buried in his off shoulder, and I watched him go down a dozen yards away.

And so I left Australia with a pig to my credit rather than the buffalo bull I'd planned so long and tried so hard to kill. But that old boar confirmed that I truly was on the road to recovery, and that alone made the whole trip worthwhile. The only way to establish closure seemed to be a return trip the following year.

By the time we reached civilization again back in Darwin, we were already making plans.

Don with the Basalt Warrior that marked
the beginning of his recovery from neck surgery.

A Tiwi bull offers a "buffalo stare."

CHAPTER NINE

Tiwi Bulls: 2004
Australia

WHEN THE GRAZING BULL'S HEAD pivoted suddenly and caught me mid-stride, bovine tranquility evaporated at once, replaced by a withering look that simultaneously suggested curiosity, contempt, and an utter lack of respect for the camouflaged figure crouched 20 yards away. I'd had considerable close range experience with the species by this time, but I couldn't decipher the animal's mood beyond the realization that I suddenly had its complete attention. And with the nearest climbing tree over a hundred yards away, he most certainly had mine.

Quartering toward me, the bull offered nothing but massive neck and forequarters, an unthinkable shot for my recurve. The next move was clearly up to him. The possibilities ranged from a charge to a snort and clatter of hoofs in the opposite direction, undoing all the effort I'd invested in the long, careful stalk. But I'd learned enough about Asiatic water buffalo to anticipate a long, tense face-off that just might end with an opportunity to slam an arrow through his ribs… if I could maintain my discipline and composure. At the moment, that *if* looked as big as the bull himself.

I don't know why animals I'm stalking always seem to become

suspicious when I'm in the most uncomfortable position imaginable, a circumstance too common to be explained by chance alone. But there I was again, weight concentrated awkwardly on one leg, back throbbing in a contorted semi-crouch, certain that any motion on my part would break the spell and result in consequences ranging from adverse to disastrous. Flies buzzed at my ears and sweat ran down my forehead as the bull slowly licked each of his nostrils so that moisture from his tongue might allow him to pick up the extra molecule of scent he needed to identify me. There was nothing to do but wait out the confrontation. As minutes ticked by beneath the blazing tropical sun, I tried to take my mind off my discomfort by reflecting on the long, tortuous path I'd taken toward this imposing ton of trouble.

As I'd learned the year before as a non-combatant, the formidable Asiatic swamp buffalo, *Bubalus bubalis,* arrived in Australia from Timor in 1828. Originally intended as a source of meat and hides, the buffalo had other ideas and promptly dispersed across what is now Australia's Northern Territory, colloquially known as the Top End. The hardy stockmen and commercial hunters with whom the buffalo shared their new home granted them abundant respect based on their size and occasionally evil temper. For nearly 200 years, buffalo stories have enlivened the legends of Australia's outback much as bear tales crop up around campfires in Alaska.

When these animals began to attract attention from American bowhunters a decade or so previously, they were initially viewed as a tune up for their better-known African relative, the Cape buffalo. With the benefit of experience, a number of observers familiar with both species (myself included) now think those priorities could easily be reversed. In terms of size, body structure, and outlook on life (and hunters), the two species are quite similar, differing primarily in the shape of their horns, which sweep backwards in graceful, glossy arcs on the Asiatic version. While their vision is only fair, their ears and noses are both excellent, and their personality can be summarized with two adjectives: *belligerent* and *unpredictable.* However, I will concede that a wounded Asiatic buffalo isn't as malignantly clever as a Cape. That doesn't mean that following up a wounded bull without firearms isn't utterly daft. It just means that it isn't quite as daft as it would be in Africa.

My personal feelings about my favorite big game species invariably depend on impressions of habitat as much as the quarry itself. No doubt this contributes to my fascination with Australian buffalo. I've lived in Alaska and spent months in the bush from Siberia to Africa, but I've never seen wilderness quite like the Tiwi Islands.

Melville and nearby Bathurst Island seem to belong to another epoch. Forget any sense of the confinement one might experience on a South Pacific atoll; Melville is as good a place to get lost as any I know. The islands are an aboriginal homeland today, and entrance to the area requires permission from the local governing council. Far more buffalo than people inhabit the island, and once you bounce off down the road from the landing strip in Snake Bay you shouldn't expect human company until you decide to bounce back. Imagine Alaska's North Slope with palms, gum trees, and haunting green cycads instead of tundra. The emptiness carries the same emotional impact.

Bill and I had set out that first morning of the hunt to stalk our way along a meandering creek bed that the Australian dry season had turned into a series of mud holes. Our quarry is called water buffalo for a reason, and we knew that as the temperature began to rise, bulls would appear from the surrounding thickets to enjoy their daily wallow. I was due at the plate, and after all the frustration my inability to hunt had caused the year before, I meant to take the first mature bull that offered a perfect shot.

We'd covered two miles by the time we spotted the lone bull grazing through the grass. The terrain was open, but every time he lowered his head to feed the dense vegetation obscured his vision, so I decided to try the stalk. Before I left the cover of the brush, I quickly rechecked my tackle: #78 recurve, 1000 gr. wood arrows made from Brazilian walnut, carefully honed 2-blade broadheads. After surgery, it had taken me months to rebuild enough arm strength to handle that bow, but I felt confident that my gear was up to the job. I'd originally planned to hunt with a set of #85 limbs, but I'd learned the previous year that precise shot placement matters more than bow draw weight, and I felt fully confident of the tackle I was carrying.

The wind held steady, and an hour's worth of cat-and-mouse eventually brought me into bow range... and the uncomfortable standoff described earlier. Somehow, I maintained my contorted position for 20 minutes without moving anything but my eyes. What happened next defines an important difference between buffalo and North American hoofed game. Even if I'd survived that kind of scrutiny from an elk or a mule deer, the animal would almost certainly have resumed feeding away from me. But when the bull lowered his head to graze again he actually continued in my direction, no doubt confident of his ability to deal with me if I turned out to be some kind of threat after all.

For bowhunters, especially those carrying traditional longbows or recurves, the problem on open country stalks usually reduces to: *get close enough!* But as the range narrowed from 20 yards to 12, proximity was no longer an issue. I needed a perfect shot angle-- dead broadside to slightly quartering away--but for what seemed like an eternity the bull refused to offer one. When he finally began to open up, the middle three fingers of my right hand tightened on the bowstring. But I wasn't ready yet: his near foreleg needed to come forward, opening up as much of his thorax as possible. And so I continued to wait, fully aware that one random puff of breeze could make the long stalk unravel at any moment.

But finally the moment of truth arrived. Concentrating on an imaginary spot the size of a nickel tight against the shoulder crease, I came to full draw while the bull's eyes remained shielded by the grass. This was no time to question one's ability or equipment, and as my right thumb knuckle hit the familiar anchor point on my jaw, I reminded myself of the countless hours of practice I'd invested in this shot and all the lethal energy stored in my recurve's graceful limbs. Then, by way of the mysterious process Eugen Herrigel describes so eloquently in *Zen in the Art of Archery*, the arrow was away.

From the moment I began to draw, I'd never doubted the outcome of the shot despite the notorious difficulty of bringing down a buffalo cleanly. My arrow vanished into the bull's ribs leaving three white fletches marking the spot I'd isolated earlier. I knew the animal was dead even if he didn't. Trying my best to remain inconspicuous, I stayed frozen with my bow arm extended as the bull spun, lurched forward, trotted 50 yards, and sank to the ground for good.

It would be hard to describe the week that followed as anti-climax. I enjoyed some unique fly-fishing and spent a lot of time with my camera. By the time we left our remote bush camp fellow bowhunters Mark Viehwig and Ed Schlief had also killed bulls, adding up to a remarkable record of accomplishment for hunters armed with nothing but sticks and string. To add to the satisfaction of the week's conclusion, Lori was waiting for me when we finally rolled back into Snake Bay. The clear winner of the IQ contest, she'd spent the week touring the New Zealand coast with Bill's wife Linda and Dan Smith's wife Lanee while we'd been living with the crocodiles. But she and I had scheduled a couple of extra days on Melville to explore the rich local waters with our fly rods, and I couldn't imagine a better way to end the trip.

After all the heat, dust, and bugs it should have been easy to say goodbye to Melville Island for the last time, but something about the austere beauty of the place and the sheer excitement of all those close range encounters with dangerous game made that impossible.

The moment I climbed into the airplane for the ride back to Darwin, I knew I'd be back.

Denny Sturgis enters the Red Zone with a Tiwi bull.

CHAPTER TEN

Tiwi Bulls: 2007
Australia

BY THE TIME I made my third trip to Melville Island I had become good friends with Lawrence Priddy, the only permanent resident of the island's remote eastern end save for his wife, Marjorie. Lawrence's complex ethnic background establishes his credentials as a member of Australia's Lost Generation. As poignantly documented in the film *Rabbit Proof Fence*, Australia's government, in a fit of cultural hubris prior to the Second World War, decided that all aboriginal children should be removed from their families and educated in English-speaking boarding schools. Having none of that, his aboriginal mother hid him in the bush where he honed survival skills most of his contemporaries were rapidly losing. This trial by fire evidently proved effective, for Lawrence and Marjorie have been living alone in the wilderness for decades, and this is the kind of country where survival does not come easily.

Lawrence had never seen a fly rod until we met during our first exploratory trip. I couldn't shoot my heavy buffalo bow then, but I could cast, however awkwardly. Many of my scouting contributions to that expedition took place near the waterline while I was carrying my fly rod. There I fell in love with barramundi, and even after years spent trotting the globe with my fly rod, they remain one of my favorite game fish.

Now I had been charged with keeping our camp supplied with fresh fish, and Lawrence signed on enthusiastically to this project. Fish swim in his blood, and no wonder. He and Marjorie only eat three things: fresh vegetables from their garden, rice from the general store in Snake Bay, and barramundi. His taste in fish is that specific. The local mangrove jack, golden snapper, and threadfin salmon are all delicious but Lawrence turns up his nose at them. On his plate, it's ocean fresh barra or nothing. On my third trip to the island Denny Sturgis killed a good bull early, but after several nights of tasty but chewy buffalo steaks--which Lawrence refused to eat--everyone in camp was ready for some fresh fish on the barby, no one more so than Lawrence.

"There's one thing now, Don," he reminded me as we slogged across the saline mud toward the tidal creek in front of his plywood and canvas fish camp. "None of this kissing them and putting them back in the water. I've got me knife."

Indeed he did: a long, wicked blade unencumbered by a sheath, more than ready to slice through a fly line or somebody's thigh in a moment of carelessness. But we'd worked this out three years earlier when, after keeping two nice barra for dinner, I'd slid the third fish I landed back into the creek. Lawrence's subsequent apoplexy provided the springboard for a long discussion about releasing fish versus eating them. The unforgettable taste of those exquisite, flaky fillets at the table that night enforced my concession to local custom. Now I was glad Lawrence had his knife. No worries, mate.

Surprisingly strong tides run along the shores of the Arafura Sea. Our plan that morning was to launch Lawrence's dinghy, fish our way up the creek on the rising water, and drift back down to camp on the ebb. Our boat did not inspire confidence. Flimsy as a tin can and not much more seaworthy, I'd learned earlier that its "slow leak", as Lawrence described it, was a relative term. Maintaining freeboard required nearly constant bailing. Operating in close waters, the porous hull wouldn't have been a serious problem except for a second issue: the ubiquitous presence of crocodiles substantially longer than our boat.

By natural coincidence, the range of the barramundi coincides almost perfectly with the range of the Australian saltwater croc, one of the few black-hatted bad guys in the animal kingdom whose behavior in the wild actually justifies its reputation. Few creatures on earth look so evil, but it's the ones you never see that you have to worry about. As we dragged the dinghy down from the mangroves above the high water mark toward the creek, we intercepted a spanking fresh set of croc tracks. The skid mark from the tail was wider and deeper than the one the boat left.

I've spent plenty of time at close quarters with dangerous game all over the world, but I'm not embarrassed to admit that "salties" scare me. Since I love fishing too much to stay away from the water, I'd developed two coping mechanisms. The first was to remind myself that I'd led a full life, and that in a worst-case scenario nothing would hurt for long. The second was to trust Lawrence's judgment. After seven decades in the bush, his crocodile avoidance instincts have passed Darwinian muster. If he saw no problem paddling a leaky, unstable boat down a muddy creek lined with crocodile tracks, I shouldn't either. Or something like that.

Underway at last, I braced myself against the gunwale and began to roll a flashy streamer in against the mangroves while the brisk tidal current swept us inland guided by an occasional paddle stroke from Lawrence in the bow. Unusually high tides had turned the current the color of clay, but I remained unfazed by the lack of visibility. Several days earlier I'd fished the same water under similar conditions and raised more than enough big barra to make me forget about the crocodiles.

But not this time. Lawrence, who has probably caught more barramundi than any man alive, offered a running commentary of explanations involving wind, weather, moon, stars, and other imponderables. I'd heard them all before and the bottom line remained unchanged: no one really understands the mysterious switch that makes barra feed voraciously or go to ground.

Two hours later, the flood had carried us up into a swamp just below the broad, salty plain separating the inter-tidal zone from the jungle. Since we weren't going back toward the sea in the dinghy until the water began to drop, I resigned myself to two idle hours of sweat and bugs, but Lawrence, obviously dismayed by the thought of another buffalo dinner, wasn't ready to throw in the towel yet.

"You've never minded a bit of a walk, eh Don?" he asked as he gave his fillet knife a few hopeful strokes from his sharpening steel.

"Never," I assured him.

"There's a creek down the way that might hold barra up above the tide."

"How far would that be, Lawrence?" I asked pointlessly.

"Not far." No surprises there, as that was the one and only estimate of distance I'd ever heard from him.

After tying the dinghy off on a snag, we slogged through a bit more crocodile habitat than I cared for before we reached the relative security of the pan. The two-mile hike down a series of buffalo pads passed quickly to the rhythm of further exposition from Lawrence upon the mysterious habits of barramundi. Finally, we crested a shallow bank and broke out upon a series of interconnected potholes stretching inland toward the trees. The first pool looked like a well used buffalo wallow. We had arrived.

"Ever catch barra here?" I asked as I studied the water.

"No," Lawrence acknowledged. "But I saw dead ones here once just before The Wet."

I had accumulated enough experience with barramundi by this time to feel less despair than a typical naive visitor armed with a fly rod might have felt in the face of such gloomy water. Like our own snook, barramundi live a catadramous life cycle, the mirror image of a salmon's. Maturing inland in fresh or brackish water, they descend to the sea to spawn, depending on high tides and seasonal storms to carry them back inland. The result is often large barra in strange places, and I'd caught them in less promising water than this.

Nonetheless, I worked my way through the first several pools without drawing a strike while Lawrence followed along and worked on his knife blade. Clouds of exotic water birds wheeled overhead, and given the silence from the water, distraction and inattention became inevitable. Hence my helpless surprise when a savage boil erupted suddenly behind my fly just as I lifted it from the water to begin another cast.

"There's fish in here!" I cried like the first fool to strike gold at Sutter's Mill.

"But damn it, Don!" Lawrence cried mournfully. "They're *still* in there!"

Focused back on the water again, I made an observation that should have occurred to me earlier. As the distance from the tide's reach increased, the water had grown progressively clearer in each pool along the creek's route into the trees. Although hardly a Montana trout stream, the pool where I'd raised the first fish looked like honest largemouth bass water rather than a mud hole. Suddenly, I knew where I had to be.

"I'm heading that way," I announced, pointing the tip of my #8-weight toward the jungle.

"I don't know, Don," Lawrence replied as his perpetual smile dissolved in a worried look. I suddenly realized that this was the first time I'd ever heard him suggest trepidation about anything.

"What's up there?" I asked, nodding my head toward the brush.

"Dunno," he answered evasively. "This and that."

Well, hell. After weeks of tromping about the island, I'd already stared down buffalo, watched four-meter crocs sink into the water I was fishing, and stepped around a king brown or two. Big barra do not fall to the faint of heart. The outback had thrown down its glove and it was now my turn to pick it up or walk away. Someday the inevitable triumph of enthusiasm over discretion in my outdoor decision-making will no doubt undo me, but not yet. I hoped.

At the edge of the trees, solar oven sunshine began to merge with dappled light. The water looked more inviting than any I'd seen yet, but obstructions along the bank made casting impossible. The smell of the sea and the noise of the birds receded as I eased forward. High above, the last of the sea breeze murmured through the treetops as dense foliage closed overhead. In terrain baked constantly by brutal tropical sun, these were the deepest shadows I'd ever encountered on the island.

Glancing ahead in search of an opening, I suddenly noticed darkness beyond what the shadows could explain. As fragments of the visual puzzle coalesced, I realized I was staring at a solitary buffalo bull. Asiatic swamp buffalo remind me of grizzly bears: no matter how many of them you've seen, the next encounter always manages to take your breath away. The irony proved impossible to ignore. After all the meticulous effort I'd invested stalking into point-blank range of one I could kill with my bow, I'd blundered into one of the biggest bulls I'd seen on the island while armed with nothing but a fly rod.

Standing in the shadows, the bull looked as black as a certain whale once looked white. I knew full well that most buffalo will lumber away at the first whiff of human scent. But, as with grizzlies, it's the other 1% that demand undivided attention. The bull stared at me and I stared back until the breeze sucked at my face and sent him crashing off through the underbrush, leaving me to wonder if I really wanted to continue this exercise.

Thirty yards beyond the buffalo, the brush thinned along the bank. As I approached and studied the geometric arrangement of trees and snags, I concluded that advancing along a fallen log across the pool might allow me 20 feet of casting room. That's when I noticed the skid marks in the mud on the opposite bank. A single shaft of sunlight illuminated the tracks well enough for me to determine that they were glistening fresh and headed toward the water. As my eyes scanned the perimeter of the pool, I confirmed that the track never came back out.

Even so, I couldn't bring myself to retreat to the security of open ground without throwing my streamer into the pool. Dissuaded from the log by the crocodile sign, I reached around a tree and flicked an abbreviated roll cast between the snags, wondering how I would ever manage to drag a big barra from that rat hole. Because of the obstructions, I could barely strip the fly the length of my rod, but as I gave it one last twitch, a huge surge of water swelled beneath it and left me staring at the Mother of All Barramundi.

This gender-specific allusion is deliberate: born male, all barra undergo a mid-life sex change, so the really big ones are ladies. Over a meter long and thick as my thigh, the fish smacked the fly and sounded as I struck reflexively... a decision that I can only say sounded like a good idea at the time. Everything snapped at once out in the gloomy warren of snags: leader, rod tip, even the dead limb I was holding for support. It was time to retreat.

"What did you find in there?" Lawrence asked as I rejoined him back in the sunlight. He'd already realized I wasn't carrying anything good for dinner but seemed to be taking his disappointment in stride.

"This and that," I replied without elaboration. At the moment, he didn't need to hear more of my stories any more than I needed to hear more of his. I had lost all sense of time back in the darkness of the jungle, but the tide hadn't. We arrived back at the skiff to find the waterline a half-mile away. Our easy Huck Finn ride back down to fish camp had vanished as definitively as the barra in the shadowed pool. We double checked the knot on the skiff's bowline and set off on foot.

Midway through the long hike back to camp, I pulled my fishing hat off to swat a particularly annoying group of bugs. On the front, the cap bore the logo of the Backcountry Flyfishing Association, a Florida group I'd addressed several times before. The words *Catch and Release* were stitched on the back There, I decided, lay the origin of my comeuppance. There's certainly nothing wrong with releasing fish (Lawrence's opinion notwithstanding) and under these wilderness circumstances there wasn't anything wrong with killing a few either. But all the world loathes a hypocrite, and I had sinned by proclaiming one standard while practicing—or at least intending to practice-- another.

Back at fish camp at last, I dug my backup rod out of the back of the truck and walked down to the creek to make one last effort to catch a barra for dinner. I took my hat off before I made the first cast.

On this trip, I had a lot on my mind beside buffalo, and no wonder.

Several months earlier, Bill had called to chat about recent events at Toomba and discuss some final arrangements for the busy season ahead at the Melville camp. After a few hunting stories, he mentioned in passing that he'd been experiencing some indigestion and had lost some 20 pounds, which he, in contrast to some of us, didn't have to lose. A warning light flashed immediately; decades of internal medicine practice had taught me that unintentional weight loss is a serious symptom, and I urged prompt evaluation. Tests revealed the worst, and by the time I reached Australia he'd been through several rounds of chemotherapy.

Bill obviously wasn't going to make it to Melville Island, but he was determined that the show must go on, and Brad, Dan, and I resolved to do the best we could. When we arrived in Townsville to head for Toomba before going on to Darwin, Linda bravely brought Bill out to the airport, ostensibly to go over some last minute checklists and hunting plans. But the visit was about far more than that, and by the time we hit the road I knew I'd never see him again.

The terrain looked oddly different when we finally arrived on the island, and it took some serious reflection to decipher my sense of *jamais vu*. A terrific cyclone had scoured the branches from the canopy overhead and the tropical sunlight suddenly flooding the under story had triggered suckers to sprout from the roots of the ubiquitous Morton Bay ash. Furthermore, late rains had delayed the usual dry season burns. The result was a luxuriant carpet of head-high foliage that looked nearly impenetrable in places. No wonder I didn't see a single buffalo during the three-hour ride from the Snake Bay airstrip to our bush camp. But as a glass-half-full optimist, I reminded myself that while the bulls might be unusually hard to spot this season, the unexpectedly dense cover would facilitate stalking to the intimate ranges we needed for quick kills. How close is that? Fifteen yards, ten, five… close enough so that hunters who have been there will never forget the experience.

I wasn't going to think about shooting a buffalo myself until everyone in our first group – Michigan bowhunters Denny Sturgis, Dick Engle, and Gary Smith – had killed one of their own, so I spent several thoughtful days fishing, taking pictures, and helping other members of our party locate good bulls and ease into bow range. Eventually Dick and Denny each had a bull on the ground, and Gary had decided that his aging shoulders weren't up to pulling a heavy buffalo bow. At the urging of my campmates, I decided to string my own bow and go hunting.

My first stalk that day unraveled courtesy of a flock of parrots. I had successfully maneuvered within 15 yards of an excellent bull when the birds overhead took exception to my presence. Buffalo are seldom as naïve as they look. At the first alarm cries from above the bull exploded in flight, never to be seen again.

Dan Smith and I were exploring a new area chosen after reviewing the topo map, and our calculations proved accurate for once. The creek bed we sought still held water, the buffalo had turned the pools into wallows, and the wallows were full of bulls… big bulls. In fact, my next two stalks went south when new buffalo appeared from the brush, wandered downwind of my position, and spooked before my original quarry offered a shot.

Finally, I spotted a heavy old bull plodding down a pad through the brush with the wind at his back. After nearly an hour of cat and mouse at close range, he still hadn't offered the broadside I needed. I finally decided to cut a wide loop around him and hope he continued on course.

Good landmarks are few and far between in this terrain, but 20 minutes later I was right where I thought I needed to be. The bad news: I wasn't. The good news: Dan had noted the landmarks more accurately than I had, and he won the whispered argument about where we were in relationship to the bull. After cutting another circle through the brush the bull's black outline suddenly appeared 50 yards down the trail, and it seemed obvious that we were on a collision course. I barely had time to back into the cycads on the downwind side of the pad and nock an arrow when my field of vision filled with buffalo.

As the bull continued toward a position that would place him broadside at three yards, he seemed to offer a target impossible to miss. But experienced hands know better, and I concentrated carefully on my anatomic landmarks as I timed my draw to match his stride. Then my heavy arrow smacked into his chest and disappeared. Seconds later, the huge animal collapsed 70 yards away.

Was I afraid of being that close to an animal that could have laid me open with a single toss of its horns? Not until I thought about it back in camp that night...

When Denny and Dick left the island with two bulls apiece, it was time to start anew. Brad, Dan, and I were operating with an unusual degree of motivation. At that point, every bowhunter who had visited the Melville camp had gone home with a buffalo, a remarkable record of which Bill was justifiably proud. In his failing voce at the Townsville airport, he'd told us how important it was to him to keep that streak alive, and medicine had taught me how important such considerations can be to people in his circumstances. The three of us vowed that if anyone went home without a buffalo, it would not be for lack of effort on our part. (Of course, Brad and Dan kindly acknowledged that my fly rod expeditions were essential to keeping the camp supplied with food.)

When Jay Campbell's first three stalks produced no shots thanks to last minute visual detection by the quarry, Dan suggested borrowing from the playbook he and Bill had developed years earlier for chital stags and red deer. While I cut a dozen thick shooters from the jungle floor, Dan produced a roll of electrical tape from his pack. When we set off again 15 minutes later, each of us carried a portable shield of foliage in front of us. When Burnham Wood comes to Dunsinane...

An hour later, we spotted a big bull feeding in the grass just above a creek bottom full of wallows. The cover looked sparse, but the morning sea breeze had just kicked in reliably from the southeast. Moving cautiously when the bull's head was down and freezing behind his makeshift green shield whenever the animal paused to survey his surroundings, Jay eventually reached a clump of cycads 20 yards ahead of the bull. From there, it was just a matter of waiting for the quarry to feed into bow range and offer a broadside.

The wind held steady throughout the long wait, and then I saw the muscles in the back of Jay's neck begin to tense. Moments later he'd reached an effortless full draw, and when his arrow buried tight behind the shoulder crease moments later I knew we'd spend the rest of the morning packing buffalo meat for its eventual distribution to the locals in Snake Bay.

Back in camp that night, the news that Jay's wife Karen had just become the first woman we knew to kill an Asiatic swamp buffalo with a longbow only made the day's events feel sweeter.

Writers sometimes make descriptions of really good hunting sound too easy. Australian buffalo are tougher than this narrative makes them sound. They possess keen senses, effective stalking requires meticulous technique, and there are no tree stands or ground blinds to aid in the pursuit. Killing one cleanly with an arrow requires sustained training with heavy bows and icy nerves at the moment of truth. See Fred Bear's *Field Notes*; he regarded his Brazilian hunt for the same species as one of the most difficult in his career. We kept on killing bulls on Melville Island because the remote wilderness terrain provided abundant opportunities, and we'd learned a lot about bowhunting buffalo. When my good friend Doug Borland suggested that buffalo must be pushovers if everyone who went to Melville got one, I pointed out that if every bowhunter in Alaska had stalking opportunities on 20 good moose a day, all of them would kill good bulls too.

When Montana bowhunter Rich Johnson killed his bull near the end of the trip, Bill's record remained intact, and by the end of the week we were done for the season. But what of the future? Melville had been Bill's project from the start and it obviously wouldn't be the same without him, but Brad, Dan, and I were still keen to keep the camp going for several reasons. We realized we'd stumbled into one of the best dangerous game bowhunting opportunities in the world, and we couldn't think of a better tribute to Bill and all he'd done for Australian bowhunting than introducing more hunters to that opportunity. But during the course of the trip we'd already learned that due to complex local political concerns beyond the scope of this discussion, that wasn't going to happen. Bowhunting on Melville Island was over for the foreseeable future.

There's a lesson in that development for all of us. I can't count the number of bowhunters who wanted to book a trip to Melville Island after they'd read one of my articles or watched one of my slide presentations, but most of them wanted to go "in a couple of years"... when the economy improved, when their kids were through with school, when their back stopped hurting, whatever. From the Soviet Far East in 1990 to Zimbabwe to Australia two decades later, I've explored all kinds of remarkable wilderness hunting opportunities that were just too good to last. There will always come a time when a couple of years evaporates as an option, so as the advertisement says:

Just do it.

CHAPTER ELEVEN

Bowhunting Middle Earth
New Zealand

BRIGHT AND EARLY one February morning, Lori, Kiwi hunting partner Kevin Low, and I stepped outside an isolated public mountain hut in New Zealand's majestic Southern Alps to nurse our steaming cups of coffee and formulate a plan for the day. Although we were only a dozen miles or so beyond the end of the road, the previous afternoon's helicopter flight through the towering peaks had carried us across enough rugged terrain to leave us effectively isolated from the civilized world. Since helicopters can't be used to transport hunters in Alaska, where I've done most of my wilderness hunting, that flight had started our twelve day hunt out on an eerie, unfamiliar note, but with good reason. I still retain a pilot's eye for bush landing options with fixed wing aircraft, and I hadn't seen a flat spot that I'd try to land on in my wildest dreams.

I knew Kevin well enough to know what he had in mind: an all but impossible trek across miles of jumbled glacial talus and over a mountain or two in search of the area's elusive tahr. I had more modest goals in mind for our first day in the bush, and after glassing the panoramic view from the hut Lori and I decided to head for a grassy plateau on a ridge barely more than a long mile away. All we had to do was hike down to the creek below the hut, follow its course downhill to its junction with a larger stream, turn back uphill, and start climbing. It looked like kid stuff to me.

Unfortunately, I'm not a kid anymore; in fact, I'm old enough to start thinking about drawing Social Security. Undaunted, we set off in high spirits. Our initial learning experience of the day came when we reached a bottleneck in the first stream's course through a tight little gorge and decided to bushwhack cross-country despite Kevin's warning about the impenetrable nature of the brush. I never thought I'd fight brush nastier than the alders in coastal Alaska's goat country, but I was wrong. By mid-morning we were bruised, bewildered, and exhausted even though we'd scarcely left camp.

But we eventually made it down to the boulders lining the second stream's route down the mountain and began to make some progress. Our second error occurred when we reached the base of a steep rockslide that led up to the plateau and decided we could climb it. By the time we realized we couldn't an hour later, our only option other than accepting defeat was to head back into the brush and keep climbing. That's when we heard the jet engines roaring up at the head of the valley, where no jet had any business flying.

The commotion turned out to be from one of the avalanches that rocked the valley regularly, as we confirmed when we climbed up on a boulder that offered a view of events. And what a spectacle greeted our eyes, as boulders the size of our house careened down the mountainside and exploded into clouds of flying rock. After vainly trying to reassure Lori that no such thing could possibly happen where we were I set my legs against the contour lines, and we were back on our way uphill.

It was mid-afternoon by the time we finally broke out on the plateau, except that we never really broke out at all. The grassy ridge turned out to be a glacial boulder field that just happened to have some vegetation growing on it. Pausing to glass at intervals, we picked our way slowly across it without seeing any game... until I turned my glasses across the valley and spotted two dark shapes at our level, but on the wrong mountain. It didn't take me long to conclude that you couldn't get there from here.

Viewed through our binoculars, the tahr were certainly spectacular animals, even though they lacked their fully developed winter manes. These stocky, agile Asian goats were introduced to New Zealand from the Himalayas over a century ago, and more tahr now inhabit Kiwi country than their native range. "They're not *that* far away," Lori pointed out after we'd watched them for a while. "I can remember when you'd already be halfway down the mountain, headed in their direction. You must be getting old."

"No, honey," I corrected her. "I must be getting smart."

By then it was time to start thinking about getting down off the mountain during the daylight. That's when I made my third tactical error of the day. When hunting serious mountain terrain it's almost always wisest to go down the same way you went up, but I decided we could improve upon our route of ascent by skirting the rim of the plateau and intercepting the creek at its origin. The first part of the plan went well enough, but we soon learned that descending the upper reaches of the creek bed meant scrambling down massive boulders that all but cried out for technical climbing gear. "I knew I wasn't marrying a rich doctor," Lori observed during one mad scramble. "I didn't know I was marrying a dumb one!"

Fortunately, we made it back to camp with our limbs and our marriage both intact, ready for another day in some of the most spectacular and challenging terrain I've ever hunted.

When director Peter Jackson set out to translate Tolkien's epic *Lord of the Rings* trilogy to film, he didn't have to look far for an appropriate location. The wilds of his native New Zealand were not only conveniently close to home—they provided an ideal setting in which to recreate the fantasy world of Middle Earth. While his films inspired worldwide interest in the natural beauty of his homeland, they also rekindled the paradoxical attitudes I felt about New Zealand as a bowhunting destination.

On our first trip there, I'd hunted by invitation on a private, fenced property. While I went home deeply impressed by the country and its endlessly hospitable inhabitants, I didn't think all that much of the hunting. Although I've always been deeply opposed to high fences here at home, I've also kept an open mind about different approaches to wildlife management in other countries where the principles of the North American Model may not apply, and I've experienced true fair chase hunting behind fences on large properties in southern Africa where wildlife populations would be difficult or impossible to sustain by other means. However, the Kiwi version was just a bit too tame and controlled for me.

The problem in New Zealand seemed to be a lack of alternatives engendered by official government attitudes toward game animals. Like other isolated island ecosystems in the vast Pacific, New Zealand supported no native populations of large mammals. All of its big game—seven species of deer, tahr, chamois, goats, and pigs—arrived courtesy of importation by its early colonists, and current government policy treats them as feral pests. Consequently, on all of the country's vast tracts of wild public land, red deer are shot commercially from the air, tahr are annihilated, and 1080 poison is treated as a legitimate wildlife "management" technique. I didn't see how this situation could lead to a satisfactory hunting experience on either side of those fences, and said as much in print.

Several dedicated Kiwi bowhunters including Kevin Low contacted me to point out that there really were abundant, fair chase bowhunting opportunities in New Zealand for those willing to work for them. Granted, these opportunities weren't going to produce easy encounters with multiple species on the same day or artificially bred red deer "trophies" with ridiculously ornate antlers, but I wasn't interested in that anyway. A too brief hunt with Kevin, accompanied by Bill Baker and Dan Smith, for free range sika deer in wild terrain while I was in country on a speaking engagement only whetted my appetite for more. This year, we finally organized the hunt I'd had in mind all along. The only question that remained was whether or not I'd grown too old to do it.

Three days into the hunt, I was beginning to wonder. I had arrived in pretty good shape for my age, an important qualification about which I could do nothing. That fall, I'd spent a lot of time working with my new wirehair puppy, and chasing wild roosters up and down the coulees of eastern Montana provides a lot more physical conditioning than sitting in a tree waiting for a deer to walk by. I did a lot of lion hunting in December, and veteran cat hunters know that a good chase can be the equivalent of a marathon. We'd spent all of January in Arizona, hunting something hard almost every day. Even so, nothing can really get you in shape for an honest high country bowhunt except high country bowhunting. Furthermore, the terrain proved to be exceptionally rugged even in comparison to Alaska sheep and goat country, which I always thought set the standard in such matters.

In fact, Lori and I were handling the steep country, thick brush, and poor footing pretty well. The real problem from the hunting perspective was our difficulty locating game. It was late summer in the southern hemisphere, when tahr spend most of their time low in the valleys holed up in the brush to get away from the heat before moving higher during the rut in May. Even Kevin couldn't find them, and since he's probably taken as many tahr and chamois with traditional archery tackle as anyone alive I didn't think our failure reflected our own inexperience with the quarry.

At the end of the third hunting day, we held a strategy meeting. Our original plan had been to spend a full week at the head of the valley in prime tahr country before hiking down the main river to a second hut to concentrate on chamois. When we decided to head downstream early, we committed ourselves to some heavy packs since we'd have to carry all the food and supplies we'd brought for the whole trip. Even so, I felt strong and enthusiastic as we set off down the steep slope toward the river bed early the following morning, perhaps because I didn't realize I was setting out on one of the longest five-mile hikes of my life.

The trail, such as it was, ran up and down constantly as it wound through the heavily glaciated terrain, and the footing was treacherous almost every step of the way. And halfway between the two huts, I almost paid a serious price for underestimating the country we'd chosen to hunt.

I was bringing up the rear at my usual slow but steady pace when I set off across a steep slide lined with crumbling rock. Suddenly, the boulder I was standing on gave way and I felt my heavy pack drag me over backwards in an accelerating avalanche. When I finally stopped bouncing, I found myself lying under a pile of rocks at the edge of a steep cliff face just above the surging glacial river, delighted to find that I was still alive and that all four of my limbs were working. Further damage assessment revealed that the ring finger on my right hand was bent backwards at a crazy angle and the same digit on my left hand wouldn't fully extend.

After securing myself and my gear against a plunge into the icy water below, I decided that the finger on my right hand was dislocated rather than broken. Gritting my teeth, I popped it back into place. I even managed to laugh at the realization that with x-rays and whatnot, that little maneuver would have been a $1000 visit to the emergency room had there been one. No wonder we can't afford our health care.

By this time, Lori had realized by some kind of telepathy that I was in trouble and hiked back up the trail to look for me. Together, we examined my other hand and concluded that I'd ruptured the extensor tendon on that side. Fortunately, Lori was thinking like the nurse she is when she's not out in the woods. "That ring has got to come off *now!*" she announced, and she was right. Employing her own bag of emergency room tricks, which involved a whole lot of spit and un-ladylike verbal encouragement, she worked the ring off just before the swelling beneath it could cut off the blood supply. It was the first time in 15 years that I'd seen my left hand without my wedding band. At that point there wasn't much to be done except set off back downriver and hope I could still shoot my bow the following morning.

The week that followed proved strenuous and fascinating. We did encounter chamois almost every day, but they had a frustrating way of showing up on the opposite side of the river, which we couldn't cross. Since we'd changed plans and couldn't carry all of our heavy supplies down to the second hut, our food stores began to dwindle. The abundant wood pigeons in the trees and the blue mountain ducks on the river were beginning to look a lot like dinner to me, but both are protected native species. I'd expected to lose some weight on the trip, but I hadn't expected to starve.

Fortunately, Kevin solved that problem for us when he made a careful stalk and an accurate shot on a mature chamois doe. He had told us previously that chamois aren't nearly as good to eat as tahr, but at that point our camp had no room for food critics. Although both sexes of chamois carry elegant hooked horns, his animal suffered from deforming horn rot, a common problem on the wet western side of the Alps. No matter; at that point we were all more interested in backstraps than trophies for the wall, and his doe served that purpose admirably.

When the helicopter returned at last for our evacuation back to the road, I still hadn't had a chance to see if I could shoot my bow with fingers buddy-splinted on both hands. Even so, I knew I'd just enjoyed one of the most memorable and challenging hunts of my career... and we weren't quite finished yet.

We'd allowed a couple of extra days in our schedule for the possibility of delays due to weather, and we finally arrived back at Kevin's home on the North Island with plenty of time to spare. Kevin is one of those rare individuals with the ability to make almost anything happen at will, and by the time I'd finished admiring the bay in front of his home town he'd already arranged to borrow a friend's boat so we could explore it the following morning.

Full disclosure, even though it may sound like heresy in hard core bowhunting circles: I was more interested in tackling kahawai, the local saltwater game fish, with my fly rod than shooting my bow when we set out the following morning. But Kiwi archers take their bowfishing seriously, and this bay has produced many of the biggest rays in their bowfishing record book. Furthermore, Lori had carried our camera rather than her own bow during most of our stay in the mountains, and she deserved a shot at something before we left the country. And so we pushed away from the boat ramp fully armed, with my 7-weight rod, Lori's left-handed recurve, and an old right-handed recurve of Kevin's in case one of us felt the urge to tackle a big ray ourselves.

The kahawai proved as elusive as the tahr had been in the high country, but rays lay everywhere in the clear water on the tide flats. Lori finally couldn't stand it any longer. As I was scanning the horizon futilely for birds working over schools of fish, she suddenly shouted, "There's one!" and we heard her recurve twang. Then the plastic jug attached to the opposite end of the line from her fish arrow was racing away across the waves as if we were reenacting a scene from *Jaws*.

Two species of rays occupy New Zealand waters, and she'd sunk her shaft into the smaller but sportier of the two: an eagle ray. Although the fish didn't weigh more than 20 or 30 pounds, it led us on a merry chase along the edge of the flat before Lori hit it with an insurance arrow and we brought it to the boat. Although I'm really not a diehard bowfisherman, I have to admit that I was impressed. "Now we need to find you a black ray," Kevin told Lori, and we set off to do just that.

Maryland saltwater bowfishing guru Rob Davis refers to any ray from his home waters that weighs over 100 pounds as a "big 'un", but in the world of New Zealand black rays that's just a baby. The bow and arrow record for that species tipped the scales at over 400 pounds. As we drifted along and scanned the water, Kevin encouraged me to stay close to my fly rod, since he frequently sees kingfish (yellowtails to American saltwater anglers, *hamachi* to sushi lovers) trailing black rays in the shallows. Accustomed to thinking of yellowtails as deepwater fish, I didn't pay much attention to his suggestion.

I should have. When we finally spotted a nice black ray cruising the edge of the channel, my jaw dropped as I saw four nice "kingies" trailing along in its wake. Pandemonium erupted aboard the skiff. I reached for my fly rod. Kevin leapt for his own bow. (It's legal to shoot kingfish with arrows as long as they exceed the legal minimum length, which these clearly did.) While we fumbled with our tackle, Lori kept her head and did the right thing: She shot the ray. A bird in the hand...

While her black ray wasn't one of the monsters the bay produces, it proved to be plenty of fish for us when it headed straight for the bottom and refused to budge. Eventually, we managed to horse it into the shallows and capture it. I even shot an eagle ray myself as we headed back toward the boat launch, and then it was time to turn back into toads and begin preparing for the long journey home to the piles of snow waiting for us there. We already knew how much we were going to miss New Zealand.

According to the conventions of the genre, stories about epic hunts in distant lands are expected to end with lots of trophies and hero pictures, and I've enjoyed my share of trips like that. But I've also been around long enough to know that you can't count on that kind of outcome when you're hunting with a longbow. New Zealand offers its own paradoxical rules in this regard. You can have an easy time of it on fenced property that contains abundant animals with big horns, but only under circumstances that don't meet my own standards of fair chase hunting. On the other hand, bowhunting the country's substantial populations of free range game means tackling rough country in search of wildlife that has deliberately been managed *against* rather than *for*. Sometimes you have to settle for stingrays.

But those are just the kind of hunts that teach you the most about yourself and produce the greatest number of lasting friendships, and I'll take that choice every time.

Don glassing tahr country.

Don with a hard earned axis deer from the alpine.

CHAPTER TWELVE

Molokai Grand Slam
Hawaii

THE PLAN sounded simple enough: drive half way up the mountain, climb for two strenuous hours, and spend the rest of the day hunting wild goats and pigs high in the alpine above the cliffs. Our troubles began the night before the hunt, when a moist Pacific air mass swept across the Hawaiian Islands, dumping sheets of rain on the highlands of Molokai. We arrived at first light to find the dirt track impassable, not that such an insignificant development would deter my old friend Doug Borland.

"We can make it from here," Doug promised as we gazed wistfully at the hunting grounds rising from the mist far above us. Those who have been afield with Doug know he doesn't really feel he's hunting unless he's crawled a couple of miles straight up.

"Why not?" I replied as I stared up at the distant basin. Having hunted the area several years earlier, I knew what gorgeous terrain lay in wait if we could make the climb. And that is all it took to convince two fools to set out on one of the longest days of their lives.

It took over four hours of relentless climbing beneath the hot tropical sun to reach the basin, but as soon as we broke out of the overgrown remnants of the trail, I knew the effort had been worthwhile.

Flush from the recent rain, a series of waterfalls cascaded over the lip of the basin. The condition of the trail suggested that no one had hunted the area for months. And above the sound of the mountain wind, we could hear the incessant bleating of wild goats rising from the cliffs below.

Since Molokai's goats are utterly inaccessible until they leave the security of their vertical escape terrain to feed, we decided to separate and hunt pigs in the forest. Wild pigs move freely up and down the mountain depending on the availability of food at different elevations, and after an hour back in the jungle, I hadn't located any fresh pig sign. Mildly disappointed, I worked my way back to the open area above the cliffs to meet Doug. That's when I saw the goats.

A half dozen young billies had left the cliffs to graze in the grass, and they were far enough from the rim so I felt I could recover one safely if I managed to shoot it. Most Molokai goats are dull brown in color, but one of these sported a striking silver coat, and I resolved to take him if possible. However, wild goats are as keen-eyed as antelope, and the open country stalk promised to be a challenge.

I used a shallow draw to work my way into position between the goats and the cliffs with a stiff wind in my face. However, the grass was only ankle high, and I ran out of cover fifty yards from my quarry. There was nothing to do but work on my tan and hope the goats fed into a more favorable position.

Fifteen minutes later, the herd worked its way over the rise into the next little draw. Checking carefully for stragglers, I circled once again and put a careful sneak on the spot I expected them to be. As I crawled into position behind a boulder, I caught a glimpse of silver hair in the crease in front of me. As soon as the goat lowered his head to feed, I came to full draw and rose to my knees. The arrow whistled through the goat's chest right behind the shoulder, and the mountain erupted in a clatter of hooves as the herd broke for the security of the cliffs. But my shot placement was perfect, and the silver billy collapsed in the open well short of the treacherous rim.

By the time I finished dressing the goat and rejoined Doug, it was already time to start for home. Wild goats are small animals, but after all the exertion of the climb, I was thankful the load in my pack wasn't any heavier. Half way down the mountain, we stopped to let Doug make a stalk on a band of big billies with long, sweeping horns, but an alert sentry spotted him and spooked the herd before he could get off a shot. That was probably just as well; by the time we reached the vehicle, both of us were nursing sore legs and wondering if we were getting too old for this kind of thing.

But there is no cure for fatigue like a cold drink and a hot meal, and Lori and Olga had both waiting when we reached Doug's condo at the far end of the island. As the memory of the long, steep miles faded, we settled into the pleasure of good company and the satisfaction of a job well done. With a pig already under my belt on a previous trip, I now had two thirds of the Molokai hat trick with my bow. Of course the remaining third – an axis buck – was the most difficult of all, but I had the rest of the week to get the job done.

All I had to do was ask my legs to get me back up the mountain one more time.

Cut off from the rest of the world by the vast reaches of the Pacific, the Hawaiian Islands form a fascinating ecosystem. Only two mammals are native to Hawaii: the monk seal and the Laysan bat. Hawaii's shortage of game on land ended with the arrival of our own species, as early settlers and explorers began to populate the islands with animals that could supplement the bountiful sea as a food source.

Wild pigs arrived with the early Polynesians, who reached the islands between 500 and 800 AD. European explorers led by Captain James Cook introduced new populations of feral swine centuries later, along with the goats that still run wild over the islands' steeper, drier terrain. The British introduced both species as a source of meat for their far-flung naval crews. The axis deer arrived in 1857 as a gift from an Indian rajah to King Kamehameha V, and with no natural predators other than man, they soon established thriving populations on several of the islands.

The arrival of these species, along with a wealth of alien bird and plant life, certainly came as a mixed blessing. Introduced mammals provided a welcome source of meat for islanders, but they also caused tremendous destruction to Hawaii's fragile native ecology. Today, indigenous Hawaiian bird and plant species remain threatened throughout the islands because of competition from hardier imports and depredation by feral goats and pigs.

Like most mainlanders, my own original perception of Hawaii derived largely from images of Oahu's crowded beaches and bustling tourist trade, none of which seemed particularly attractive to an outdoorsman who values wild places. Fortunately, back when I lived in Alaska, Anchorage bowhunter Doug Borland introduced me to the island of Molokai and his native Hawaiian friend Walter Naki. I soon learned that Hawaii contains some of the wildest terrain in North America, along with truly unique bowhunting opportunities for anyone with the determination and stamina to tackle it. I took a nice boar on an earlier trip, and after attending the PBS convention in Seattle, Doug and I flew on to Molokai with our families to enjoy some badly needed sunshine and let me work on the challenge of completing the Molokai hat trick.

I didn't expect the goat to be much of a problem. It's not that Molokai's wild goats are particularly easy: they inhabit dangerous terrain and are sharp enough to be a real challenge with the bow. But there are plenty of them, and a bowhunter who targets goats can expect plenty of opportunities for one to make a lethal mistake.

The axis deer were another story. Highly wary and possessed of keen senses, they prefer thick cover where they enjoy every possible advantage in the contest between predator and prey. As a child, I eagerly read the Indian hunting stories of Col. Jim Corbett, and remembered how the axis deer alerted him to the presence of tigers with their noisy alarm barks. Doug is one of the best bowhunters I know, but it had taken him several trips to the island to kill his first buck. On the other hand, another hunting partner killed an axis buck on his first trip to Molokai that is still the unofficial island record with the bow.

I knew it could be done. All I had to do was do it.

It has taken two full days for our legs to recover from the demands of that first trip up the mountain, but Doug and I are finally ready to make an assault on the alpine again. Walter is with us this morning and as always I am delighted to be hunting with him, because of his unfailing enthusiasm as much as for his intimate knowledge of the island. Fortified by coffee and pastries from the bakery in the sleepy village of Kaunakakai, we bounce up the mountain in the vehicle at first light. Layers of jungle unfold beneath us as we drive, and it occurs to me that there is really no place on earth I'd rather be.

The rig gains as much altitude in twenty minutes as Doug and I managed in two hours the day I shot the goat, for which I am grateful. It's not that I'm lazy; I'd just rather invest my legs in the hunt. When we finally run out of road half way up the mountain, Walter hops out and wisely decides to hunt right where we are. Incorrigible to the end, Doug talks me into setting off up the mountain in search of a trail that may or may not exist. Question my judgement if you will; if I had a problem with that kind of suggestion, I would have stopped hunting with Doug Borland years ago. Just think what I would have missed.

Two hours later, we break out of the brush and enter the alpine, where we split up to hunt our way along the ridge in opposite directions. Pig and deer sign abounds. Layers of wet scud are blowing across the ridge from the north, but the visibility is sufficient to let me spend an hour glassing the open basin below. The country looks empty. Wind and drizzle have kept the deer bedded in the brush, where they will be all but impossible to locate. It's an El Nino year, and like everyone else I decide to blame this mysterious weather pattern for my troubles. I wonder what we're all going to do for excuses when the water temperatures in the mid-Pacific return to normal.

Finally the weather grows seriously inhospitable, with enough gusty wind and horizontal rain to send me scrambling for cover. The visibility drops to a matter of yards, leaving me little choice but to hunker down in the lee of a rock and wait out the storm. Soaked to the skin and shivering vigorously, I can close my eyes and imagine I'm hunting sheep in Alaska. So much for the notion that a Hawaiian bow hunt is just another trip to the country club.

I'm about to turn around and grope my way back down the mountain when the ceiling lifts, revealing the vast alpine basin once again. Although it's hard to be optimistic about finding any deer, the country is just too inviting to ignore, and there is always a possibility of stumbling across a pig in a sheltered lee. The breeze has shifted with the passage of the front, leaving me with a steady uphill crosswind. Wiping the rain from my face, I set off to circle the head of the basin and peak over the edge of each little draw in hope of finding a pig rooting in the bottom.

After traversing a steep side hill and slogging across a swollen creek, I ease up to the edge of the first pocket. Suddenly, brush breaks uphill as a tawny form bounds from the top of the ravine. My scent has spooked a bedded axis doe. At the sound of her alarm bark, two bucks explode from the foliage right underneath me and sprint up the opposite side of the steep draw, where they freeze and stare in her direction. Suddenly, I realize they are unaware of my presence.

Fingers shaking, I ease an arrow onto the string. The best buck is nearly 40 yards away, quartering slightly away and facing uphill. That's a long shot for me, but my draw and release feel effortless and the arrow looks perfect as it arcs across the draw and smacks into the deer's flank. As the buck wheels and tears off up the mountain, I am briefly concerned that I have hit him too far back. In fact, considering the shot angle, the placement is ideal, and I watch him collapse mid-stride in the grass 60 yards farther up the hill.

Walking up to the dead buck evokes complex emotions. I have hunted a lot of striking animals around the world, but the deer's exquisite white spots and perfect velvet antlers make it difficult to remember one more beautiful. Axis deer don't make many mistakes, but this one did, and I can't help wondering if I really deserved to kill him. A long, carefully conducted stalk would have felt more satisfying, but I stuck it out on the mountain and made the shot I had to make,

[114]

and in the end I decide to stop beating myself up and enjoy the feeling of accomplishment.

Of course, my day isn't over yet. By the time I've boned the deer, the visibility is back down to nothing. I take a wrong turn somewhere in the fog and wind up having to bull my way uphill through dense brush for an extra hour to reach the trail, all while balancing 80 pounds of venison and antlers on my back. Half way back down the mountain, I crest a rise to find a huge black boar rooting in the trail 30 yards in front of me. I have the wind and plenty of cover, but after a moment of consideration I come to my senses and shout the pig off the trail. I have what I have come for today, and it never pays to be greedy.

Back at the vehicle, Walter greets me with a grin. No wonder; he has pigs stacked up like cordwood and managed to miss a buck as well, all within sight of our parking place. And when Doug finally comes down off the mountain and joins us, he tells of stalking the two biggest pigs he has ever seen on the island. "What a day!" someone finally suggests when all the stories have been told for the second time, and no one disagrees.

Pigs, goats, axis deer… from the coarse to the sublime, Molokai offers the bowhunter a little bit of everything. Throw in some fishing, unspoiled beaches, and the opportunity to enjoy the sun and surf with your family, and it's easy to see why the island has become one of my favorite destinations.

Just don't make the mistake of thinking the hunting is going to be easy.

Section III

FAR NORTH

FAR NORTH

THE TENDER AGE at which I fell under the North's powerful spell stands as a tribute to an earlier generation of writers. From Jack London to Russell Annabel, I read them all, and their descriptions of the untamed land lying between my house and the North Star seemed to have been created just for me, as personal as a handwritten invitation. As a slightly older kid, I began to nibble at the edges of this vast domain on family canoe trips to Ontario and Quebec, brave expeditions--in my young mind at least--during which I learned to love the magic of a loon's haunting cry and the eerie calm of mist rising slowly from a black lake's glassy surface. Whenever we returned from wherever we'd been, the rest of the world always looked a little bit smaller and less exciting. I was hooked.

In fact, to borrow from the parlance of angling, I'd flat out *swallowed* the hook. I always promised myself I'd live in the Far North someday. Never one to worry about practicalities, when I sniffed out an opportunity to move to Alaska's Kenai Peninsula in 1980, I took it. Accompanied by my now ex-wife, son Nick (barely out of diapers), Sky (still the best hunting Lab I've ever owned), and a pair of horses, I set off up the Alcan brimming with naivety and *North to Alaska!* spirit, a perfect set-up for cheechako blunders and my own due measure of disappointment.

The blunders didn't take long. I spent the first night of my Alaska hunting career shivering on a glacier near Prince William Sound. I found out the hard way just how big an Alaska moose really is when

[119]

it's dead and how quickly a squirrelly tailwind can eat up the length of a gravel bar when you're trying to land a Super Cub. The problem was simple: like most new arrivals, especially those who think they've got the outdoors all figured out, I didn't show the country sufficient respect. But I learned, even if the process took some time.

And the disappointments followed as well, a point I've reluctantly had to enforce to another generation of the Alaska bound. Alaska's limited road system virtually guarantees crowds anywhere others can reach by vehicle. As hunting Alaska has become an increasingly commercialized enterprise, even readily accessible bush locations have started to see their share of crowding. And the crowds aren't always pleasant. While some of the finest outdoor sportsmen (and women) I know are Alaskans, some of the worst are too.

But anyone with sufficient perseverance should be able to reach beyond all that, and I did. The results proved worth the effort, for in its unspoiled state there's simply nothing like the wilds of Alaska to inspire and challenge. Even after more than three decades of familiarity, I still get goose bumps at the sound of a wolf howling or the sight of a brown bear lumbering across the tundra. I suspect--and hope--I always will.

Of course the North includes more country than Alaska, as if our own Last Frontier weren't enough. Two of the most memorable expeditions of my life took place on the Russian taiga, and only the fact that I've described those bowhunts in book form before (in *Longbows of the Far North*) prevents me from including a chapter on that fascinating country here. But I have included a chapter on northern Alberta, and would have included material from British Columbia, Labrador, and Quebec—all locations that offer their own unique versions of bowhunting our continent's wildest northern reaches—had space allowed.

And if I've done my job well enough, perhaps another wide-eyed kid will read what follows and dream, just as I did 50 years ago. I can imagine no greater satisfaction as a writer.

CHAPTER THIRTEEN

Return to the North Slope
Alaska

NONE OF THE WORLD'S SEAS arouses a feeling of spookiness quite like the Arctic Ocean. While the narrow gap between polar ice and shoreline largely prevents the development of heavy seas, the odd combination of confinement and expanse still manages to chill the soul. There's just so much cold liquid and so little of anything else, as if the observer were perched upon the rim of a giant martini. As Doug Borland and I deplaned at Barter Island's rough gravel strip, I turned to the sea and sucked in a long, cold breath. Finally, after two long decades, we were back on the edge of the world again.

Doug, a longtime Alaskan, had made two pioneering trips into the area we planned to hunt, both in the company of the late Jay Massey. Through lots of good old-fashioned intelligence gathering, they'd located a pocket of rams deep in the heart of the Brooks Range, far enough from the nearest place to land an airplane that no one in their right mind would consider hunting there. But their efforts had earned them a just reward: three large Dall rams for two longbow hunters on two trips, a measure of sheep hunting accomplishment seldom equaled.

Inspired by Doug's stories, I'd made one trip into the area

myself, accompanied by my father, just before I left Alaska. But nature treated us less kindly. First, a blown-out river kept us from reaching our original goal. Then, just as I located some rams in a different drainage, a savage polar storm system dumped several feet of snow on our heads and kept us confined to our backpack tent in survival mode for days. Even so, when we finally emerged cold, tired, and hungry, we both agreed the North Slope had provided us with one of the most memorable trips we'd ever taken. During the months of planning that preceded our return that August, I had to wonder which version of the arctic awaited us this time.

Our arrival in the tiny village of Kaktovik did not offer much promise. Days of strong northwest winds had pushed the polar ice right onto shore and a dense layer of clouds lay against the hills to the south, rendering mountain flying impossible. Experienced Alaska hunters eventually learn to be philosophical about the weather, but after three days of burgers, old paperbacks, and satellite TV, we realized we were running out of hunting time, especially since we faced two long days of hiking each way to and from the sheep country. Finally, we decided to fly up the valley as far as the ceiling allowed and look for a place to land. If we found an acceptable gravel bar, we'd push ourselves to make up for the time we lost, and if we didn't we'd head home and forget the sheep for another year.

Fortunately, we were flying with legendary North Slope pilot Walt Audi. Although my own instincts left me pessimistic as we loaded our gear into the 206, Walt found a seam in the weather that let us cruise upriver, albeit at an altitude low enough to let us count the rocks in the streambed below. As we neared the drainage we planned to hunt, an accommodating gravel bar appeared beneath the wings and moments later Walt rode the aircraft to a rattling stop. It was too late to worry about the weather or the snow covering the peaks. Finally, we were going sheep hunting.

In fact, Doug was going sheep hunting... I was more or less along for the ride. Since I was a non-resident by then, Alaska law prevented me from hunting sheep without the services of a guide. Caribou season was open, but the Porcupine caribou herd is highly migratory and most of the animals had already moved east into Canada. I hadn't even brought a bow along on this trip, and I admit that my hands felt strangely empty as we cached our backup supplies and readied our packs for the long hike ahead. But as designated photographer, I was carrying a full supply of camera equipment in my pack, as well as a 12-gauge in case Doug had an opportunity to stalk a grizzly. Somehow, all the extra weight on board made the absence of my own bow a little easier to accept.

There are basically two routes from point A to point B in the Brooks Range: along riverbed gravel bars or by way of caribou trails at higher elevation. Gravel bars offer the advantage of good visibility and a gradual grade, at the cost of bruised, wet feet. But the trails along the side hills offered a lot of unnecessary up and down, so we set off upstream along the braided creek without any real effort to keep our feet dry. By the time we finally ground to a stop for the night ten miles farther into the mountains, my feet felt numb from constant immersion in the creek's frigid water and my overloaded pack seemed to be cutting its way through both my shoulders. But somehow, being there again made it all worthwhile.

The North Slope is just that kind of place. Few locations on Earth remain so profoundly wild, even by Alaska's standards. Many hunters making their first trip to Alaska return dismayed by the incessant drone of float planes in the autumn skies and the plethora of camps that sprout in popular areas during hunting season. No such worries for us--the size of the country and its distance from civilization saw to that. When we finally slogged into our planned campsite the following night, Doug recognized the remains of an old fire ring he and Jay had used 20 years earlier, the first subtle sign of human presence we'd seen since leaving the river. In this day and age, the affirmation of wild places' capacity to endure provides a feeling of satisfaction greater than any set of horns I've ever put on the wall. As we settled into camp, I experienced a feeling of contentment not even my aching muscles could compromise.

We spent the next several days searching for sheep. Although the weather had broken, the storm had already taken its toll. The high basins where Doug and Jay once found rams lay carpeted in snow. The footing proved difficult, and few objects are more difficult to spot against a white background than white sheep. We glassed a number of ewes and lambs at lower elevations and watched a group of three-quarter curl rams cross the creek below us, but the big boys remained elusive.

In order to cover more ground, we split up each morning and headed for different drainages. As much as I enjoy Doug's company this approach met with my approval, since the wildness of the Brooks Range is best appreciated alone. I felt oddly at peace with my unfamiliar status as a non-hunter, and realized that I really do see wilderness differently when I'm not carrying a bow. One afternoon, a fine bull caribou wandered by in the creek bottom, a lonely straggler from the teeming herds that had passed through a few weeks before. I didn't even appraise his headgear critically or pick an imaginary spot behind his shoulder as he passed, and as he disappeared into the tundra to the east I wondered if I'd ever seen a caribou so clearly.

Finally, we had to admit that the rams just weren't there. Doug ascribed their absence to the weather, but I wasn't so sure. Twenty years is a long time, and a bad winter or a pack of wolves can be all it takes to shuffle nature's deck completely. But I knew Doug had a lot of emotion invested in returning to the area where he and Jay had hunted once, and I didn't dwell on these observations. In the end, we simply agreed to start packing back down the valley, to look for rams at lower elevations and try for a grizzly along the river where we expected to find the bears searching for food.

Late that afternoon, Doug alertly spotted a lone sheep picking its way across a jumble of scree above us, and as soon as I had the animal in my glasses I could tell it was a ram. Only full curl rams are legal in this area, and this one looked close. Without a spotting scope, neither of us could make the call for sure. I suggested we drop our packs and start up the mountain for a better look, but after further study through his binoculars, Doug declined. It was certainly not a large ram, and even if its lamb points brought its horns to full curl, it wasn't the sheep he wanted. The choice was his alone to make, and I respected his decision even if it wasn't necessarily the one I might have made myself.

Later that afternoon, we stopped beside a deep pool for a badly needed breather. When I glanced into the crystalline water, I saw dozens of brilliantly colored arctic char turning deep in the current. Laboring into camp beneath heavy packs earlier in the week, I'd accused Doug of packing far more food than we needed, but by this time we were down to a little salt, a couple of tea bags, half a stick of butter and a handful of pancake mix. But I'd brought along a few flies and a spool of tippet. While I whittled down a willow pole and rigged up, Doug started a willow twig fire on the bank, and by the time we departed we'd gorged on delicious char prepared with – you guessed it – salt, butter, and pancake mix. I can't remember what happened to the tea.

We'd left extra food at the landing strip, always a wise idea in the Bush, where weather often delays scheduled pickups for days. But with the nearest tree over a hundred miles away we had no means to secure our supply from bears, and the thought of returning to a raided food supply was almost enough to make me cry. When a ptarmigan popped out of the brush thirty yards away, Doug nocked a blunt-tipped arrow and shot, but the bird waddled off unharmed, leaving us to slog on downstream toward the river and hope.

We'd left our little cache in a long line of willows next to the river, and as we entered the brush I jacked a slug into the shotgun's chamber in case we encountered a raiding grizzly grown territorial. But the bears had overlooked our waterproof bag, and as soon as we shed our packs, pitched the tent, and gathered a bit of firewood, we dumped its contents out on the tundra and took inventory. After a week of skimping over freeze-dried nothing, this sudden embarrassment of riches practically took our breath away. To this day I can't decide if we were more excited by the six-pack of beer or the two cans of Spam.

Ordinarily, gravel bar fires north of the tree line leave little to recommend, with willow, either green or rotten, the only available fuel. But high water the previous spring had left the bars in the main river littered with brush fragments that had baked dry in the arctic summer sun. Before long we had a real fire crackling, and after considerable debate we opted for Spam slices topped with melted cheese smothered in black beans and rice. I've dined at my share of 5-star restaurants over the years, but I can't remember a meal I've enjoyed more.

I awoke early the following morning thinking about grizzlies. Doug and Jay had only run into a few during their trips, but they'd spent most of their time at higher elevations. When the weather forced my father and me down onto the river bottom, we saw grizzlies every day even without making any effort to look for them. The bears aren't very big this far north, but they are among the most beautiful representatives of the species I've ever seen, with honey-blond coats and contrasting dark markings on their faces and feet. With our sheep hunting behind us and a day left before our scheduled departure, I felt confident Doug might still get a crack at a one.

And it didn't take long to locate a candidate. As we rolled out of our sleeping bags and brought the coffee water to a boil, movement across the river caught my eye and moments later we stood glassing a lone boar working his way across the tundra. But at this latitude, bears have already entered their period of hyperphagia by late August, traveling incessantly in an effort to bolster their metabolic reserves prior to hibernation. By the time we mobilized our gear and crossed the river, the foraging bear had a long head start up the mountain. Despite wide-open terrain and a brisk uphill sprint on our part, once the bear disappeared over the ridge ahead of us, we never saw him again.

And so this challenging trip's conclusion found me perched high on a hill in the sun scanning the valley for something that wasn't there, a fitting end to a wonderful journey that involved far more hunting than finding. The fascination of the Far North derives in no small measure from its unpredictability. Had we visited this valley a few weeks earlier during the caribou herd's annual migration, we would have found ourselves in the middle of a North American Serengeti, as thousands of fresh tracks reminded us daily. Now the country had swallowed its bounty whole, and long days of determined glassing and hiking couldn't produce any quarry bigger than an occasional ptarmigan.

But from the very start, our trip had been about more than killing game. Jay's untimely death and my father's advancing age insured we'd never hunt these mountains with them again, but we owed them both the honor of remembering what we'd done together there before. Had the country changed during the interval since we'd seen it last? Not really, give or take nature's shell game with the missing rams. Had we? Well, sure... the hills seemed steeper, the packs heavier, the way at least a little longer. But we came and we saw, and even if we didn't conquer, we proved we could still do the things that really matter.

And you don't need to bring horns home to appreciate that kind of satisfaction.

Postscript: A decade after this trip, Doug returned to the valley again, this time accompanied by Montana bowyer Dick Robertson and his son Yote, who had established Alaska residency while working in Dillingham. Since an Alaska resident can serve as a guide for a first-degree relative, all three were legal sheep hunters. Both Dick and Yote killed magnificent rams, with self bows no less, and Doug might well have taken one too if they hadn't already accumulated as much meat as they wanted to pack 25 miles back to the river.

Don glassing the tide flats.

CHAPTER FOURTEEN

Too Close for Comfort
Alaska

GET CLOSE could serve as a universal mantra for bowhunters. Proximity to the quarry defines the bowhunting experience and distinguishes it unequivocally from hunting the same game with firearms. Over the years, I've found myself remarkably close to a number of wary big game animals through a combination of skill, circumstance, and luck (with heavy emphasis on the latter). Some of those encounters left me with nothing but a good story, like the time I missed a sleeping Hawaiian boar from a range I can't admit in public. But one fall, a black bear on the Alaska coast taught me that the mantra isn't infallible. It really is possible to get *too* close!

Not that I hadn't been plenty close to bears before, both black and grizzly. The first black bear I ever killed up north was feeding in a fall berry patch when I spotted him on the open tundra. When a long stalk left me out of cover and beyond bow range, I spent well over an hour lying in the rain hoping the bear would eventually close the gap for me. When he finally wandered past my hiding place, he was so close that he showered me with water when he shook his coat as I drew. I always assumed that was the closest shot I'd ever take at a bear. Little did I know.

Fall visits to our second home in Southeast Alaska tend to be social affairs as much as hunting trips. With a house full of family and friends that year I'd spent days serving as fishing guide and camp chef, but the company was so enjoyable I didn't mind. But by the time bear season reopened on September 1, I felt ready for a little quiet time in the woods. After making some excuses, I rounded up my gear and set out into the inevitable rain.

I wasn't really hunting bears that afternoon. While fishing a nearby river for salmon the day before, I'd noticed a Sitka blacktail buck feeding on the tide flat near the river mouth. Deer season was open, but I was armed with nothing but a fly rod at the time. The deer was no monster, but I had a house full of guests eager for venison and packing a "meat" buck across the tide flat would be a lot easier than hauling one down a mountain through the alders. Since it's usually easier to locate bears than bucks in Southeast Alaska, I decided to return to the area and look for the deer.

The tide had barely started to build and the low water made the hike across the flat easy, but I knew I'd have to conclude my hunt soon or face a miserable slog around the advancing flood on my way back out in the dark. Flights of teal whistled past as I made my way to the corner of the flat where I'd seen the buck the day before, making me long briefly for my shotgun and one of the Labs kenneled unhappily back in Montana. Lost pink salmon floundered in the tide pools. Despite the drizzle, the terrain was so full of life that I scarcely registered disappointment when I couldn't find the buck.

I'd carried my 4-piece fly rod in my pack, and I finally decided to hike out to the river and look for fish before starting back ahead of the tide. From the riverbank, I glanced downstream toward the bay and noticed a black dot outlined against the kelp-strewn rocks. The bears should have been far upstream chasing fish on their spawning beds, but I'd studied this area countless times without noticing this spot before. My binoculars quickly confirmed that the object was a mature black bear. So much for my deer hunt and the salmon.

With a favorable wind blowing off the bay, I quickly set off to narrow the gap. The next time I spotted the bear, he was continuing in my direction with the breeze at his back, an uncharacteristic lapse on his part. As the animal disappeared from sight again, I realized that he had reached a fork in the road: one potential route would take him up the river to me, the other along a narrow tidal creek draining part of the flat. A summer's worth of accumulated grass made movement noisy despite the rainfall and I realized that I would have to get in front of the bear and let him come to me. With the animal hidden by the terrain, I faced a critical choice. My instincts told me he would turn up the creek rather than continue along the river, so I hustled across the flat to set up an ambush.

Ten minutes later, the bear appeared heading toward me up the tidal drain; I'd won that mental coin toss. As I nestled behind a bank in a side channel the situation looked perfect, since the bear would offer a 10-yard broadside if he continued on course. Instead he inexplicably veered away from the drain and began to noodle around in the grass 40 yards away and comfortably out of my range.

He had discovered a prize left behind by the tide: a dying pink salmon that he gnawed on for several minutes. Despite the temptation to stalk closer, I've developed great respect for bears' hearing over the years and I knew that I'd never make it across the noisy mud and grass undetected. My only recourse was to wait.

To my pleasant surprise, the bear turned and headed back in my direction once he'd finished off the fish. When he disappeared from sight behind the bank, I shifted into position to take the shot when he wandered by. And that is when the afternoon really began to grow interesting.

Although the slosh of his footsteps in the mud confirmed that the animal was now within bow range, I still couldn't see him because of the bank between us. Expecting my anticipated broadside, I continued to wait… but no bear. Suddenly I noticed two black ears protruding above the bank I was hiding behind. The bear was directly above me, about six feet away.

It's hard for anyone but an experienced bowhunter to

understand how it's possible to be that close to an animal with no shot opportunity, but there I was. Unable to think of any way to better my lie, I simply held my ground and waited. Two beady eyes appeared beneath the ears and I narrowed my own to slits in order to avoid direct contact. After a full minute of close range scrutiny, the boar finally bolted back to his initial position across the creek.

That's it, I thought… but was it? The bear had never smelled me thanks to an unusually steady wind, and he'd remained in the open rather than heading for the security of the nearby jungle. I decided to hold still and await developments. Five minutes later, the bear turned back in my direction, and, as Yogi Berra once remarked, it was *déjà vu* all over again. Once more, he disappeared from sight. Once more, I heard footsteps approaching. Once more, he failed to appear broadside on schedule. And this time, when those ears poked over the bank on top of me, I faced a serious decision.

We all know—I hope—that frontal shots with a bow on anything bigger than turkeys are generally a terrible idea. The solid ring of bone formed by the spine, shoulders and sternum shield the vital area almost perfectly. But *if* you know the anatomy there's a way to do it: right on top of the suprasternal notch, the dip at the top of the breastbone just below your Adam's apple. Trouble is, the target is very small and the angle must be perfectly straight, which is why no one should consider it under ordinary circumstances.

Which these were not, for three reasons. First, the bear knew I was there (even though he didn't know quite what I was) and had returned anyway. Coupled with the slow lateral rocking movement of his head, his behavior told me this was a bear with an attitude. Second, I was now within what I call swatting distance, the point blank range from which any large animal can cause injury if startled. Third, the orientation of his ears told me that he was facing me directly at a range from which even I can hit a target the size of an orange. Hence my decision: if he continued over the bank, I was going to draw and kill him before he ran over me.

And this time, rather than blowing back across the creek, he kept coming. As first his head and then his neck hove into view, I felt my right hand reach anchor. When his chest followed suit, I rose from my knees to provide my arrow with a path straight down the middle of the bear and then I released. Two welcome sights registered at once. First, my arrow disappeared to the nock right where I wanted it. Second, the bear vanished behind the bank rather than starting a fight. By the time I scrambled up to where I could see, he was dying 20 yards away. Reconstructing the shot, I determined that the animal had been three feet from the tip of my arrow when I released.

My problems weren't over yet. The animal lay dead well below the tide line and even after field dressing him I couldn't budge the carcass. With seawater advancing rapidly I knew I didn't have time to skin him, so I dug a length of line from my pack, threw a basket hitch around a boulder and tied the bear off to my impromptu anchor. That worked like a charm, and the bear was right where I left him at low tide the following morning.

For the record, my #72 recurve sent the broadhead through the bear's heart and liver (and a lot of other things) before it lodged in a ham. Am I recommending that shot selection? Absolutely not. But all rules are made to be broken as long as you know when and how… especially if the target is a bear that's too close for comfort.

A load of moose heads down the Moose John.

CHAPTER FIFTEEN

Moose John Adventure Alaska

WHENEVER I go back to Alaska, it doesn't take long for me to start looking at the terrain with a pilot's eye again. In the bush, you don't construct airstrips--you discover them, and as soon as Ernie Holland dropped the flaps on the Citabria and began to descend, I could see that he'd found a dandy. The strip on the upper Moose John lies tucked away gracefully between the mountain and the trees, a thousand feet of smooth, hard gravel that no one but an experienced pilot would ever have noticed in the first place. For years, this little strip and the base camp beside it have served as a staging area for bowhunters eager to explore the river that Ernie, Doug Borland, and the late Jay Massey pioneered and elevated to legendary status years ago.

Doug, Ernie, and I had planned this trip for a year, but despite the size of the bull I saw just downstream from camp on the flight in, it was hard to pretend it was all going to be about moose hunting. Even in the enormity of Alaska, Jay's absence would linger over all of us. When sudden family health problems forced Doug to cancel at the last minute, my regrets over his absence only heightened my own sense of purpose. This float would be an opportunity to reflect on the country and all our friends living and dead who had passed this way before. Now that Ernie had taken over the responsibility of running Moose John Outfitters, it was time to close the circle. Whatever game came our way would only be a bonus.

The hills above camp beckoned the morning after my arrival. Free at last of Alaska's same-day-airborne constraints, I felt ready to hunt. There were lots of chores to be done but Ernie knew how eager I was to explore the high country after two days of travel, and he kindly encouraged me to string my bow and go hunting. After an hour of climbing, I found myself high on a ridge glassing a stunning artist's pallet of fall colors spread out before me. Ancient caribou trails traced the contours of the hills, remarkable testimonials to the economy of motion. Somewhere in the tundra below, a ptarmigan croaked. Then a glossy black dot appeared from the brush on the opposite side hill. The bear seemed intent on the berries underfoot, and after double-checking the wind, I began my stalk.

Half an hour later, I lay comfortably on a carpet of lichen while the bear fed in my direction just out of bow range. The sky lay clear and still overhead and the sunshine practically sparkled off the bear's prime fall coat. When he turned broadside and lowered his head 30 yards away, I almost rose and drew. But I have a lot of respect for the toughness of bears, and with circumstances in my favor I elected to wait for him to offer a closer shot. Then the wind faltered and the bear's head shot up, and he set off across the hill in a stiff-legged threat display that made me briefly question the wisdom of stalking bears without carrying a firearm. My stalk was over, leaving me to wonder about passing up a shot I probably would have made without difficulty. But in my experience if you have to wonder about a shot, it's one you should decline.

By the time I finally trudged back down the hill, I'd stalked two more bears without releasing an arrow. Despite a recent week of elk hunting, my legs felt the strain of the long day. Nothing really gets you in shape for hunting Alaska other than doing it. For reasons I've never been able to explain, the mountains somehow seem steeper there, as if the sheer loneliness of the place makes the contour lines edge closer together.

But the day wasn't over yet. After discussing my hunt, Ernie and I hiked upstream to a deep pool where the warm afternoon sun had spawned a heavy mayfly hatch. The water ran so clear that we could see the grayling holding against the rocky bottom from which they rose delicately to sip flies on the surface overhead. We quickly rigged our fly rods and spent the next hour catching some of the biggest grayling I've ever seen in my life.

The next four days passed easily, as time always does removed from the distractions of our allegedly civilized life. Getting the regular hunters onto the river and preparing base camp for the long winter ahead kept us pleasantly busy. But there was also plenty of time to climb the hills in search of bears and wade the river for grayling, as well as to remember my own reasons for leaving the north 15 years earlier, a decision now mixed paradoxically with equal measures of contentment and regret.

Finally the time came to move on. We spent a long morning packing our equipment down to the river, inflating rafts, and lashing our gear as efficiently as possible to the rowing frames. As a veteran of many wilderness float trips, I knew how critical it was to load properly. If our rafts couldn't accommodate what we had in the beginning, how would they ever carry another thousand pounds of moose meat? Then we pushed off into the clear current at last and bade our homey base camp good-bye for the season.

It wasn't just the relief from the long climb up the mountain every day; the feeling of liberation felt intoxicating in its own right. Nature doesn't offer a lot of free rides, but a hundred-mile trip down a wilderness river surely qualifies as one. Suddenly I didn't have to do much of anything in order to let as much of Alaska as I could absorb slide by. As long as we kept the rafts straight in the current, the country simply rose up to greet us.

There is an easy way and a hard way to camp as you float down a typical Alaska river. The easy way--out on the gravel bars--offers the advantages of good visibility, limited distances to carry gear, and convenient flat ground for tents. Setting up camp in the black spruce is the hard way, but it pays off whenever the river comes up and floods the bars below the banks. Jay always advocated camping high in the spruce no matter what. Maybe I'm just lazy, but unless weather and water conditions suggest otherwise, the easy living out on those gravel bars has always suited my own tastes perfectly. With the Moose John running low and clear and no weather on the horizon, I didn't have to argue too hard to convince Ernie we should spend our first night on easy street.

I was sound asleep and snoring comfortably when Ernie roused me from my dreams. "Shut up!" he whispered urgently. "He's right outside the tent! Keep that up and you'll have him right on top of us!" Assuming we had a grizzly in camp, I sat up in the dark to listen. From the other side of the tent's flimsy fabric, I could hear the unmistakable grunt of a rutting bull moose. As Ernie later recounted events, he woke up to the sound of the bull grunting in perfect cadence to my snoring (which more than one tent mate has described as world class). After a hurried discussion, we elected to let the bull pass on down the bar undisturbed and hope we could call him back in for a shot first thing in the morning. Of course, we never saw him again.

That decision represented a mental error on my part. Accustomed to the concept of legal shooting hours in most states, I'd totally forgotten that there are no such regulations in Alaska. Because of the long periods of twilight during hunting season at Alaska latitudes, if you can see it, it's legal to shoot it. With clear skies and a full moon overhead, I might well have felt comfortable with a shot on a point blank moose. At least those who have shared tents with me before will derive appropriate satisfaction from learning that the same racket that ruined their sleep served quite well as a nocturnal moose call. Over coffee the next morning, we reminded ourselves that we were on the Moose John, the moose rut was on, and we'd had the good fortune not to ruin a long float trip by killing a bull so soon, a rationalization that sounded great at the time.

Moose hunting reminds me a lot of flying airplanes: long hours of routine punctuated at unpredictable intervals by more excitement

[138]

than you ever thought possible. After three more days on the river, Ernie and I had the routine part down pat. We would float to the downwind edge of a likely willow bar, walk into the brush, call, and wait. Bull calls, cow calls, furious raking with an old moose scapula against the trees… we tried them all. While fresh sign lay in wait at every stop, nothing responded to our earnest entreaties. That didn't mean we were experiencing bad moose hunting; it meant we were experiencing typical moose hunting. In our optimistic moments we told ourselves that the biggest bull in the world stood just around the next bend. The rest of the time we reminded each other that a dead moose was the easiest way we knew to turn a relaxing float trip into a whole lot of work.

On an Alaska moose hunt, small game can provide a welcome means of staying sharp in the field as well as supplementing the dinner menu. Spruce grouse proved abundant, and whenever we floated past birds graveling up on the bars, we took time out to bag a few. As my confidence in my shooting grew, I wondered about some of the opportunities I'd declined while stalking bears in the high tundra. But you can't second-guess those decisions, and I chose to let the delicious taste of pan-fried grouse serve as its own reward.

Then one evening we floated around a bend to find three rafts pulled up on shore ahead of us. Ernie knew they belonged to Bret DeBernardi, Brad Hayes, and Tim Hansen, an eager party of young bowhunters he had put on the river a week before. As we pulled into shore to look for them, I felt a sudden surge of elation at the sight of a moose rack lying on the gravel bar just beyond their rafts. In the fading light, it took my eyes a moment to realize that there was still a moose attached to the antlers.

As the happy trio emerged from the brush, the story unfolded. They had been hunting their way down-river much as we had. On this particular gravel bar, in contrast to all the others, their calls had produced an immediate series of grunts in reply. As they set up, three different bulls eventually emerged from the brush to investigate. One finally walked past Bret at five yards, at which point he drew his longbow and shot it through the chest. To make matters even sweeter, the bull collapsed in plain sight with nothing but a few yards of open gravel between his deathbed and the rafts, as sweet a place to drop a big moose as any I've ever seen.

Our own moment of excitement came the following morning a mile or so downstream. We awoke to a pleasantly brisk morning and I set off into the muted early light to hunt my way along a willow-lined oxbow behind camp. When I returned two hours later, I was startled to see Ernie standing on the bar beside the rafts holding two sticks beside his head, swaying gently, and grunting like a wild man. *That boy's been out in the bush way too long,* I told myself as I studied the comical scene.

Then I heard another resonant grunt rise above the gurgle of the current. As I watched in awe, a huge bull stepped out of the trees on the opposite side of the river. Ernie, it turns out, had inadvertently drawn his attention by chopping firewood and then coaxed him in with a series of bull calls. Wild with the imperatives of the rut, the bull ignored our brightly colored rafts and the fire crackling on the bar in order to concentrate on Ernie's calls and impromptu head-bobbing display. Now all we had to do was figure out a way to convert the bull's bad judgment into a shot opportunity.

As soon as Ernie realized I had returned to the bar, he motioned for me to try to move in for a shot. I decided I should wait to see what the bull meant to do since I would almost certainly have a shot from my present position if he came across the river. Admittedly that seemed unlikely, for a sheer, steep bank lay between the bull and the current. But as I watched in amazement, Ernie offered another series of grunts and the bull plunged straight down the bank and into the stream.

Broadside at a range of perhaps 45 yards, the bull looked like a huge target, but I knew better than to launch an arrow at that distance. For a moment, he looked ready to come right across the river and into camp, but he held up at the water's edge despite our best efforts to call him forward. Finally, I realized that this channel of the river was only 25 yards wide, and I would have an excellent shot if I could make it to the waterline. But as I started forward, the bull turned to fix me with a befuddled stare and suddenly the spell broke. He clamored back up the bank and disappeared into the trees, and although I took a raft across the river and spent several hours trying to call him back in, we never saw him again. And that, as they say, is moose hunting.

We spent the next several days letting the current ease us on downstream toward our eventual return to civilization. Late-run silver salmon slid by beneath the rafts like crimson torpedoes. Wolf and grizzly tracks lined the sandbars. We grunted and moaned and beat the willows at every bend but the bulls remained hidden somewhere in the enormous reaches of brush that lined the river bottom. Then suddenly it was the night of September 25, and another season on the Moose John was over.

That evening we prepared a generous evening meal and sat around the campfire reflecting on the trip. Wouldn't a moose rack have looked nice lashed to the front of one of our rafts? Well, sure... but that hardly meant I felt disappointed. The Alaska interior is hungry country, and sometimes you have to put a lot of nickels in the slot machine to hit the jackpot. And for each of us, the trip had been about so much more. Years ago, Ernie had started out here as a pilot and novice bowhunter; now he was running the show. And I couldn't keep from thinking about all that had happened since I first went north to live two decades earlier. A lot of water had passed downstream since then, in more respects than one.

And then we raised a glass to Jay and talked about all he had done for both of us. In the course of one's life, there are a few--but very few--individuals who actually change the way one lives and for us, Jay Massey had been one of them. He might be gone now but his legacy endures, and in the end that realization was all we needed to take home.

Don with a cold weather Alberta buck.

CHAPTER SIXTEEN

Northern Lights Bucks Alberta

THE WALK ACROSS THE FIELD made me feel as if I were back in Alaska: bitter cold air that turned my breath to ice, the pistol shot sound of branches popping in the cold, the chilly light in the southeast sky as the sun circled warily beneath the horizon. But the clincher towered far overhead: shimmering curtains of northern lights bright enough to burn the moon shadows from the snow. Of course I'd seen the aurora shine like that before... but never while hunting whitetails.

I was three days into a return trip to Alberta's legendary Edmonton Bow Zone, hunting once again with my old friend Jeff Lander. Two years earlier, El Nino weather had made for pleasant but largely unproductive hunting as unseasonably warm temperatures delayed the whitetail rut and allowed the bucks to remain nocturnal. This year, zero degree weather and bone chilling layers of ice fog had challenged our endurance while the switch that governs the rut remained stubbornly locked in the off position. But it was only a matter of time and we knew it, and the size of the bucks that inhabit the rolling farmland outside Edmonton made them worth the wait.

Strapped into my tree at last, I kept a lonely vigil as the sun crept above the skyline to the south. Suddenly I saw three does leaving the field, headed in my direction. Oozing into shooting position in case a buck happened to be following, I felt the cottonwood begin to vibrate in response to my shivering. As they passed by 30 yards away, I mentally gauged the feasibility of a shot at an imaginary buck and concluded that it would have been out of my range under such difficult conditions.

Several minutes later, I detected another flicker of movement against the snow. The latest arrival turned out to be one of the Bow Zone's ever-present coyotes. Fluffed out in his winter coat, the big dog seemed to have "Back Quiver" written all over him, but in typical Wily Coyote fashion he detected some warning cue the does had missed and turned back well short of bow range. Not even some encouragement from the mouse squeaker Pat Cebuhar had given me the last time we hunted Kodiak together could change his mind.

Just as I decided I had reached the limits of my endurance, I heard the sound of hoofs on snow behind me. Once again I asked my gelled muscles to ease me to my feet. Whatever was picking its way through the brush sounded big, but as I turned slowly toward the shooting lane, I felt an uncommon degree of anxiety. In fact, I felt so cold I wasn't sure I could bring my bow back to full draw. In the end, my concerns proved academic. As the sound of the approaching animal swelled through the chilly air, I finally saw the outline of a moose lumbering through the brush. Since Jeff had a moose tag, I duly noted the sighting and began the long tedious process of climbing down from the tree once the huge animal had passed.

Aurora borealis, moose, and whitetails... what a combination.

Usually when I travel to hunt, I do so in search of animals I can't pursue close to home. And there are certainly plenty of deer in the woods right around my house. But there aren't a lot of *big* deer; suspect genetics and Montana's four-week rifle season pretty well eliminate that possibility. And as Gene Wensel told me many years ago, big whitetails might as well be a species all their own, at least from the bowhunter's perspective. While I've never been one to care about scores or record books, the sight of an outsized whitetail buck affects me even more profoundly than an encounter with a big bull elk or moose. Beamy, heavy-racked bucks are always worth traveling for, and no whitetail destination I know excites the imagination quite like the Edmonton Bow Zone.

While a few of my regular hunting partners consider tree stands boring, I find them an endless source of fascination simply because of the opportunities they provide to observe the world around us. Often these observations involve the animals we hunt, and much of my own firsthand knowledge of game derives from otherwise uneventful mornings and evenings aloft. But non-game species provide their own share of entertainment, sometimes including our own.

The afternoon after my encounter with the moose, I climbed into a tree at the edge of a field beside a strip of cottonwoods connecting two large woodlots. The configuration of the cover and abundant sign made the stand location a natural, and I entertained high hopes for the evening hunt. As does began to appear at prime time, I noticed a vehicle turn off the gravel road and enter the field a half mile away. After spinning a wild series of loops across the snow, the car continued in my direction, and I soon heard the dull thud of heavy metal bass rise above the sound of the engine. Clearly, this wasn't going to be my night.

Indeed. The perimeter of the field must have been two miles in circumference, but the car eventually wound up right under my stand. I wondered for a moment if there had been a miscommunication with the landowner and I was about to receive a chewing out, but it immediately became clear that the driver was completely unaware of my presence. As the car slid to a stop, he stumbled out and began an amateurish moon-walk across the frozen stubble to the beat from the boom box. Then the bong came out. "Man!" he bellowed to the empty woods after a long, greedy drag. "Is this some great shit or what?"

Struggling to contain my laughter, I thought up several snappy replies. (*Yeah, but you should have been here last week.* Or, *That's what the Mounties said when they busted the guy who sold it to you.*) But sometimes it's best to let sleeping dogs lie. My evening hunt was already ruined, and it didn't seem worth getting shot out of my stand by some paranoid kid who couldn't figure out why the trees were talking back to him. He soon departed, and even though I hadn't seen a buck I left the field with a certain winner in the Crazy Things I've Seen While Hunting contest.

Later that evening, Jeff and I visited our friends John and Cindy Schneider for dinner, giving me an opportunity to look at the great antlers from the buck John had killed with his self bow the previous season. While the venison simmered over the stove, John showed us some awe-inspiring videos he'd made late that summer in the fields beside his house. If I've ever seen a 200-inch whitetail, it was the buck on John's video. "He's still out there in the swamp," John assured me. "And you're hunting him tomorrow."

"But John!" I protested. "You've been campaigning that buck all season! I can't just march into your backyard and try to sneak him out from under you."

"I'd love to see you kill him," John replied, and he meant it. When the hunting is all over, that kind of sportsmanship and generosity surely means more than the size of any horns.

After a quiet sit the following morning, John and I met back at his house, warmed up over a welcome cup of coffee, and set off into the woods on a brief scouting mission. A hundred yards into the cover, we found a huge, fresh scrape located in a natural funnel between a field and the bedding cover. Twenty yards downwind from the scrape, a large conifer offered an ideal stand location and we quickly went to work. Again, John insisted that I take first crack at the new stand, an effort that ultimately proved unproductive.

The following day, it was my turn to insist that John hunt the scrape. That evening, Jeff dropped me off at a stand along the edge of a large wood lot where I had rattled in a small buck earlier in the hunt. The cold had abated somewhat--which meant that it was five above instead of five below--and as I settled into place for the evening I felt pleasantly relaxed and comfortable even though my hunt was winding down. As I studied the terrain and concentrated on the sounds of the woods behind me, I considered the likelihood that I would leave without killing a deer and accepted it stoically. One does not hunt the Bow Zone because it offers lots of opportunities at game, but to enjoy the possibility of an encounter with an exceptional buck.

Just as the sun kissed the distant horizon, I saw a deer emerge from the cover 300 yards away. I no longer carry field glasses when I hunt whitetails, since I decided years ago that they are really nothing but a distraction in a tree stand. I could tell the deer was a buck, and it looked significantly larger than the little 4-point I'd had under the stand earlier. As the deer worked its way across the field and disappeared into the adjoining wood lot, I realized I wasn't going to get a better look without offering a bit of encouragement.

All good sets of rattling antlers have a story behind them and this one was better than most. The horns had come from the same wood lot I was hunting. Jeff and his daughter Rachel had each found one of the matched set the previous spring, and as I hung my bow on a convenient branch and reached for them I felt as if I were handling some family heirloom. Could such intangibles possibly matter to the buck? I only knew that they mattered to me.

I've seen bucks respond to rattling antlers in many different ways, none more exciting than the flat-out charge, a phenomenon I get to experience once or twice a season back home if I'm lucky. This proved to be the night. At the first ring of tine on tine, the buck exploded from the cover on the opposite side of the field and began to trot straight in my direction. There was no doubt at all about where he was going to wind up, and I needed to be ready to deliver the goods when he arrived.

When the buck dipped down into a crease in the field, I swapped the antlers for my recurve and moved my feet into what I hoped would be the optimal position for a shot. When he reappeared, I enjoyed my first good look at his headgear. While obviously a nice deer, I suppose I'd been jaded by all the real monsters I'd seen on local walls over the course of the week, and for a moment I felt myself hesitate. Finally the voice of reason prevailed: this was a big deer carrying six points on each antler, I was due to leave the following day, and the sight of him prancing all the way across the field in response to my rattling felt mesmerizing. He was asking for an arrow, and I would have been a fool to deny the request.

But not at the price of a marginal shot… Twenty-five yards out, he turned broadside and glared down into the brush behind me in search of the big fight, staring right into my face in the process. I remained motionless. Slowly, the buck worked his way toward the fence line to my right. After offering a series of inquisitive grunts, he turned and passed in front of me just over fifteen yards away, and when he stopped and stared down into the brush once more I picked a spot, drew, and released.

When I reflect back upon animals I've killed over the years, I'm struck by the fact that what I remember most vividly usually isn't the shot but the recovery. This buck proved no exception. The deer spun at the moment of impact and I was pleased to see the broadhead protruding from his off side, confirming complete penetration. I have my share of weaknesses as a bowhunter, but I've always prided myself on an accurate first assessment of my hits. My impression was that the arrow had struck the deer an inch or so high and back of the spot I'd picked, but still well below the spine and in front of the diaphragm. As the deer made a quick hundred-yard dash back along the edge of the field and into the brush, I expected him to drop in plain sight. He didn't.

With good tracking snow on the ground, I still anticipated little difficulty. After climbing down from the tree and organizing my gear, I waited until the light had all but faded from the sky and set out simply to confirm his track and assess the blood trail. With blood sparse at best, I marked the track where it entered the woods and walked out to meet Jeff on the road.

Jeff's daughters Rachel, Kirsten, and Lisse were due to meet us in camp for dinner, which gave us a good excuse to give the trail the two-hour rest it deserved. Rachael desperately wanted to return with us, but the thermometer had already plunged back below zero and she was poorly dressed for what might turn into a long, frozen hike through the woods at night. Over her protest, Jeff and I reluctantly vetoed the idea. I hope she's forgiven us.

The brilliant light from the full moon disappeared rapidly as Jeff and I returned to the trail. Predictably, my flashlight failed at once, leaving us to work with Jeff's alone. Once inside the trees, a riot of fresh deer tracks forced us to rely on scant traces of blood to stay on the trail. Suddenly, I began to have second thoughts about the hit, and when Jeff's flashlight began to falter I made an executive decision to leave the trail until the following morning. Given the frigid temperature I wasn't concerned about the meat, and the thought of bumping a wounded deer from the circumscribed patch of woods made the risk of losing some venison to the coyotes seem minor.

After a long, sleepless night, we returned at first light. Jeff set off to walk around the wood lot to check for exit tracks while I returned to the original trail. Moments later, I came across the buck lying barely 10 yards from where we'd turned around the night before, the victim of a perfect double-lung hit. I have no doubt that he'd been dead by the time I first climbed down from the tree. And we hadn't lost a scrap of meat to scavengers.

Antlers are marvelous, but friends are more so. This hunt wouldn't have been possible without Jeff's knowledge, John and Cindy's hospitality, and Rachael's contribution of just the right rattling antler. When the horns have been mounted and the venison consumed, those are the qualities that endure.

The view down the barrel.

CHAPTER SEVENTEEN

The View Down the Barrel Alaska

I'D BEEN OUT in the Bush so long I didn't know what day it was anymore, but I did know it was crunch time.

The wind had risen out of the west overnight. Forty-knot gusts had made the skiff run across the lake wet and dicey, and if the storm kept building we faced the possibility of being unable to make it back to camp on the other side. But the real problem lay in the thick tangle of alders in front of us: a large brown bear that might or might not be dead.

The challenge began the evening before, when I spotted a large boar working his way down the beach with the wind at his back while diving for the late run red salmon migrating along the far side of the lake. Five of our six hunters had already tagged out on good bears—one with his bow, four with rifles—so Wisconsin bowhunter Bob Shultz had me and my fellow guides Bob May and Ernie Holland all to himself. Bob May has probably had as much brown bear experience as anyone in Alaska, but he had never backed up a bowhunter and was eager to do so. Consequently, I stayed behind to watch the bear and offer hand signals while Ernie ran the two Bobs across the lake and dropped them off in position for an ambush.

This looked like another ideal situation similar to encounters we'd been experiencing all week. Both of the rifle hunters I'd guided had taken their bears from 20 yards or less, and I'd been within bow range of another half dozen brownies without even trying. But this particular bear hadn't grown old by being dumb. After Ernie dropped the others on the beach, the bear took a long, hard look at the boat and stepped into the alders, never to be seen again.

But I'd already spotted another bear approaching from the opposite direction and began to give hand signals to that effect. Matters really grew complicated when yet a third bear appeared and set off on an apparent collision course with the second bear and the hunters, who were by then hidden in the grass above the beach. I knew they couldn't see either animal and did my best to convey the situation to them, but I wasn't sure my hand signal vocabulary was extensive enough to describe the developing events.

The last bear to appear reached the concealed hunters first. Although not as big as the first of the trio, he looked like a solid boar and I hoped Bob would choose to take him. When the bear suddenly whirled and disappeared up the bank and into the brush I knew he had shot, even though rain and distance kept me from evaluating the hit.

By this time, the second bear, still out of sight from the hunters, was closing fast from the opposite direction. Ernie made a valiant effort to haze him away with the skiff, to no avail. Ernie reached the hunters just ahead of the bear, but even a warning shot from his .375 had no effect on the animal. After a tense standoff, the bear finally continued up the beach leaving everyone with a case of jangled nerves.

By the time I reached the scene in our second skiff, Bob May had made a cautious approach to the alders where the wounded bear had disappeared only to be backed off by a menacing series of growls. I convinced everyone that the best immediate course of action would be a retreat to the beach to analyze the situation and consider our options. Bob Shultz was certain that he'd seen his arrow pass all the way through the bear and was happy with its placement, with one caveat: at the exact moment he released, the bear had turned slightly toward him. "Might be a little far back," he conceded. We all knew what that meant.

Several factors complicated our decision-making. Steady rain promised to eliminate any blood sign overnight. Furthermore, deteriorating weather meant that we might not make it back across the lake the next morning. Unaccustomed to bowhunters, Bob May was all for settling matters then, one way or another. Ernie was ambivalent. I argued strongly that the most likely result of going in immediately would be a bullet hole in what should have been a bow-kill (with several even less pleasant outcomes possible as well). Bob Shultz later thanked me for holding sway.

And that's how we came face to face the following morning with one of the tensest situations a bowhunter will ever have to face.

I dislike any mention of firearms in bowhunting stories, where they occasionally appear when a bowhunter shares a camp with gun hunters or decides to finish up an awkward situation with a rifle. But they do have one legitimate place: when the quarry truly qualifies as dangerous game.

Despite extensive African bowhunting experience including face time with most of the Big Five, I've never even touched a backup rifle there. I've also had considerable experience with Asiatic water buffalo in Australia, but always relied on my wits and judgment rather than firearms to keep me out of trouble with them.

Which brings us to North America, where I think only one big game species (other than the seldom hunted polar bear) really qualifies as dangerous game. Sure, black bears, cougars, and wild hogs are all *potentially* dangerous but none triggers screaming alarms in my brain, and I've hunted all three for decades armed with nothing but a bow.

Ursus arctos is another matter. Whether classified as a coastal brown bear or an interior grizzly, these animals are large, aggressive, and unpredictable. I've carried backup rifles for bowhunting friends in Russia and Alaska, and still guide seasonally for Master Guide Bob Cusack on the upper Alaska Peninsula. Those experiences have taught me plenty about bears, the outdoors, and myself, and a lot of that knowledge translates readily to personal bowhunting situations. (In Alaska, a commercial guide cannot hunt at all while conducting a hunt. What a pity; I'd have a house full of brown bear hides if it were otherwise.)

One interesting observation… A bear hit with a *properly placed* arrow is usually less trouble after the shot than one hit in the same place with a rifle bullet. Charges after the shot are less likely, and recovery distances are often shorter. I attribute this apparent paradox to the tremendous fight or flight response triggered by the noise and impact of a rifle shot.

I can also tell you that having played both roles I find it much more stressful to be the guide carrying the rifle than the hunter carrying the bow. Given the vastly superior stopping power of a large caliber rifle, that conclusion also seems paradoxical. But when push comes to shove, it's the guide with the rifle who will have to take the responsibility and make the hard decisions, sometimes instantly.

Responsibility and hard decisions? That sounds almost as bad as a real job.

So there we were. Bob May felt that he had an accurate fix on the growling he'd heard the night before and we decided to start with a careful sweep through that area. After a long, anxious night Bob Shultz was willing to help any way he could, but he didn't argue when we pointed out that the best place for him was out on the beach and out of the way.

Ernie and I agreed later that this was the nastiest piece of cover we'd ever entered in search of a bear. In addition to the usual alder jungle, ferns and grass tall enough to hide a crouching bear covered much of the ground. The search resembled a military operation more than a bowhunt, with just one of us moving at a time while the other two established fields of fire through the alders and provided cover. An hour of this left us with frayed nerves, soaked clothing, and no sign of the bear.

That failure provided me the opportunity to do what I should have done in the first place, which was to back off and think like a bowhunter. I asked Bob to replay the shot and mark where he'd seen the bear disappear into the brush as closely as possible. My search of that area soon produced his intact arrow lying in the grass. The rain overnight had almost washed it clean, but I could see enough traces of blood to convince me it had passed through the bear's chest. And while the rain had eliminated any possibility of a blood trail, I could pick out enough broken fern stalks to follow the animal's track with confidence. With Ernie on one side of me and Bob May on the other, I kept my eyes glued to the ground while my friends provided cover. Ten minutes later, the faint sign in the grass had led us straight to the bear, stone dead from a pass through at the base of both lungs. The boar had gone less than a hundred yards.

Breaking camp the following day felt bittersweet. A high pressure system had pushed away the rainclouds, leaving the tundra's autumn colors sparkling in the sunlight. It would have been fun to stay in camp for a few more days just to fish, or to see if Ernie or I could kill a bear of our own with one of our bows. But after two weeks in the bush we were all ready for a hot shower, and, still reeking with grease from all those big bears, I didn't need to skin another one for a while. The decision to break camp proved wise. A huge storm system blew in the following day, and it became impossible to fly for over a week.

I still felt wistful as we broke down the tents and began to haul all the gear to the shore. As usual, I told myself that I was just too old to keep doing this for another season. And as usual, I knew that I was lying.

Section IV

ALONG THE BORDER

ALONG THE BORDER

I'VE ALWAYS BEEN INTRIGUED by the country along our southern border, in part because of my own ancestry. Both my parents are Texans. My father's father settled in the Brazos Valley, where he was a member of the last generation of horse and buggy country doctors. That's an interesting story of its own, but his home lay a bit too far north to qualify as border country.

My mother's family, on the other hand, originally moved to Texas by covered wagon and established a large ranch south of San Antonio. Unfortunately, long before I came along her father had lost the place to a combination of wine, women, and song, with a heavy emphasis on the first two. He separated from my grandmother when my own mother was just a child, and my maternal grandmother became the only one of my four grandparents I ever knew. I've always felt the emptiness of my family tree, and I suppose that whenever I return to that country now I'm searching for missing pieces of my own past as much as I'm searching for game.

No matter where you hail from the border country feels different, perhaps more distinctly different than any other corner of our vast and complex nation. Now more than ever, basic Spanish is often essential if you want to get anything done. The stark beauty of the desert terrain and the magical quality of the light beg for attention from the camera lens. Adapted to an arid environment in which browsing animals can mean quick death to a plant, the flora sports an array of thorns that will immediately earn the visitor's respect. The bird life is fascinating, as the region contains many species found nowhere else in the country. And there's always a remote chance for a glimpse at a desert sheep, an ocelot, or even a jaguar.

Newcomers will have to learn to adapt to the demands of the desert environment. As an Alaskan accustomed to wet feet and horizontal rain, I had to re-program my instincts to reflect the fact that the biggest threat to survival wasn't too much water but not enough. Then there is the matter of illegal alien traffic. The vast majority of these people are simply fleeing poverty and looking for work, but there's always the chance of stumbling into somebody's drug deal. Along the Arizona border, where we now spend a month every winter, you won't have to walk far along any dry wash in the backcountry to find trails of human footprints headed north. I watch my back there as carefully as I do in Alaska bear country.

But it would be a mistake to let thorns, heat, and paranoia compromise one's impressions of this great country. There's just too much to see and do there, and I plan to take even greater advantage of those opportunities in the years ahead.

CHAPTER EIGHTEEN

The Song Lines
Mexico

DEFINING THE FEEL OF NEW PLACES by their bird life has become an old habit. Tonight along the dry arroyo, green jays dance through the thorns like revelers at a masked ball. High above the mesquite, a caracara sails past on a magic carpet of warm air, its dark plumage somber as Death in a Bergman film. The roadrunner skittering along at the edge of my vision might look like a cartoon character, but I know it's hunting too, searching for something to skewer with its pointed bill. *Beep, beep,* my ass. This is the desert, not Disney World.

One by one, I tune out these distractions and concentrate upon the sounds of the darkening brush ahead. Because they are built close to the ground and frequent thick cover, pigs are one of the few creatures that make more noise than we do when they move through the woods, engaging in apparently pointless vocalization and feeding with the table manners of, well… pigs. All this means they're often easier to hear than to see, which is how I learned that the nasty strip of thorns along the bank of the arroyo contains at least one of the things I have come to find. All I need to do now is close the gap to shooting distance.

After several minutes of intense auditory scrutiny, another soft, reedy grunt rises from the brush somewhere ahead like a single note from an oboe. The evening breeze feels gentle as a sleeping baby's breath, but I am careful to keep what there is of it in my face as I slowly begin to ease forward. Finally I can hear the faint rustling of brush against hairy flanks barely ten yards away. But the thorns guard their secrets well. There is no way to stalk deeper into the thicket, much less shoot an arrow through it. All I can do is wait and hope the pigs emerge into the open before the evening light fails completely.

But that never happens. So close and still so impossibly far away, the game remains inside its own zone of safety while the last of the color drains from the western sky. But by the time I give up and set off through the mosaic of cactus and moon shadows toward camp, companionship, and dinner, I have accepted matters with resignation. I knew all along that finding what I came for here would not prove easy. At least I can enjoy the satisfaction of being right.

Just to the north across the Rio Grande, lies my mother's people's country. My maternal forebears arrived by covered wagon in time to endure their share of the violence that simmered along the border throughout most of the 1800's. My grandfather made a hard living there until he lost both his ranch and his family in a fog of alcohol and general misbehavior years before I came along. All I have left of him is a scattering of faded photographs showing a rugged prototype Marlboro man, usually posed with a lot of big, dead whitetails. Despite his distant reputation for belligerence and erratic ways, I have always regretted the apparently unbridgeable gap of space and time that separates us.

Although my mother left the border country years ago and never returned, she took with her hints of what she left behind: the soft drawl apparent to everyone but me, the Spanish idiom that worked its way into my own childhood vocabulary, fireside recollections of south Texas history, a taste for all things *picante*. These are the clues that have finally led me back. The bows and arrows are merely excuses. I need to see and feel the places I came from, to search for things that have been lost longer than I can imagine. But as on any hunt, only the act of looking is assured. What I find depends upon both circumstance and the effort of the search.

Our friend Ricardo provided the immediate impetus for our trip. An enthusiastic outdoorsman and dynamic young businessman of dual Mexican-American citizenship, he kindly invited Lori and me to visit his family ranch and address a business banquet in Nuevo Laredo. Realizing that this wouldn't be the usual outdoor crowd I address a dozen times a year, I worked up something new for the presentation: *Hunting, Wildlife, and Cultural Values in the New Century.* But on the night we cleaned up and headed to town, I suddenly realized just how much that sounded like the work of a pipe-smoking pretender wearing a tweed jacket with leather arm patches. "Think I can get through this?" I whispered nervously to Lori.

"You'll do fine," she assured me. I only wished I could share her confidence.

As an admitted social cynic, I decided years ago that when people back home greet each other with hugs and kisses it's usually because they want something. But that night it didn't take long for me to check my skepticism at the door. Down here, people greet one another effusively because they're glad to see them. When they say *mi casa es su casa*, they mean it. It's enough to make you think. Up north, we build stout walls against the cold and eventually exclude more than we ever intended. Along the border, people seem as open and accommodating as the architecture of the homes they inhabit, and Lori and I quickly yielded to the spell of their hospitality.

In front of the podium at last, I took a deep breath, discarded all my prepared notes, and launched into a series of hunting stories as if I were entertaining friends around a campfire. When you do this kind of thing as often as I do it doesn't take long to tell when you're engaging the audience, and that night we all felt like family in a matter of minutes despite the size of the crowd. By the time I had finished, those who hunted all wanted to go hunting and those who didn't wanted to know more. The best questions come from the women in the audience, an aside that provides a special measure of satisfaction. In the course of my travels, I usually can't wait to get out of town and back to the bush, but not that night. Before anyone realized it midnight had come and gone, but nothing had turned into a pumpkin. Conversation flowed like wine as my own rusty Spanish began to flex its muscles. Everyone seemed to have an invitation to extend: to hunt, to fish, to share what they had to share. Never mind the game that eluded me earlier. I felt as if I had finally found something of value after all.

But I couldn't keep myself from studying the faces of our new acquaintances, wondering whose relatives might have crossed paths with my own. Had anyone's grandfather hunted deer with mine, bellied up to a bar with him, shared in his triumphs and despair? Despite the evening's familiar ambience, the past guarded its secrets as carefully as the brush had guarded its own the night before. I was still on the trail of something never meant to come easily.

A successful search for something we badly want to find seems the best way to conclude our haunted, richly textured visit, and Lori has provided us with just the opportunity we need for closure.

Her recurve drove the cedar arrow into the buck's side at last light the previous evening. She felt confident about the hit, but after an extensive discussion of what she saw as the deer tore off through the brush, I decided that the arrow might have penetrated only one lung. With a crisp, cool sky overhead, we chose to leave the trail until morning. And yes, the buck was a nice one, a 5-point according to our western vocabulary, a 10-point according to Ricardo's: the kind of deer you search for until you haven't got any looking left in you.

Now as the three of us assemble at the site of the shot and ease slowly off through the brush with the early light behind us, we feel joined by our common purpose, like astronauts, or sailors in dangerous waters. The morning will end in triumph or disaster, with no possibility in between. We all want this buck so badly we can taste the longing in the back of our throats. We will proceed together as a team, joined in an unstated promise to share equally in the outcome of our search no matter what the result.

[164]

At the edge of the brush 50 yards from the spot where Lori released her arrow, a running track appears on a patch of barren dirt and that's enough to get us started. Ten yards farther ahead, one tiny crimson droplet glistens from a prickly pear on the right side of the trail, correlating perfectly with Lori's recollection of her arrow placement. Three trackers make an ideal team in difficult cover, with one marking the last sign, another working meticulously ahead on hands and knees, and the third casting about like a bird dog searching for clues in unlikely places. In just this fashion we leapfrog ahead, ignoring the thorns that insist on exacting their toll for our passage. Finally Lori discovers one end of her arrow, broken off a hand's width below the fletches. This important piece of evidence convinces me the deer is lying dead somewhere in the vast sea of scrub ahead of us, ours to track down or lose to the coyotes.

The next hundred yards require an hour of painstaking work to cover. Each drop of blood feels like a gift, while the increasingly lean intervals between them remind us harshly of all that lies at stake. I can feel Lori begin to recoil from the possibility of failure. Then Ricardo and I round a thick clump of prickly pear from opposite directions and simultaneously come upon the buck, serene in death's repose, antlers glistening in the morning sun.

One of the things I enjoy most about bowhunting big game is the finality of its conclusion. Catching big fish or shooting a lot of birds can be gratifying, but somehow those activities always feel soft and reflective in the end. Not so with bows and arrows: you either get what you tried to get or you don't, and this time we got it. But after the long, difficult track the sense of accomplishment pales before the sense of relief. The outdoors has no more satisfying conclusion to offer.

As Lori kneels to examine the buck, she turns, picks momentarily at the dirt, and rises with an exclamation almost as joyous as the one she shouted when Ricardo and I announced our discovery. In her hand lies a perfect flint arrow point, a pre-Columbian relic left behind by an anonymous Coahuilatecan hunter back when our own ancestors still thought the world was flat. And suddenly, indescribably,

I feel whole again.

Australian aborigines mark their world with song lines, mental paths through space and time composed equally of terrain, history, and myth. Invisible to outsiders, they lie across the outback as obvious as paved highways to those who have learned the trick of seeing them. Now, finally, it's my turn. The deer, the arrowhead, and Lori's obvious delight have somehow closed the circle. There are those you get to love and those you don't, and the long trail has taught me to appreciate my wife as surely as it has taught me why I was never meant to know my grandfather. The sense of dislocation that has troubled me ever since our arrival has eased at last.

The thorns seem unable to bite us now, and dragging the deer back through the cactus to the road feels as effortless as ice-skating across a pond on a sunny winter day. Utterly comfortable in our shared company, the three of us laugh with the understanding of elders and the enthusiasm of children. We have all found what we have come for, and for the moment at least, nothing can take it away.

Lori with her borderline buck.

CHAPTER NINETEEN

Brush Country
Texas

AS ALWAYS, the senses tell the story: the soft murmur of doves filling the air, the brilliant flash of a cardinal in the trees, the pungent smell of mesquite, the sharp prick of thorns reminding the visitor of the old Lone Star caveat *Don't Tread on Me,* even though the original warning applied to the country's fauna rather than its flora. Who but Texans could put a coiled rattler on their national flag? This afternoon the oppressive burden of the summer heat on the longest day of the year makes us feel trapped inside an oven. No one ever recommended hunting south Texas in June, but we planned the trip around our fly rods and the redfish that prowl the flats in the nearby Gulf and brought our bows along almost as an afterthought. Now, dealing with more heat than I've felt since a torrid October week in Zimbabwe three years earlier, I have to wonder if we've pushed things a bit too far.

But there's the pond right where our hand drawn map says it should be and there are the hogs to go along with it: a sounder two dozen strong, each bristly pig dripping with fresh black mud. Never one to ignore a golden opportunity, Lori declares her intentions as the hogs scatter back into the brush. Sitting in a ground blind atop a cooler full of ice sounds like just the thing to her, and it's a hard proposal to argue.

Thirty minutes later she's settled into place while I load my daypack, check my bearings, and set off into the cover determined to do this my own way.

Despite the merciless heat, it feels good to be back in the brush country. The property we're hunting belongs to our friend Ricardo, but I have deep, distant roots here too. For me, hunting the brush country always means more than bows and arrows. It's about coming home to a home I never really knew.

Several hundred yards into the cover, it occurs to me that the welcoming committee has some work to do. The local plant life all seems determined to bite before it's bitten, and after a careless encounter with a cactus my right buttock feels like I've just been on the receiving end of a branding iron. But the hogs evidently see things differently. The prickly pear is ripening and the pigs have been smashing the plants apart to get at the succulent purple fruit. With fresh sign everywhere, I force myself to ignore the irritating sting in my rump and concentrate on slowing down the pace and keeping the breeze in my face. Heat, thorns, and lost family ties aside, I'm here as a hunter today.

A dated local aphorism describes south Texas as hell for women and horses, heaven for cattle and men. Pigs belong in the second category and the brush country supports two kinds. The diminutive javelina is the native son, and I still find them fascinating animals even though I've killed enough of them to make me feel casual about taking another unless I need it for dinner. The feral hog is the interloper, introduced to the brush country by settlers and fortified with infusions of Old World bloodlines until it became the genetic mish-mash that characterizes wild *Sus scrofa* throughout the species' vast modern range.

As an unofficial charter member of the Ham Slam club I've learned a few things about hunting pigs over the years, principles that apply whether you're hunting feral hogs in the Hawaiian highlands or bush pigs in the jungles of Africa. Pigs crave thick cover, where their thick hides allow them to move freely through thorny brush and their weak eyesight leaves them at relatively little disadvantage in the eternal contest between predator and prey. Hunting them where they live means using your own ears and nose as much as your eyes, and after another hundred yards through the pucker brush, sure enough. The rich barnyard aroma of swine brings me to a halt and then a soft chorus of grunts rises above the background chatter of the birds overhead. It's time to go into stealth mode.

Edging laterally across the breeze to get in front of the pig sounds, I nock an arrow and wait. Suddenly a dark form appears in the mesquite, inbound and closing. An industrial strength hog in the 250-pound range, the animal looks intimidating. But for better or worse, I learned to switch off the second part of my own fight-or-flight instincts years ago, an attitude I may well pay for some day. Thinking shooting lanes, shot placement, and barbecue, I watch eagerly as the animal continues into bow range.

But being close to hogs and killing them are two different things, and as the boar shuffles by a dozen steps away I just can't visualize a clear route for my arrow through the brush. Tense with frustration, I almost try to punch a shot through the tangled mesquite as the hog passes broadside, but I've been at this too long for that kind of judgement error. The hog and I both deserve better, and I know it even if it doesn't. Then the animal hits my scent line and plunges noisily back into the thick cover where he might as well be on another planet, and it's time to take a deep breath and go find another one.

This country enjoys a history far more profound than my family's own. Some of the oldest Native American artifacts ever identified come from south Texas. After Lori found the flint point lying next to her fallen buck the year before, I had a jeweler friend incorporate that special artifact into a necklace pendant to remind us of where we had been together and of those who hunted there before. And tonight as I start to ease back into the breeze, I find myself letting my ears and nose do the hunting once again, freeing my eyes to wander across the ground underfoot.

Unfortunately, my downward attention concerns more than arrowheads. This is serious snake country and the memory of the rattler we saw driving in at midday refuses to go away. We've got plenty of rattlesnakes back home, but not like that one: longer than I am tall, thick around the middle as my calf. I remember my mother telling me how my grandmother used to sit her down on the ranch house porch every morning while she walked through the yard killing snakes to make it safe for her to go out and play. In deference to the heat and the need for silence, I've left my heavy boots and snake chaps back home in Montana, and the thought of blundering into one of those six-foot dragons unprotected is almost enough to make me turn tail and run.

But not quite, not with this much pig sign around. After guzzling down the contents of one of my water bottles, I detect more hog noises above the sigh of the breeze. Once again I manage to move in front of the pigs only to be denied a shot by impenetrable brush. But no one ever said stalking this country was going to be easy.

An hour later, I'm drenched in sweat and out of water, which as any desert survival expert can tell you is not a good situation in this kind of heat. I need the contents of the cooler back at Lori's ground blind a lot more than I need another frustrating encounter with the hogs, but absent reliable landmarks I'm reduced to dead reckoning in order to find it. I've always enjoyed a good sense of direction—an instinct today's generation of GPS-packing hunters may never know—but I have to admit that the eventual appearance of the green trees surrounding the pond where I left Lori looks like a life ring floating on an empty sea. I try to whistle to avoid startling her as I approach but my whistle disappeared along with the last bottle of water.

"You look dead," Lori announces as I stumble to the blind.

"I feel worse," I assure her. Unable to tell her about my encounters with the pigs until I've re-hydrated, I burrow into the ice chest and guzzle cold tea until my head begins to throb. As it turns out, Lori's seen pigs too, but none within bow range. Muscle tone restored at last, I drop my trousers unceremoniously and invite her to put her nursing skills to work on the cactus thorns imbedded in my butt.

And we're still in that admittedly comical position when the next group of hogs arrives, headed toward the wallow. "Want to take some pictures?" I whisper as I ease slowly toward the ground.

"No!" she whispers back. "I want to break some ribs!"

I should have known better than to ask. Shifting slowly out of her way, I resist the urge to remind her of what we both already know. The heat will not allow for any prolonged blood trails and her shot will have to be perfect. But inside 20 yards, Lori has become deadly with her recurve and at the twang of her bowstring the closest boar wheels and tears off after its companions with bright fletches sprouting immediately behind its shoulder. The blood sign confirms the impression of a perfect hit and 70 yards later we're exchanging congratulations over a stone dead pig.

As much as I'd like to spend the last hour of light searching for a hog of my own, our circumstances won't allow for any distraction. The thermometer back at our rented vehicle reads 107 in the shade and in that kind of heat meat care becomes an immediate priority. Suddenly I feel like Hemingway's Santiago watching the sharks circle his marlin. But we've done our homework, and a walk-in locker is waiting to receive the goods back at our motel. Moving quickly, we heave the hog off the ground beneath one of the trees near the pond, tie it off, and set to work. Half an hour later we're ready to start down the dirt road with a cooler full of pork resting on the back seat behind us. A *vaquero* appears out of nowhere, giving me an opportunity to practice my rusty Spanish as I explain our presence. After a friendly wave we're underway at last.

But we're not home free yet. The Border Patrol maintains an intimidating presence in this part of Texas, with good reason. While stalking, I came across numerous tracks and signs of illegal aliens headed north on foot across our friend's ranch. As soon as we swing onto the highway, we pass a patrol car. Moments later it's beside us, and then the blue lights begin to flash. Once we've pulled over beside the road, the agents ignore Lori behind the wheel, but they have all kinds of questions for me: polite questions, to be sure, but pointed, basically humorless, and delivered in Spanish. For once, I take pains to reply in my own native tongue. "What do you suppose that was all about?" I ask Lori when we're underway again at last.

"Have you looked at yourself lately?" she replies with a laugh.

Pivoting the rear-view mirror in my direction, I have to admit she has a point. I'm dark to begin with, and after a long afternoon of dust and sun I look enough like someone who's just crossed the border on foot to justify any Border Patrol agent's suspicious instincts. It's enough to make me pause and think about the human tracks I saw while stalking and about those who made them: desperate individuals willing to risk their lives for a chance to labor at jobs most of our own kids would consider beneath them. Life along the border raises all kinds of questions, and the answers don't always come easily.

Back in Montana the following weekend, the troops have gathered in our kitchen for what I've billed as a south Texas surf-and-turf: fly-caught redfish and sea trout from the Gulf and a roasted hindquarter from Lori's hog. Someone's complaining about the heat outside; the thermometer reached the upper 80's that afternoon. Listening to the sound of the roast sizzling in the oven and remembering what it took to get it there, I don't want to hear about it.

While our friends settle in for a serious discussion of last season's misses and next season's hopes, I excuse myself discreetly and call my folks back home in Seattle. I do that several times a week now that my parents are getting along in age and seem several sizes smarter than they did back when I was a rebellious teenager. With the brush country still fresh in my mind, I pepper my Mom politely with questions. Where exactly was the ranch where she grew up? What was the country like back when she was a kid? But she doesn't know... doesn't know or isn't telling. Too many years have passed and her own childhood memories have always been burdened by conflict appropriate to someone who grew up with a father more interested in raising hell than raising kids.

And so these questions remain for me to answer. Once again, I plan to return, to go back and look again. As always, I'll take my bow when I go.

CHAPTER TWENTY

The Fork Horn
Texas

ASKED TO SCOUT A LOCATION for a sequel to the great Sergio Leone spaghetti westerns, I'd be hard pressed to beat the Circle Ranch deep in west Texas's aptly named Sierra Diablo. It's all there, from mesquite to loneliness to desert grandeur, just waiting for a cast of misfit Italian actors to twitter away in lip-synched English while Clint Eastwood chews on his cigarillo and tries to decide who dies next. From dust to tumbleweed, the relentless wind always finds something to push around while the soaring buttes stand defiant in the face of all that entropy. There aren't enough adjectives in the dictionary: spectacular, desolate, eerie, and awesome all come readily to mind, but none of them, even in combination, do the terrain justice. What a place to hunt mule deer.

Like Blanche DuBois, I have always depended on the kindness of strangers. Granted, by the time I visited the area last December, ranch owner Chris Gill was certainly a stranger no longer although it hadn't always been that way. We'd met several years earlier through a rich circle of mutual friends united by interests in fly rods, shotguns, books, food, and natural history, common ground sufficient to trump differences in profession, personal background, and geographic choice of residence. Under the right circumstances none of those things matters, and finding those circumstances and heeding their call became something of a preoccupation for all of us. During the course of a pheasant hunt at our place in Montana, Chris had asked if Lori and I would like to come visit the Circle Ranch in December when the season was open for mule deer and quail. Talk about an offer I couldn't refuse...

Hence my solitary presence at the bottom of a steep-walled, rocky canyon as crystalline desert light began to flood the sandstone amphitheater from the east. The degree of loneliness felt just right. Lori and our friends were fixing breakfast several miles away across the hills, present and reachable by foot should I need them, as safely removed as citizens of another planet if I didn't. And as is so often the case when I'm bowhunting seriously, at the moment I preferred solitude to even the best of company.

Only a blockheaded visitor could fail to appreciate the subtle biodiversity of high desert habitat. Diversity of species, however, does not necessarily correlate with their density, and as the lights went on and I started to glass, the long, winding canyon began to feel oddly empty. That illusion derived from the natural and regrettable human tendency to focus attention only upon what we seek. As a student of natural history, I knew that my search for a big mule deer buck was compromising my appreciation of everything from cacti to roadrunners, but for the moment I didn't care. Sometimes the mind of the student must yield to the heart of the hunter.

Part of the pleasure of hunting open country derives from what I think of as intimacy at a distance. In most terrain suitable, say, for Alaska moose or Montana elk, goings-on at the ranges I was glassing wouldn't matter, either because thick cover would prevent me from seeing anything or because it would be impossible to reach it if I did. Not so that morning; the canyon lay there for my pleasure, offering virtually unlimited visual access to its secrets, which is why the complete absence of deer during the first two hours of shooting light felt like such a personal rebuff.

But then, suddenly, there they were: a half dozen pale gray forms ghosting along the edge of a draw a half mile up the canyon.

They disappeared into a terrain fold before I could glass antlers, but one deer's body looked distinctly larger than the rest, and with the December rut in progress I felt certain the group had to include a buck. While I congratulated myself on accomplishing the first necessary step in the pursuit of open country game with the bow--seeing it before it saw me--I also acknowledged that a lot more challenges lay between me and venison.

An hour later I eased slowly along the lip of the draw, glassing carefully between every step. Patience earned its reward when I spotted an ear flickering above a clump of brush on the opposite side hill. Dropping back over the skyline for cover--and carefully avoiding the prickly pear as I sought a location to sit--I soon had the whole six-pack accounted for: two mature does, three small bucks, and a splendid, heavy-beamed 5x5, the kind of buck I could hunt my home county in Montana for several seasons without seeing.

When in doubt, sit and study... The buck was clearly unapproachable to bow range in its current position, and would have been even without five extra noses and ten extra eyes and ears arranged about him like a Distant Early Warning system. But the bucks were plainly interested in one of the does. The three smaller boys took turns engaging in mock battle while the Boss followed his lady friend about the hillside, lip-curling and posturing. Sufficient testosterone can make any male vulnerable--a principle that applies to humans as well as mule deer.

But I still wasn't ready to commit to anything foolhardy. Again, patience won out when the worried doe stopped browsing and angled in my direction with all four suitors in tow. I lost sight of the whole menagerie when they descended below the eclipse, but rather than risk detection by advancing for a better look, I decided to trust my intuition. After deciding where I though the doe would likely reappear, I settled in behind a nearby yucca to wait.

And 30 minutes later, lo and behold... The doe popped over the hill and wandered by at frog-gigging range. Certain that the bucks would follow in good time with *el grande* likely in the lead, I assumed a kneeling position with an arrow on my string and tried to ignore the discomfort the sharp rocks underfoot produced.

For one solid hour I remained motionless, thinking about desert ecology, unfinished writing projects, and the buck scheduled to heave into view at any moment. But like a bride abandoned at the altar, I finally had to face reality: the son of a bitch had stood me up. After a quick break to massage knotted muscles and dig a few thorns out of my hide, I eased forward, waiting for an explosion of hoof on rock that never came. Finally, an explanation: all four bucks lay bedded on the opposite side hill, soaking up sun like kids beside a swimming pool as if girls were the last thing on their mind.

Where was a little testosterone when I needed it?

Three nights later, I still hadn't released an arrow, but I had learned a lot about bowhunting desert mule deer.

Setting up a blind at a water hole offered one obvious solution to the challenge of stalking the open terrain, but I just didn't feel like it. This wasn't a matter of snootiness: I've ambushed game at watering points before and no doubt will again. I just found wandering around in the desert too fascinating to resist. I wanted to see, hear, and smell as much as possible during our stay, and I wasn't going to accomplish that mission sitting still.

Montana visitors often ask me how I ever manage to kill antelope with a bow by stalking. My first response is always the same: find antelope in the right terrain. After three days spent watching tremendous bucks in unapproachable positions on open cliffs and hills, I finally decided to heed my own advice. Brushing off my Spanish, I questioned Evidencio, the head cowboy at the ranch, who had taken an obvious interest in my determination to hunt with a bow. He told me of a remote canyon that contained lots of trees along its bottom, as well as plenty of deer. That afternoon, Lori and I set off by jeep.

As soon as we began to hike along the canyon floor, I liked what we saw. Washed out creek beds and scattered stands of juniper and pinyon provided better stalking cover than anything we'd seen yet. Lori was licensed for javelina but not for deer, and we soon spotted a group of desert pigs climbing the wall of the canyon. Studying the terrain, I noted a sheer vertical rock wall just above them. "Don't worry," I said. "No way they're going up that face. They'll settle down and start to feed just below it."

The pigs, however, were on a mission. To our amazement, they somehow picked their way up through the cliffs. When last we saw them, they were headed over the top of the mountain through terrain that would have challenged a desert bighorn. How they managed to climb so adroitly on their stubby little legs remains a mystery.

A mile farther up the canyon, Lori alertly spotted two deer on the side hill ahead of us. My glasses confirmed that both were bucks, neither huge but one perfectly respectable. Better yet, they were browsing their way steadily down to the canyon floor and good stalking cover. While Lori climbed a rock outcropping to keep track of their progress, I entered the dry wash in the bottom of the canyon to begin my approach.

My only concern was the wind. Although basically favorable, the canyon's complex topography had caused the breeze to falter and swirl several times already. Nonetheless, the wind held steady as I eased up the dry creek bed intent on relocating the deer before they saw me. At one point I thought I might have gone too far, but suddenly an antler glinted in the brush ahead and I forced myself to reduce the pace of my approach even further.

Fifteen minutes later, I was in the best position imaginable. The smaller buck had just crossed the creek bed unaware 20 yards in front of me and his big brother was about to do the same. Sliding an arrow onto my bowstring, I eased toward the shelter of a conveniently located boulder and waited for what seemed a certain shot.

Of course, that's when the wind betrayed me. One moment, I had everything and nothing the next. At the first suggestion of breeze on the back of my neck, the smaller buck exploded from the brush and bounded back up the hillside with his partner in tow. I watched them stot their way uphill and stop a hundred yards away, deriving no solace from the realization that the hunt would have ended there for a rifleman. I could only recall the conclusion of my earlier conversation with Evidencio: *Es muy difícil con arca y flechas.*

Lori chose to sleep in the following morning, the last day of our hunt, and I could hardly blame her. The long, hard miles had accumulated rapidly enough for me … and I had a deer tag in my pocket. Encouraged by all that we had seen the night before, I set off in the dark for the distant canyon and a natural crossing route at its head where we had found abundant sign.

The dramatic arrival of shooting light reflected from the canyon's walls found me nestled down behind a pine, hunting with my eyes rather than my legs. The canyon floor held plenty of cold air and the first hour would have passed slowly and none too comfortably except for the dramatic beauty of my surroundings and the abundance of unfamiliar flora and bird life. Then motion caught my eye on the sunny side of the canyon's walls. A doe was moving briskly across the hillside, and my glasses eventually revealed four bucks in pursuit. Three carried unremarkable headgear, but the fourth was another story: a splendid 5-point rack on one side, a deformed, palmated club on the other. I'd never seen a mule deer quite like it.

Again, I elected to observe rather than rush ahead prematurely. After an hour's worth of mule deer whoopee, including an actual breeding of the doe by the big buck, all the deer bedded down except for one of the losers in the contest to reproduce. The disgruntled buck eventually ambled downhill in my direction and disappeared into a gully. With an abundance of brush and shadow for cover, I easily advanced within a hundred yards of the bedded deer and began to study the situation like a difficult problem on a chessboard.

I had the wind, and I even had enough cover on the side hill to attempt a stalk on the big buck. Two problems remained. The first was the doe, lying down right in the middle of the only route I could take to the deer I wanted. The second was the missing buck, location unknown somewhere between my position and the rest of the deer. I studied the terrain until I felt I knew every rock and bush on the hill by name, always reaching the same inevitable conclusion: I just couldn't get there from here.

That's when the missing buck reappeared, walking slowly downhill toward me. A quick glance through my binoculars confirmed what I already knew: this was not a very big deer. But as Aldo Leopold once pointed out, trophies are measured in effort, not inches. After days of hiking, climbing, and glassing, I felt ready to close the circle. Utilizing the cover, I began to ease laterally toward a bush between the deer and where he appeared bound, resolved that if he gave me the right shot, I would take it.

Moments later, I had my bow arm up as the buck rounded a tree 20 yards away and stopped, staring at me intently. Convinced that I was something but uncertain what, he took a step in my direction and went on point while I tried to become part of the brush. He stood well within my range, but with a bow a frontal shot at a big game animal is simply something thou shalt not do, the way thou shalt not covet thy neighbor's wife (black bears at three feet excepted). For five long minutes our standoff continued as I struggled to hold the shakes at bay. Finally, the deer seemed to accept me. As he turned broadside, I waited until his head went behind a bush to come to full draw, and when he reappeared, I picked a spot on his chest and released.

And when I walked up to the dead deer 150 yards from where I'd shot him, I realized how much more this forkhorn meant to me than any number of animals I've killed that were far larger according to conventional "trophy" standards. Thanks, Aldo; I needed that.

That evening, with the dead buck dressed and hung in the barn, Lori and I set off for a walk in search of javelina, quail, natural beauty, and one last encounter with the marvels of the high desert. Less than a mile from the ranch house, I noticed a cluster of does in the creek bottom with a solitary deer standing on the hillside above them. The first glance through my glasses almost made me lose my composure. "Treat yourself to a good look at that buck," I whispered to Lori. "You'll never see a bigger mule deer."

A heavy, perfectly symmetrical 5x5, the inside spread of the buck's rack would have accommodated a yardstick easily. The deer was built like a bull moose. Fresh from pursuit of the does, his tongue protruded from his lips like a Labrador retriever's on a hot summer day. If I'd still had a deer tag in my pocket, I would no doubt have been seized by a desperate need to acquire what stood before me. In the event, I was free to enjoy the sight, and dream of next year.

For that, among a great many other things, I had the forkhorn to thank.

Don with a West Texas mule deer.

CHAPTER TWENTY-ONE

Desert Light
Arizona

MY FIRST EXPEDITION to the Arizona desert took place so long ago that I can barely recognize the lean, mean guy with the jet black beard staring back at me from the few scratched slides that remain as my only photographic record of the trip. Ray Stalmaster and I arrived in Phoenix mid-January that year, leaving a swirling Montana blizzard behind us, and headed for the remote reaches of the San Carlos Reservation near the New Mexico border. A long day of travel by back road (and I use the term *road* loosely) took us into the heart of some of the wildest, most remote terrain I've ever encountered in the Lower-48 States. We only saw one other human being during the week we spent in the desert, but he deserves a brief digression.

Our first two days of spot-and-stalk javelina hunting taught me a lesson I've since relearned hunting these intriguing desert pigs from Arizona all the way to Texas and Mexico: You have to spend a lot of time trying to spot before you get to do any stalking. Javelina are sparsely distributed animals, and there's a whole lot of desert to hide them.

After a lot of glassing from the ridge tops I'd seen plenty of fascinating wildlife other than javelina, including a few scattered cattle that acted so spooky I wondered if they'd turned feral generations earlier. Occurring singly rather than in herds, they acted wary as whitetails. Over the course of a dozen encounters with them I noted that I wouldn't have been able to kill a single one with a rifle if I'd been hunting them.

So imagine our surprise when we rounded a bend in the two-track running along the floor of the canyon and nearly ran into a cow hog-tied in the middle of the road. A half-mile later we came across a second, and then a third. "I'd sure like to meet the gang of cowboys dragging those things down out of the hills," I commented.

A mile later, we did. The crew I imagined working with carefully coordinated teamwork turned out to be a lone rider. He and his mount, the toughest looking quarter horse I've ever seen, bore bloody scarlet crisscrosses from the thorns on every inch of hide that wasn't covered by leathers. The wrangler had just finished tying off another steer when I pulled over and offered him his choice from our cooler, where the last of our ice supply had finally melted into lukewarm water. "What are you going to do with them now?" I asked as he drained a beer in two gulps.

"Got a stock trailer over the hill," he replied as he swung up into the saddle and disappeared back into the brush. I come from country where you see rodeo buckles in every bar you enter, but ever since that encounter I've had to wonder how many of the guys wearing them know what a *real* cowboy looks like.

After another hour of fruitless glassing the following morning, I spotted a flicker of movement a hundred yards below me. Moments later, I had a dozen javelina feeding uphill in my direction. With a steady uphill thermal in my face, the stalk didn't consist of much more than edging laterally across the side hill to get in front of the pigs. The shot could have been measured in feet rather than yards, and after an easy blood trail I was packing my first javelina down the mountain to camp. That night we agreed that javelina ribs grilled over an open mesquite campfire sound a lot better than they taste, and that the desert was so much more appealing than Montana in the winter that we should return every year.

And for a while, I did, although that was a long way to travel just to shoot one pig. I probably should have become serious about desert deer hunting before I did, but it didn't take me long to discover Arizona's desert quail, and since I love my shotgun and bird dogs as much as I love my bow, I devoted most of my time on those early return trips to quail hunting. Then I got busy with my lion hounds back home in the winter, other destinations beckoned when I did decide to travel, and I just plain forgot about the appeal of the desert and all it has to offer for over a decade.

A variety of factors finally induced me to return. Although Lori and I had been married for a dozen years she'd never hunted the desert, and I knew she would love it. We had both grown serious about our photography, and I know few settings that offer better opportunities for the camera. A number of friends from Montana had started to snowbird south to homes near Tucson, so we had plenty of places to stay. Our old friend Doug Borland was due in the area on business, and I knew I could rely on Doug to log some long miles with me in the desert. Finally, I'd decided that it was time to get serious about killing a Coues deer with my bow.

The sleek little desert version of the whitetail first described by the military surgeon Elliot Coues enjoys a reputation as one of the toughest big game quarries on the continent. And that's not all it has going for it. In contrast to many of North America's most highly regarded trophy species, you don't have to win a lottery to draw a tag, or hire a guide to make the hunt. Arizona archery deer tags sell over-the-counter, and the vast majority of Arizona Coues deer live on public land. As the originator of the Blue Collar Super Slam, these factors made Coues deer an appealing quarry for me.

At the beginning of that trip, Doug, Lori, and I spent a week north of Tucson proving that Coues deer deserve their reputation. The terrain lent itself well to classical spot-and-stalk hunting, which Doug and I both enjoy, and a lot of climbing and glassing revealed no shortage of deer including some excellent bucks. To no one's great surprise however, spotting them and getting within bow range proved to be two different things. I blew a potential opportunity on our first morning out when I moved too soon after rattling at the head of a brushy basin, only to spook a heavy-racked buck that was obviously coming my way in response to the horns. Other than that it was nothing but distant fleeting glimpses and a lot of useful knowledge about the area and the terrain to be filed away for another season.

When Doug finally had to return to Tucson on business, Lori and I decided to head south, visit our old friends Mike and Nancy Hedrick, and work out our accumulated frustrations on some quail. Although it was a poor year for the two desert quail species (Gambles and scalies), Mearns quail populations were thriving in their mountainous live oak habitat, which also happens to be prime Coues deer country. After several days with Mike and Nancy, we'd enjoyed some great dog work, missed a few quail, and killed a lot more... and I had located several remote waterholes with abundant deer sign around their edges.

By this time, I'd received e-mail communications from Greg Munther and Dave Petersen, who had been hunting Coues deer nearby earlier in the season. Greg had killed a very nice buck... after sitting for 17 days beside good waterholes. With our clock running down, I knew I'd have to be both lucky and good to pull a buck out of the hills in the time that remained.

After giving the three most attractive looking waterholes I'd located due consideration, I decided to tackle one that didn't have the most abundant sign. But it was in a secluded location with plenty of good cover, and it was small enough to offer a shot at almost any deer that came in. A tree large enough to hold a stand stood just above the edge of the water, but I'd decided I was going to do this from the ground, so I hiked in before dawn the following morning, cobbled together a blind from fallen branches and debris, and settled in for what I expected to be a long but relaxing day.

I spent most of the morning trying to sort out the unfamiliar bird life visiting the waterhole and working on some overdue medical reading. I admit that I'd started to nod off in the midday sun by the time I suddenly heard sloshing noises from the water in front of me that

[184]

sounded larger than a bird but smaller than the range cattle that had wandered by occasionally. Opening my eyes and aligning them with a gap in the leaves that made up the front of my blind, I realized that I was staring at the haunches of a deer less than ten yards away.

Then a glimmer of sunlight flashed from an antler. The Arizona season is bucks-only and I'd already decided that I should take any legal Coues deer, since it would be a first of species for me and we had so little time left to hunt. But as I reached for my bow and oozed slowly into shooting position I realized that this was more than a barely legal buck. I was looking at a heavy, symmetrical 4x4 that most trophy rifle hunters would have been delighted to shoot. And after four hours versus 17 days… take that, Greg!

But the fat lady had yet to sing… I was nearly at full draw as I came up over the limb forming the top of the blind and realized that I had a serious problem courtesy of a simple mental error on my part. As careful as I'd been with most aspects of my makeshift blind construction, I'd left a large, dead branch from the oak tree that formed one corner of the blind hanging down in front. Of course the buck—head down and near foreleg extended as if he were trying to commit suicide—stood directly behind the branch. I just couldn't visualize a clear route for my arrow through the obstruction.

But my blind was serving its primary purpose well, and the deer obviously had no idea I was there. He had to leave somehow, and if he went back out the way he came (I could see fresh tracks in the mud to my right) I'd still enjoy an easy shot opportunity. And even if he exited in the opposite direction, I still should have had a reasonable chance to make some venison.

But it was the deer's day and not mine. When he finally departed he walked straight away from me, keeping the offending branch perfectly aligned between us. With every step he took I waited for him to veer off course enough to give me an ethical quartering away shot, but that never happened until he was nearly 40 yards out. At that point (remember that I *always* confess my misses) frustration overcame me and I released an arrow that probably should have stayed on the rest.

Fortunately, it sailed harmlessly over the buck's back, which is why I can laugh about it now.

There's a moral to every story, few more obvious than this one. The dead branch that saved the deer contributed nothing to my ambush, and it took me no more than fifteen seconds to break it down and get it out of the way once the buck had sped off never to be seen again. Granted, I'd built the blind in the dark, but I still should have noticed the branch. I'd convinced myself that there was no way a deer could get into the waterhole and back out again without offering me a shot, and I fit the data to the theory rather than the other way around. People who analyze human error have a name for this kind of mental system failure when it occurs in an operating room or an airplane's flight deck. I'm just going to call it stupidity and promise myself to do better next time.

For there most definitely will be a next time in Arizona. At the time of this writing, Lori and I have already rented a place there for the month of January, which should allow plenty of time to pursue everything we plan to pursue with bow, shotgun, and camera alike. Rocky, the older of my two Labs, has turned into an excellent no-slip upland retriever and our new German wirehair puppy will be ready to get started on quail. I'll probably buy another javelina tag; a decade has passed since I shot one.

And I'll be damn careful to trim my shooting lanes the next time I set up a ground blind for Coues deer.

Don and Doug Borland hunting Coues deer country.

Section V

COAST TO COAST

COAST TO COAST

MY GLOBETROTTING INSTINCTS have more to do with enthusiasm for new places, people, and wildlife that finding new quarries to pursue or different heads to put on the wall. To the extent I went for the hunting, it was because it was different and not because it was better. Credit the principles of the North American Model of Wildlife Conservation, which have continued to allow our country to offer some of the best hunting opportunities in the world despite an increasing human population, habitat insensitive politicians, and our society's relentless and sometimes pointless busyness.

And you don't have to set off to remote corners of the country like Alaska or Hawaii to find them. Whitetail enthusiasts need look no farther than our own upper Midwest to find the biggest bucks in the world. Re-introduced wolves notwithstanding, the Mountain West still offers great elk hunting, and top end predatory big game species like black bears and mountain lions thrive there as well. The high plains hold plenty of pronghorns. And so on…

However, those destinations and the game that calls them home receive plenty of attention in the outdoor press, so I'm going to offer a different view in this section, by exploring lesser known opportunities in places that don't spend as much time on center stage.

We'll range from Florida's palmetto swamps to the Eastern Shore of Maryland before heading all the way west to California. There won't be a lot of "trophy" heads at the end of the day, but we'll meet more new friends and explore some wild habitat in surprising places.

Those considerations kept the journey exciting for me even when the goal of the hunt was nothing more glamorous than wild pork on the barbecue or a boatload of giant rats, and I hope they do the same for you.

CHAPTER TWENTY-TWO

Big Lizards
Florida

"HAVE YOU BEEN convicted of a crocodilian offense within the last ten years?"

The question left me momentarily confused. I'm used to supplying all kinds of information when applying for a hunting license – birth date, Social Security number, height, weight (yeah, I sometimes lie about that one) – but *crocodilian offense*? I finally realized what the nice lady behind the counter at the Brevard County courthouse was asking me and replied with an emphatic, honest *no*. Fifteen minutes later, my wife Lori, local fly-fishing guide Don Perchalski, and I were all officially licensed as assistant alligator trappers operating under the aegis of our old friend Don Davis, who had drawn the gator tags in Florida's annual lottery.

Gator season didn't open until a half hour before sundown the following night. While Don D. (yes, the presence of three Dons on the team made for some confusion) went back to work, Don P., Lori, and I headed to our assigned gator area to scout, work some kinks out of our tackle, and do a little fly-fishing. An hour later, we slid Don's skiff off the trailer and began to run across the tannin stained waters of the St. Johns River to see what we could see.

The St. Johns is a fascinating body of water for several reasons of interest to outdoorsmen. It is one of the very few major rivers in the country that flow from south to north. It marks the southernmost limit in the range of the American shad, and coincidentally we'd spent some time on the lower river that spring fly-fishing for shad with the two Dons and our old friend Flip Pallot. And as students of bowhunting history know, the St. Johns was home to the Thompson brothers during the remarkable period chronicled in the classic *Witchery of Archery*. And here we were, about to embark on a hunt in this fabled setting for a species utterly unfamiliar to Lori and me. My home states of Montana and Alaska hold a tremendous variety of game species, but alligators are not among them.

That afternoon, we tried to locate some gar to give our bowfishing tackle a test run on live game, but had to settle for shooting at lily pads when the gar failed to appear. We then ran the whole length of our permit area and were mildly disappointed when we only saw a handful of small gators. "There was another open season here a week or so ago," Don pointed out, "and public land gators get worked over pretty hard. Hopefully, they're all just hiding back in the brush with the high water." That explanation sounded logical to me, and we spent the rest of the afternoon catching bass and bluegills on popping bugs.

Lori and I were suffering from scrambled systems, since we'd just arrived the night before from a two week stay in Africa. Since I knew we wouldn't be able to sleep anyway, I'd scheduled a snook expedition that night with our friend Scott Cormier, another fly-fishing guide and budding bowhunter. After saying goodbye to Don P. at the boat ramp, we headed south to meet Scott and then stayed out through the wee hours of the night catching enough big snook to mollify my concerns about missing the Montana archery opener even if we never saw an alligator.

Pleasantly jet-lagged and exhausted from our late night excursion, we awoke at Don D.'s house the following afternoon with just enough time to work on our tackle and think about gator hunting before I was scheduled to give a presentation to the two Dons' local fly-fishing club that evening. Regular readers know that I am definitely *not* an expert bowfisherman. If I lived in a place where I could shoot fish I liked to eat – or big game like alligators – I would devote more time to acquiring those skills. But Montana doesn't offer much to shoot at in the water but carp, and one mid-summer carp expedition per year is usually enough for me. I had to admit that I was going into that night's hunt as a virtual beginner.

Twenty three species of crocodilians inhabit the tropical and semi-tropical waters of the world. Despite occasional well publicized alligator attacks in Florida, only two pose a regular threat to humans: Africa's Nile crocodile and the saltwater croc of the Indo-Pacific. Angling adventures have provided me plenty of contact with both, while casting to tiger fish in Africa and barramundi in northern Australia. The Australian "saltie" is a protected species and I've never hunted African crocs, but my own interest in Florida gator hunting arose when I spent a lot of time with the African version on the lower Zambezi River. They're legal game there and I decided I wanted to shoot one, but since none of our African friends had any idea how to go about it with a bow, I decided I should learn the ropes on something a bit smaller and less aggressive. When I mentioned this interest to Don Davis, who has had plenty of experience with Florida gators, he applied for the tags, and there we were.

The natural and political history of the Florida alligator is a fascinating story in its own. Gators were exploited commercially for their meat and hides as far back as the 1800's. Their take was completely unregulated until 1943, when a four-foot minimum size was established. The gator population continued to decline in the face of intense commercial pressure however, and the state closed the gator hunting season completely in 1962. Poaching remained rampant, and the alligator was named to the first federal endangered species list in 1967. Alligator numbers then rebounded dramatically. The species was re-classified from endangered to threatened in

1977, and in 1980 the state's Alligator Management Program allowed regulated hunting again, with no demonstrable impact on increasing alligator numbers.

That sounds like a terrific wildlife success story and it is... unless you are one of the increasing number of Floridians who wake up in the morning to find a gator in the swimming pool. The state now issues about 4,400 public land alligator permits, but professional hunters licensed by the state kill around 11,000 "nuisance" alligators per year. As is so often the case when humans and high end wild predators interact (witness the number of "problem" cougars killed in California since that state's misguided ban on lion hunting), it's difficult to balance the interests of preservation and public safety. Florida seems to be striking a reasonable compromise with its gators, and I was happy to be doing my part.

With the wildlife management issues understood to my satisfaction, it was time to think about my tackle. The bow was no problem; my favorite #72 recurve was in our luggage from Africa. By coincidence, an old patient from my former medical practice had decided to give up bowhunting that year because of shoulder problems, and he'd given me an astounding assortment of old arrows and broadheads including some heavy glass shafts and unidentifiable (by me) fish points I'd lugged all the way to Africa and back. Properly rigged with safety sliders, I felt confident they would do the job. I knew that line management would be a key issue and I'd settled on a mid-size reel attached to my bow with a strap-on gadget adaptor. Friends had told me I'd have to use heavy line for gators, but my angling experience has taught me that you can land a marlin on 16-pound test tippet if you're careful enough, and I went for length rather than weight.

I wasn't wild about the idea of trying to manage a float while I was handling the bow, since shooting heavy fish arrows in the dark is tough enough without such distractions. I addressed this problem by pulling a loop of line through the back of the reel and having a float on a short line ready to attach to the loop with a heavy angling snap swivel. If the gator made a big run, I'd rip the gadget adaptor off the bow while another member of the team clipped the float to the loop and threw the whole thing over the side, reel and all.

I've talked to bowhunters disappointed after alligator hunts with guides who insisted on using bang sticks before bringing the gator into the boat. I have a lot of respect for gators and realize that "dead" ones can wake up and wreak havoc in a small skiff, but a gator taken with the aid of a bang stick just isn't a bow kill. Fortunately, ours was a bow-only gator team, and that part of the plan was clear. If I got a gator to the boat, I'd slam a sharp broadhead down through the base of the neck just behind the skull and sever the spinal cord. There would be no firearms of any kind aboard.

After more preliminary planning than I'd invested in any bowhunt for years, it was finally time to go gator hunting.

Dusk has already yielded to night by the time we ease Don P.'s skiff into the water, and the St. Johns looks like a ribbon of thick, black ink. The temperature is in the comfortable shirtsleeve range, with just enough breeze to keep the bugs at bay. There is only one more boat trailer in the parking lot, so we should have plenty of water to ourselves. As we idle away from the ramp, Don D. breaks out a Mag Light and sweeps it along the shoreline ahead. Hot damn! We're hunting alligators.

"Do you want to hold out for a big one?" Don asks.

"No way," I answer as I fiddle with the heavy arrow. "Matter of fact, I don't want a big one. I don't have much room for a hide and I won't be able to take much meat back home."

"Gator!" Don hisses. "See him?"

I don't, and that perplexes me since decades of saltwater flats fishing have left me with pretty good eyes for things in the water. As Don rambles on about a quarry I cannot identify, it takes me a minute or two to define the problem. Your eyes have to be aligned perfectly with the flashlight beam in order to pick up the characteristic red glow reflected back from a gator's retinas. Once

I've figured this out the first gator becomes obvious, as do a half dozen more along the shore. Don P. was right on our scouting trip. They were here all along.

But they've also been hunted earlier this year, and getting within bow range turns out to be a lot harder than it sounds. Time and again those red eyes simply disappear as we begin to close the gap. By our fifth or sixth unsuccessful approach, we've begun to develop some of the teamwork we'll need to close the deal. The whole process reminds me of fly-fishing for sailfish, which requires at least four people who know what they're doing to produce a hook-up: one to run the boat, one to man the teaser, one to clear the deck when the sail breaks water, and finally the angler with the fly rod ready to cast. In our case, Don P. is poling the skiff silently, which has to be a huge advantage over earlier hunters dependent on outboard motors. Don D. is manning the light while Lori stands by to handle the line after the shot. All I have to do is get the fish arrow into a gator.

After more than a dozen unsuccessful approach attempts, Don D. alertly spots gator eyes way back in the brush along the bank. Evidently the cover makes this one feel more secure, because this time the glowing red eyes remain stationary as Don P. eases the skiff into bow range. "How big?" I whisper.

"Six feet," he guesses aloud. Perfect.

But things are never easy with a bow. The gator is protected by a warren of overhanging branches. Although Don P. has me just over a dozen feet from the target, I can't see a way to thread an arrow through the obstructions. Motioning with my hand, I ask him to move the skiff's bow to the right. Now I've got a narrow hole to shoot through that will get my arrow over the largest obstructing branch... but because of the angle, I can no longer see the gator.

I've thought this scenario through earlier. I am ordinarily highly conservative in my shot selection, and during our recent trip to Africa I drove a couple of PH's crazy by turning down shots they thought I should have taken. But this is a different story. There are really only two possible outcomes when you shoot a fish arrow at a gator: a clean miss (no harm, no foul), or an arrow embedded in the gator (and it doesn't really matter where). Thus emboldened, I make my best guess as to the critter's position back in the hole, draw, and release.

And I soon appreciate an important realization: the most exciting moment in a gator hunt comes when you reach for the line after a shot, feel movement, and know that you have one on. The brush makes this hit especially chaotic, since we have to get the line running freely or risk giving the arrow a chance to pull out. Fortunately, Don D. and Lori are all over that chore, picking the line out of the brush like a backlash on a casting real. With Don P. maneuvering the boat like the pro he is we're eventually back in open water, following the surging line down the St. Johns.

Luckily, Don D. has had plenty of experience with this part of the game. The trick is slow, gentle pressure on the line; trying to horse the gator up to the boat usually leads to disaster. Don works the gator through several close approaches followed by strong runs just as if he were playing a big fish on light tackle, while Lori adeptly keeps the line in order. The critter hasn't gone nearly far enough to make me think about attaching the float to the line.

Then the alligator is suddenly lying on the surface beside us, oddly placid even though it's capable of taking off again at any second. By this time, I'm comfortably rearmed and ready for the opportunity. Carefully visualizing the sweet spot at the base of the skull, I draw and release once more. The arrow passes completely through the gator, which shudders briefly and goes limp. Voila: bang stick by Magnus.

Still not taking any chances, Don D. compresses the gator's snout while I make a dozen tight wraps around it with a roll of heavy electrical tape. An unnecessary precaution as it turns out; the fish arrow is lodged tightly through the ribs just behind the foreleg and the finishing shot has completely severed the spine as intended. Except for some paper work and skinning (gratefully assisted the following morning by Don P.'s taxidermist son, Justin), my gator hunt is as over as it can be.

What to make of this bold venture into one of bowhunting's most obscure corners? Prior to the hunt, I really didn't know how much I would enjoy shooting an alligator. Well, I enjoyed it a lot. The setting was dramatic, the hunt challenging, and I went home with a gorgeous hide and a bunch of delicious gator meat. Perhaps the most interesting aspect of the hunt was the element of teamwork it required. I do plenty of hunting on my own, but I don't see how I could hunt alligators without friends.

Fortunately, we have some good ones.

Florida gator: a face only a mother could love.

CHAPTER TWENTY-THREE

Replacement Barbecue and the Grand Slam of Trash Florida

I'D ALWAYS BEEN CURIOUS about the origins of the term *barbecue*. The word looks vaguely French and I thought it might have appeared in our own South courtesy of Cajun influence, but I'd never seen a similar French root word. Turns out the term originated among the indigenous Arawak islanders of the Caribbean and came to our own southern shores courtesy of early Spanish explorers. Nowadays, the term has been corrupted to refer to virtually any means of cooking meat over wood or charcoal, but in the heart of the South folks still treat the concept with respect, none more so than my old Floridian bowhunting partner, Don Davis.

"Indirect heat is the key," Don explained that first night in camp as we set up the barbecue prior to departing for our evening hunt. Elaborately crafted from sections of oil drums, the camp barbecue unit certainly looked up to the task as Don rubbed down the pork shoulder and stoked the coals.

Six years had passed since we'd last hunted with Don, but an invitation to speak at the annual Traditional Bowhunters of Florida get-together had provided another welcome excuse to escape a cold and snowy Montana March. We were a week early for turkeys this time around, but we'd planned a fly rod assault on the local snook, and the hogs in Florida's surprisingly wild interior are always in season.

And Lori and I found a few that evening. I actually had tension on my string when a large, gray boar emerged from the palmettos at last light, but the shot didn't feel right and I never released. As the inky southern night descended, we returned to camp to rendezvous with Don, trade stories, and rip into the barbecued pork, which proved done to absolute perfection. After a long, mouth-watering meal, we carefully put the leftovers in the cooler and went to bed dreaming about the pulled pork sandwiches we planned to enjoy once we'd worked up an appetite again the following day.

The next morning, we rose in the dark to calm weather, stars overhead, and a scene of minor disaster. Camp raiding raccoons had visited as we slept, and somehow the masked rascals had tipped the cooler over, opened it with their paws, and devoured everything inside including the leftover barbecue. Since we didn't feel like driving back into town to re-supply, this discovery provided a powerful motivation for our morning venture into the scrub. Never mind the big boar I'd spotted earlier; I wanted more pork for the barbecue.

Still feeling the effects of a long day's travel, Lori chose to sleep in, so I headed across the creek bottom by myself. As dawn broke gloriously behind me, I spotted several groups of pigs feeding in the field nearby, including the same boar I'd nearly killed the night before. Since the grass in the field only stood ankle high, I planned to parallel the hogs and try to ambush one when they left the field for the dense cover along the creek.

The first group to head my way didn't include a hog over a hundred pounds, but I knew from previous experience that smaller pigs make ideal eating. Scrambling to reach a position just downwind of their point of exit from the field, I nocked an arrow and momentarily lost track of the hogs as they filtered into the scrub. But suddenly an 80-pound boar was shuffling through the grass in front of me 20 yards away, and I came to full draw. For a moment I thought he was going to reach an impenetrable tangle of briars without offering a shot, but then he hesitated with his near front leg forward and I sent the cedar shaft whistling into his armpit tight behind the elbow. Nothing goes down quicker than a well hit pig (and nothing can be tougher to track than one hit unfavorably). The heart-shot boar staggered ten steps and collapsed in plain sight, sparing us a potentially nasty recovery.

The hogs still in the field seemed unaware of his fate. With the first pig safely accounted for, I continued to parallel the feeding hogs and actually passed up a point blank shot at a second pig of about the same size. But the gray boar that I wanted hadn't grown old by acting stupid, and he eventually trotted off into the jungle without ever passing an ambush point that he couldn't first inspect with his nose or his eyes.

Back in camp, I cleaned and dressed our eating hog while Don fired up the barbecue again. Dense hickory smoke was still issuing from its seams when we set out again that night. Lori wound up making a long stalk on a large group of pigs at last light. No shot resulted, but it was hard to feel too disappointed. We were thinking about supper more than trophies, and Don's masterwork at the barbecue met our every expectation.

Do I wish I'd managed to anchor that big boar? Well, sure... but as consolation prizes go, our replacement barbecue proved hard to beat.

Situated on ten thousand acres of prime central Florida wilderness, Don's hunting camp had already become one of our favorite getaways. Although I used to visit Florida as a kid to fish every spring, for most of my adult life the state had been little more than a waypoint en route to destinations as diverse as Africa, South America, and the Caribbean, and the Miami airport frankly has little to recommend it. Years earlier, Don had introduced us to a slice of Florida that few visitors ever even see, a vast swath of roadless swamp and palmetto large and complex enough to lose even an experienced outdoorsman. (In fact, Don and Lori still insist that I *was* lost there once, even though I simply wanted to experience the sounds of the swamp in the dark by myself that night.)

I've commented upon the way warm climates seem to bring out the best of human social instincts in an earlier chapter, and Don's hunting camp represents another prime example of that principle. If not quite an actual family, the dozen-odd hunters with whom Don shares the place at least constitute a tribe, and they quickly welcomed Lori and me into their circle on our first visit. The terrain and wildlife proved fascinating to visitors from the Mountain West, especially during the winter when our home lay covered in layers of white. And we never found any shortage of game. I didn't need to travel to Florida to hunt whitetails (in fact, Don quickly became a regular November visitor at our place), and because of scheduling complications I never got to hunt the Osceola gobblers there nearly as much as I might have liked. But the hogs alone were always worth the trip, especially when combined with some fly rod time on the nearby Indian River Lagoon, and small game and various varmints were always abundant.

The latter were very much on our mind the following evening as we tore into my barbecue hog. I still couldn't believe the coons had managed to open the cooler and pick our pockets so cleanly. Suddenly the Coleman lantern overhead flickered and died, plunging us unexpectedly into darkness and silence, which we all three maintained by some mutual unstated agreement. By the time I reached for my pack and the headlight it contained, pots and pans were beginning to rattle over by the barbecue. "Grab your bow," I whispered to Lori. "It's payback time."

The raccoons had already given us an ample demonstration of their determination and intelligence the night before, but those aren't their species' only character strengths. Anyone who has ever hunted them in classic fashion with hounds knows how incredibly tough and aggressive they can be. I've seen big boar coons back down blueticks that have dozens of cougars under their belts. If coons were the size of bears, you wouldn't be able to walk through the woods safely at night. Ordinarily I'm content to leave them alone unless I'm training my lion dogs, but these camp raiders had started the conflict in the first place and I knew we'd have no peace until we set some limits for them.

When I heard the nock of Lori's arrow snap onto her bowstring, I flipped the switch on my headlight. Soft, blue light flooded the cooking area, revealing a whole posse of coons swarming over the barbecue trying to get at the pork inside despite the heat. A more dedicated small game enthusiast than I am, Lori never needs encouragement in the face of an opportunity like that. At the twang of her bowstring, a soft splat followed by an outburst of angry growls and hisses rose from the table beside the barbecue as coons scattered in all directions. One down, I thought to myself.

By this time I'd realized that the local scavenger population had learned all about the fine southern cooking that took place in camp. Attracted by the sounds of food preparation and conversation, they simply waited until the lights went out and then went to work on whatever goodies they could lay their paws on. With that in mind, I suggested that we defer the trail on Lori's coon and repeat the process all over again. While Don refueled the Coleman, I served up our second round of pork and beans. "Guess it's time to turn in!" I yelled into the darkness ten minutes later as Lori nocked another arrow and Don killed the lantern.

Within minutes, dishes began to rattle all over again. When I turned my headlight back on a real prize waited among the coons: an especially large, silvery possum. Our only New World marsupial, possums have always fascinated me and not just because of their unique biology. When my father was growing up poor during the Depression his corner of northern Texas held virtually no big game, and he and his friends regarded possums as prized quarry. Although I'd grown up listening to him tell stories about his childhood adventures chasing possums with his hounds, I've never lived where possums live and in fact had rarely even seen one. I'd always told myself that if I ever had an opportunity to kill one with a bow, I'd take it to the taxidermist just to remind me of all those fireside stories I'd enjoyed as a kid.

Lori didn't have time to consider all this personal rationalization, but she didn't need to. As soon as I pointed out the possum among the scurrying raccoons she had an arrow on its way. And when the critter sprawled over on its back a few moments later, it wasn't playing possum; it was dead.

Meanwhile, one of the coons had scampered up a huge live oak towering over the cooking area. With Lori's possum secure I turned my headlight beam upward, revealing a pair of eyes a long way up what looked like a very tall tree. "You can do it!" Don urged as he handed me my bow.

I'm glad he thought so. My broadhead struck the branch the coon was standing on with a mighty thwack, leaving the cedar shaft vibrating like an Indian arrow in the side of a covered wagon in an old western movie. Unwilling to donate another arrow to the tree, I lowered my bow and began making excuses. Long shot, poor light, too many branches... but Don wasn't buying it.

"Watch this!" he said as he reached for his recurve. The shot that followed deserved a gold medal. The dead coon hit the ground with a thud, and the following day Don even got his arrow back.

Over coffee prior to our hog hunt the following morning, a caffeine driven thought occurred to me. "Honey," I said to Lori, "you've already got two thirds of the Grand Slam of Florida Trash."

"The possum, the coon..."

"The armadillo!" I added, filling in the blank. That was all the encouragement she needed to set out with Don in search of some possum on the half shell.

I've always held that hunters shouldn't kill anything without being able to articulate a reason for doing so, even for species considered varmints, whatever that term means. I'd justified the previous night's coon as a combination of deterrence and revenge, the possum as a tribute to my own family history. The armadillo could have been more problematic. I'm a brave and adventurous eater and Judge Woody Woodson, the camp patriarch, had always assured me that there was nothing wrong with barbecued armadillo, but I wasn't so sure. Fortunately, it didn't have to come to that. Before we left Montana, a friend had put in an earnest request for an armadillo to mount, and that was all the encouragement Lori needed.

The good news: Lori got her armadillo. That was also the bad news. When I met up with her and Don an hour after sunrise (and another fruitless encounter with my big gray boar), she was happily carrying her prize by the tail. Lori can field dress a deer almost as quickly as I can, but since this was a taxidermy specimen she deferred the knife work to me. At least that was the excuse she came up with, and it worked. Sort of.

My first impression of the armadillo skewered on Lori's arrow like a shish-kabob was that she'd shot a 15-pound cockroach. After a career as a schoolboy trapper I'm fairly handy with a skinning knife, but even after several minutes of careful study I had no idea where to begin. The project looked better suited to a band saw than a knife blade. I finally appealed to Don, but it turns out that he's too smart to shoot an armadillo and had no more experience skinning one than I did.

"Suppose we give it to Woody for barbecue?" I finally suggested.

"We can try," Don replied, and with that the Grand Slam of Trash faded into history.

Almost. Fleshed out carefully and salted down, Lori's possum hide made it back home in fine shape. My friend mounted it with a hook in its prehensile tail so that Lori could move it around the house at will. After a few glasses of wine she's even been known to surprise dinner guests by showing up at the table with it hanging from her neck. My only enduring contribution to the record of events was the arrow stuck high in the tree (which proved impossible to climb), where its bright yellow and white fletches remained plainly visible for years to anyone seated at the camp dinner table.

Don has never been reluctant to inform the curious just how it got there.

Lori glassing the green hills of California.

CHAPTER TWENTY-FOUR

Green Hills of California
California

WE ALL KNOW CALIFORNIA, or at least we think we do. Hollywood, glitter, and more bad ideas than most of us care to imagine...does that sound like a place anyone would want to hunt?

But it turns out that California, like New York, Washington, and, increasingly, my own home state of Montana, could easily divide in two like an amoeba. In California, the goofiness generally lies confined to urban centers between San Francisco and points south while the rest of the state includes some spectacular wilderness, abundant (albeit often mismanaged) game, and folks who think a lot like the rest of us despite the loud and highly visible antics of their neighbors. All of which goes to show that it pays to keep an open mind...

Our visit that spring depended upon a combination of fortunate incidental circumstances. First--no surprise here--my fly rod, as I was working on some material about Bay Area striped bass for an angling publication. Second, our friendship with Charlie Bisharat and Shane Harden, two enthusiastic bowhunters and striper fanatics from the Sacramento area. And third, the good graces of a friend back home: Katie Wier, the lovely and capable RN who shared the nursing duties in our medical office with Lori and whose father happened to live on a working cattle ranch in northern California that supports good populations of wild hogs. In return for the hospitality Shane and Charlie had shown us on their home water, I finagled an invitation to visit for a few days of pig hunting and off we went.

Despite three college years in the Bay Area a long, long time ago, I had never seen anything like the version of California waiting for us when we pulled into the ranch and touched base with Katie's hospitable father. An unusually wet spring had turned the hills as green as Ireland at its picture postcard best, and a colorful riot of wildflowers carpeted the ground. After a quick orientation session, we pitched our gear in the bunkhouse, strung our bows, touched up some broadheads, and set off toward what I had readily acknowledged all along might be nothing more than a walk in the woods.

An hour later, the four of us sat on a ridge glassing a long, meandering valley that at first seemed to contain nothing but herds of the spookiest range cattle I'd seen since my first Arizona javelina hunt. Beautiful as the scenery looked, every garden has to contain at least one snake, in this case the poison oak that literally covered the hillsides. Since this attractive but noxious plant doesn't grow in Montana Lori had no previous experience with it, and I carefully pointed out its characteristic leaves so I wouldn't have to spend the next two days running back and forth to town for antihistamines. Then a flicker of movement caught my eye on the valley floor below and my binoculars soon confirmed our first hog sighting.

The contrast between the pigs' glossy black coats and the lush green foliage surrounding them reinforced memories of spring bears on the tide flats of coastal Alaska. The group of six appeared to include at least two mature boars and after more back and forth courtesy than the situation really warranted I finally convinced Charlie and Shane to set off on the stalk.

With shadows creeping down the hills on the western side of the valley, the witching hour was already at hand. We'd no sooner lost track of our hunting partners than Lori alertly spotted more pigs. Since they were far enough away from the first group so that an approach wouldn't interfere with our friends' stalk, we shouldered our packs and set off in pursuit. Twenty minutes later, we were in excellent position above the hogs, which included one mature boar and a large, dry sow. But I didn't trust the wind, although it had been blowing gently up the valley all afternoon.

"I think the breeze is going to switch and suck back downhill as soon as the air starts to cool," I explained to Lori. "We've got some time; let's wait it out."

That weather prediction proved accurate, but before we could make our move on the feeding hogs we faced another complication as something--probably Shane and Charlie--spooked a group of cattle and sent several dozen head stampeding up the draw toward the pigs. Suddenly my patient analysis of the wind meant nothing as nervous hogs began to trot up the hillside. With the calm, carefully measured approach all experienced bowhunters prefer rendered impossible, we double-timed uphill in pursuit.

The bad news was obvious, but the good news was that the hogs, although rattled by the cows, still had no idea we were there. With Lori the designated hitter, we worked our way across a series of narrow draws just behind the pigs with her in the lead. Finally, I watched her come to full draw ahead of me, although the terrain made it impossible for me to see her target. As soon as she released, an angry squeal rose above the breeze and I scurried forward only to be greeted by a large and obviously unhappy pig.

Lori was still 20 yards away and couldn't see the animal from her position. Nocking an arrow of my own, I made a quick decision. If the pig turned and opened up, I meant to take the shot for two reasons. First, I thought Lori had likely hit it and our House Rules call for hunting partners to fire at will in case of uncertain hits. Second, this pig clearly had an attitude problem that needed correction. So when the animal turned broadside at the top of the ridge, I drew quickly and took a shot I probably wouldn't have tried under different circumstances.

Because of the animal's position on the ridge, I couldn't tell quite where my arrow had struck although the shot felt perfect.

Scrambling uphill, I saw my bright yellow fletchings hanging from one pig's armpit as the group departed, an ideal place to hit a hog. I counted noses when the running pigs emerged from a nearby line of trees and came up one short. Coupled with the remains of my arrow, which had obviously passed through something important, and abundant blood sign, I felt certain we would quickly find the animal down.

"I only shot because you hit it," I explained to Lori as we regrouped and eased toward the trees ahead of the fading light.

"But I missed!" she replied, and there lay her clean arrow to prove it.

As if this information wasn't surprising enough, I quickly spotted a large pig standing under a tree a hundred yards away, obviously unaware that it was supposed to be dead. Our glasses failed to reveal any sign of injury, but I felt certain this had to be the animal I'd shot. When it bedded down, I faced a hard decision but eventually decided to make another stalk. I still felt confident that my first arrow would get the job done, but this was a meat hunt and I didn't want to risk losing prime pork to warm temperatures overnight. When the animal stood up at 30 yards, my second arrow whistled through the center of its chest and dropped it for good in a matter of yards.

The field dressing chores took place in the dark, and the autopsy wasn't as conclusive as we might have liked. The animal proved to be a large dry sow with four solid inches of fat packed beneath her hide. Although my first broadhead hadn't hit the heart, placement and penetration still looked excellent. I can only surmise that because of the steep upward angle of my first shot, the shaft passed beneath the near lung. In any case, the results proved two things: wild hogs can take a hit, and, as Shakespeare said four centuries earlier, all's well that ends well.

I wish I'd known about the hogs 40 years earlier, back when I was apparently the only hunter on the Berkeley campus. Most of the hunting I did during my college days took place on trips back home to Washington, although I did find time to harass some of the blacktails in the Berkeley Hills. My bowhunting skill level was better suited to pigs than wary deer back in those days, and a hog like the one just described would have made a tremendous addition to my impoverished student larder.

All of which serves to illustrate the value of questioning assumptions. Fish and game turn up in unexpected places, a principle my travels have only reinforced. And sometimes the greatest satisfaction derives from finding it in places no one else has bothered to look.

CHAPTER TWENTY-FIVE

King Rat
Maryland

ONE OF THE FASCINATING ASPECTS of bowhunting is the variety of experience it provides, and small game is no exception. One spring a few seasons back, Lori and I took advantage of a gracious invitation to visit the Traditional Bowhunters of Maryland and address their annual banquet. While it was the off-season, hosts Mike Mongelli and Gene Widemyer knew how much we love to spend time outdoors during our travels. We originally planned to do some saltwater fly-fishing in Chesapeake Bay, but cold weather made us abandon that idea. Then someone suggested a nutria hunt.

Unfamiliar to most westerners, the nutria is an oversized South American rodent originally brought to this country by fur farmers. As is so often the case with biological imports, this one sounded like a good idea at the time. Nutria inevitably escaped into the wild where they multiplied rapidly, threatening the ecological balance of many delicate southeastern wetlands. Today they thrive in the saltwater marshes along Maryland's beautiful Eastern Shore, much to the concern of conservationists who justifiably think this habitat should be supporting native waterfowl instead of giant, alien rats.

On the afternoon before the TBM banquet, Lori and I joined

a group of enthusiastic Maryland bowhunters at a boat launch on a tidal estuary deep in the Blackwater Wildlife Refuge. The weather felt pleasantly brisk and I appreciated the smell of the sea after the long, cold winter back home. We had seen two nice flocks of turkeys on the drive in and the cry of migrating geese filled the air, but we were interested in less conventional game. Tony Sanders and Bob Bartoshesky had kindly supplied Lori and me with a quiver full of well-traveled arrows, and we felt eager to put them to good use.

After launching the two skiffs Rob Davis and Bruce Golt had trailered along, Lori, Tony, Bill Wyland, and I hopped in with Rob while Bruce and the rest of the crew headed off down the river in his boat. An outgoing tide hadn't left us much water to work with, but Rob managed to run us up into a narrow channel that led to one of his favorite nutria haunts. After tying up the boat and fighting our way through a hundred yards of high grass, we broke out onto an open tide flat that reminded me so much of Alaska's Cook Inlet that I almost found myself looking for brown bear tracks in the mud. Finally, I had to admit that I had absolutely no idea how to go about hunting nutria with a bow.

"Still hunt along the edges of the channels," Rob advised. "If you see anything that looks out of place in the water, assume it's a nutria." A sage, grizzled veteran, Rob seemed a reliable source of insight and I took his counsel to heart. After a final equipment check, we fanned out across the marsh to begin our search for King Rat.

While I still didn't know quite what we were looking for, it felt so good to be outside in pleasant weather that I didn't much care. A pair of black ducks sailed by overhead with their wings set, reminding me suddenly of my boyhood days in upstate New York, where black ducks offered a challenging introduction to the world of waterfowling. The black duck rarely travels west of the Mississippi, and I hadn't seen one in years. After slipping and slogging across several hundred yards of marshy tussocks, Lori and I reached a narrow tidal channel. As we studied its glassy surface, I noticed a sudden bulge in the water fifty yards away that could only have been made by a swimming animal. "Go for it!" I told Lori, but she had been looking in the other direction, and since she hadn't seen the disturbance she encouraged me to make the stalk.

I circled wide through the grass, but when I eased my way back to the water the channel looked empty. As I stood and studied the situation, I noticed a bit of debris floating on the surface several yards away. Remembering Rob's advice, I watched it for several minutes before concluding it was a stick. I should have watched it longer. As soon as I stepped forward, the water boiled and I realized I had just squandered a point-blank shot opportunity.

Fortunately, Lori was about to make up for my mental lapse. Just as I turned back in her direction, I heard her recurve twang and watched her fletches tear off down the channel in a scene reminiscent of *Jaws*. While the excitement in her voice suggested she had just arrowed a bull elk instead of an overgrown rodent, it was hard to blame her. In fact, I wanted to see one of these mysterious creatures in the hand just as badly as she did.

After enough splashing around to anoint both of us thoroughly, we finally recovered her prize. I have to admit that for sheer blood curdling bad looks, it's hard to imagine anything quite like a nutria. From its curved, orange incisors to the tip of its naked, scaly tail, Lori's looked as if it had emerged straight from a nightmare. Accustomed to muskrats, beaver, and mink from my boyhood trapping days, I found it hard to imagine that shaggy coat of hair appealing to any furrier. "Congratulations!" I told her. "I'm sure I'll never kill a better one."

Just then, we looked up to see Tony Sanders stalking intently along the edge of a pond a hundred yards away. As he drew and released, he turned and flashed a thumbs-up sign across the grass. Ten minutes later, he connected again, making him the only hunter to double all afternoon.

I hardly ever shoot animals I don't plan to eat, but our Maryland hosts had already assured us that nutria is quite palatable, at least once it has spent enough time on the barbecue. When we finally regrouped to begin the long slog back to Rob's skiff, Tony carefully field dressed our haul. I have to admit that the inside of the nutria looked more appealing than the outside, and I actually found myself looking forward to the idea of a nutria dinner.

The tide was still out by the time we made our way back to the boat and it took some effort to get back to the main channel. But Tony and I poled while Rob jockeyed the outboard and we finally managed to turn upriver toward the launch. By the time the second boat reached the ramp, darkness had started to fall, the evening had turned pleasantly cool, and Lori and I finally realized just how tired and hungry we felt after our long afternoon in the marsh.

On the drive back to Annapolis with Gene and Tony, we passed a waterfront restaurant with a sign that said "Fresh Oysters" and "All You Can Eat", two terms that should never appear together in front of hungry Montanans who miss the sea as much as we do. Despite my genuine interest in the table quality of nutria, the choice proved easy. As long as *someone* planned to eat them – and they did – I knew I could opt for seafood with a clear conscience. Besides, I was the guest speaker. While Gene and Lori ate dinner in reasonably civilized fashion, Tony and I plonked down our money at the oyster bar and set out to see who could do the most damage. I'm not sure who won the contest, but it certainly wasn't the restaurant.

By the time Lori and I left Maryland two days later, we had some wonderful editions to the catalog of friends and experiences that represent the true benefit of the traveling outdoor life. One of the endlessly fascinating aspects of bowhunting's appeal is that the animals you pursue don't necessarily have to be large or imposing. It is enough that they be interesting inhabitants of interesting places, a description that can apply to the ground squirrels in your own front yard or giant rodents in a distant corner of the country.

Section VI

HOME AT LAST

HOME AT LAST

LIFE HAS TREATED ME WELL, not least in terms of where I live. Two portable professions – medicine and writing – have allowed me to make that choice deliberately and I've never regretted the decision to locate in Montana. The country here is captivating, offering a mix of mountain and prairie habitat, and its inhabitants still demonstrate a fundamental regard for their neighbors. Within a short drive of our home I can enjoy good bowhunting for whitetails, mule deer, elk, antelope, cougar, bear, and turkey. Factor in fine wing-shooting and the best trout fishing in the country and it's easy to understand my enthusiasm. Rarely does a day go by that Lori – unlike me, a local native – and I don't thank our good fortune for the opportunity to live where we do.

Of course there are drawbacks to any location. Winters here can be challenging, a euphemistic term I find difficult to keep in mind when pipes are freezing and the track that connects our home to the county road has been blown in for days. Metropolitan amenities lie a long way away. The economy is moribund, a fact of life in the remote Mountain West I've dealt with by ignoring. Writing has given me an opportunity to indulge my only expensive taste – travel – and as long as I can buy broadheads and feed my family (with a lot of help from Lori) I've never cared much about all the rest. Good thing.

From the outdoorsman's perspective, Alaska is the only part of the country I know that can rival Montana for the adventure and variety it provides. I loved the years I spent there and that experience changed my life forever. Nothing can rival the flavor of wilderness that only the far north can provide. But almost everything worthwhile there demands an expedition, a major stumbling block to a man with a family and a day job. When I conclude a phone call from one of my Alaskan friends by telling them I'm about to slip out the door and hunt whitetails until dark, wistful sighs on their part always follow. Life in Montana seldom makes me face hard choices between work and family on one hand and the outdoors on the other, a simple fact that largely explains my decision to return here over 20 years ago.

When our kids are in the cute and cuddly stage, we long to keep them that way forever even when we know we can't, and the same impulse applies to the places we love most. And Montana is changing. Growth is inevitable, winters and lack of money notwithstanding, and more people always mean fewer wild places. Driven by the impulse to turn easy out of state money into trophy ranches, new arrivals do not always share traditional western values, including many of those celebrated in this book. Conflicts between landowners and outdoorsmen – the subject of a long essay in its own right – have made ready access to prime game habitat on private land a thing of the past for many. Sadly, it's hard to avoid the impression that I've already seen this country at its best.

But it's still my home, and the more I see of the world, the more I appreciate it. In the end, that may be the most valuable lesson I've learned in all my travels. As much as I love Namibia and Australia, I'll probably never live there (although my perspective might be different if I were 22 instead of 62). But when I wake up in the morning, walk out onto the deck, and look at the deer grazing in the field below the house, I know I'm living right where I should be. If it took a million miles of travel to prove the point, the effort was worthwhile.

And even if the impulse to roam – to see new country, face the challenge of new wildlife, and meet new people – drives this volume, it would be impossible to put those experiences into perspective without providing some insight into the place I return to at the end of every journey.

[224]

CHAPTER TWENTY-SIX

Two for the Gipper
Montana

THE TRANSFORMATION from deer to cougar took place with remarkable speed that year. Despite a great season in Montana that included a big tom turkey, a 6-point bull elk, and a nice antelope, I hadn't killed a whitetail, largely because of the time I'd spent helping Lori try to fill the mountain goat and bighorn sheep tags she drew that year. The Sunday after Thanksgiving, the last day of deer season, I sat in a favorite stand below the house until dark. When the last shooting light finally drained from the western sky and brought the deer season to a close, I trudged up the hill and started to get ready for lions, organizing my pack, locating winter survival gear, and loading chains, scoop shovels, and the dog box into the back of the truck. Then I finally set the alarm for 3 A.M. and tumbled into bed to dream of round tracks and try to forget about rutting whitetails for another year.

I awoke to find a welcome skiff of fresh snow carpeting the ground outside the door, the first I'd seen in weeks. Nature seemed to be making amends for my unfilled deer tag, since tracking conditions couldn't have been better. The hounds greeted me enthusiastically at the kennel as if they knew their time had finally come, while Rocky, then an eager young Lab, howled plaintively when he realized I meant to leave him behind. As I wound down the hill toward town to meet hunting partners Rosey Roseland and Mike Bentler, a wide, heavy 5-point whitetail materialized from the falling snow and headed across the draw toward the stand I'd sat the previous night. I hadn't seen that buck all year. I mentally tipped my hat to him for surviving another season and hoped we'd meet again.

An hour later, the lights of town lay far behind. Plainly visible beyond the headlights, Jupiter glowed like a beacon in the dark, beckoning us forward into the hills. As we entered cat country at last, I began to relax and let the dots and dashes of the tracks filtering past play across my retinas. Like spotting bonefish on a saltwater flat, identifying lion tracks takes place at a nearly subliminal level, and my skills felt rusty after the long layoff since the end of the previous season.

I wanted a fresh track for reasons that went well beyond the usual excitement of opening day, the opening day of anything. Mike had hosted us that year during a fantastic week of whitetail hunting at his Iowa home, and Rosey and I, who have taken our own share of cougars, were eager to express our appreciation for his hospitality. Mike had spent a week hunting with us the year before only to be undone by a frustrating series of lion chases that somehow fizzled in the end. In terms of snatching defeat from the jaws of victory, we'd set new standards for cat hunting. Mike was too philosophical a bowhunter to care, but he deserved an honest lion as much as anyone we'd ever taken out, and we badly wanted him to get one in the special way you sometimes want things for your family and friends even more than you want them for yourself.

Then there was the matter of the dogs. The previous years had not been kind to our kennels. Drive, Axle, and Charlie were gone, and Moose had retired to the rug in front of the stove at Rosey's house. At one point the year before, we'd been down to his Harley and my Beau, two youngsters with lots of potential but not much else.

Then disaster shuffled the deck when our old friend Larry Schweitzer experienced a bout of chest pain on a lion hunt. Despite a clean health history, one thing led to another. A few days after his last cat hunt, he underwent cardiac surgery and a few days after that he was dead. Once the shock settled, his widow Kathy asked Rosey and me to take his two young Walkers, Zeke and Little Joe, and treat the dogs as Larry would have wanted.

Joe barked and Zeke didn't, and since I live in the country where yapping hounds don't matter much (not that Lori always agrees), Little Joe went home with me. A bad experience with a Walker years before had left me with a preference for blueticks and black and tans, but out of respect for Larry I meant to make this new canine relationship work. I've learned over the years that whether the quarry is lions or pheasants, the process (if not the bag) goes better if you take time to get to know your hunting dogs and treat them as friends. Little Joe proved easy enough to like, and a summer's worth of training left me happy with his place in the kennel and confident in his ability at the tree, if a bit uncertain about his nose. All we needed were a few good cougars to help sort out the rest.

Our kind of hunter, Mike was more interested in the beauty of the mountains in winter and the excitement of the chase than skull sizes, and he made it clear that he'd be happy to take any mature cougar. Rosey and I appreciated his enthusiasm, since our young pack desperately needed to experience a chase. When the first set of cat tracks flashed by in the half-light, I stood on the brakes and we all piled out eagerly. The track belonged to a mature female by our reckoning, which was not a problem, but the fluff it contained confirmed that it had been left early the previous night. After a brief discussion, we decided to forge on in search of something fresher.

We left the hills several hours later without finding what we sought, planning to check a couple of lowland crossings on the way home. As I drove through the sunlit landscape, something caught my attention in the snow beside the county road. The message passed straight from my eye to my brake foot without ever passing through my brain, a silent testimonial to years of tracking experience. I wasn't even sure what I'd seen at first, but as I backed down the road, the story became clear. A lion had crossed the road in the middle of a jumbled deer trail, and the track hadn't been there on our way in.

At this point, the county road ran through private ranch property where we had not obtained permission to hunt, and I didn't relish wasting hours trying to run down the landowner. Then Rosey remembered that a mutual friend had recently purchased a piece of ground down the road that bordered the large BLM tract the lion had headed toward. From the top of the hill, I contacted him by cell phone and obtained enthusiastic permission to set off from his place. This may be the only time in my life I've actually found a cell phone useful.

An hour later, we were hiking the side hill through the big woods on public property in search of the track. The cat could have done any number of things, but we felt confident we'd likely cut the track again between the road and the ridge top. By the time we finally did, I felt myself sweating pleasantly from the exertion despite the chill. We unleashed Harley and Joe, and when they set off up the hill in full cry we released the other two dogs and stood back quietly to listen.

I immediately disliked what I heard: too much disorganization, not enough focus. Rosey and Mike set off on the cat track while I followed the dogs. Several hundred yards of tracking confirmed our worst suspicions, as my partners stood on a solitary cat track while I followed a riot of canine footprints behind the trail of a running deer. For a houndsman, this situation represents the ultimate embarrassment. As we chugged uphill after the wayward dogs I could feel the outrage in Rosey's voice, while my own reaction tended toward shame and disappointment. "I can't believe you drove 1200 miles to help us train our bonehead dogs," I apologized to Mike as we churned through the snow on top of the worst looking set of tracks imaginable.

But as in all outdoor endeavors, there is no substitute for a positive attitude in the face of adversity. Sometimes a breakdown like this spells the end of the day (or the end of the week, for that matter), but all four dogs eventually circled back and let us catch them. After a brief but intense discussion of their evil ways, we led them back uphill on their leashes and cut the track again. This time we walked it out for a mile or so until the dogs were straining wildly against their leashes.

Those who have known the dubious pleasure of leading hounds through thick cover and steep terrain will know how we felt by the time we finally decided to let them run the track again.

The dogs seemed to know they had one chance for redemption, and they made the most of it. An hour later, we stood beneath a towering ponderosa with all four dogs barking treed, and Mike had his cat. Those who dismiss cougar hunting as too easy might have had a case if they'd seen nothing but the hour before the actual shot.

But now you know the rest of the story...

Anticipating Mike's visit, Rosey and I had taken the entire first week of lion season off from work, and Mike isn't the kind of hunter who gets lazy just because he's filled his own tag. So the following morning, the alarm exploded at 3 A.M. all over again...

By unstated agreement, I was due at the plate. Rosey and I have hunted together for decades without ever having to discuss--let alone argue--such matters. I hadn't killed a cat personally in seven years, despite treeing dozens. Some of those cats fell to friends who had never hunted lions before and the rest lived to hunt again, proving that cougar hunting, like trout fishing, can successfully be practiced as a catch-and-release sport. During that time period, Rosey had killed two good toms. I'd been there for one of them and had provided a crucial bit of intelligence for the second. Now my time had come around again, and after countless long miles focused on the chase rather than the kill, I felt ready to string my own bow and take a cat.

But not just any cat. Unlike Mike, I enjoy abundant opportunity to hunt mountain lions and could almost certainly fill a lion tag every year. Under such circumstances, selectivity makes sense for reasons that have nothing to do with skull measurements, or cougar steaks for that matter. Waiting for a good tom heightens the challenge and prolongs a process I happen to love. And with a whole season ahead of us, I didn't feel like ending matters prematurely.

That attitude explains our reaction to the first two sets of tracks we cut that morning. We found them all on public land and both looked fresh enough to chase, but after following them out under the canopy and studying their toe pads in the crisp layer of new snow, we just couldn't make either of them look as if it belonged to a mature tom. Once again, we headed down out of the mountains mid-morning to check the area we never reached the day before.

As we crossed the corner of an old friend's ranch, my foot was halfway to the brake when Rosey's shout filled the cab and we slid to a stop in a clatter of coffee cups. This time the track looked plenty big enough, but it appeared to have been left early the night before. Studying the terrain below us in the direction the cat had taken, Rosey spotted an even set of tracks crossing an open field a mile away, and through Mike's binoculars we convinced ourselves that they belonged to our lion.

The tracks headed toward a thick, timbered basin on a ranch whose owners I did not know. With the sun beating down relentlessly upon the remains of the track, we drove through the hills toward the ranch house while I tried to make myself look presentable, not always an easy task as those who know me recognize. Finally, I pulled a wool cap down over my unkempt hair, strode bravely up the steps to the front door and introduced myself to the ranch wife, hoping I'd once done some member of her family a favor in the local hospital. "You want to hunt *lions*?" she asked when I stated our predicament, and I braced myself for the worst. "We've been waiting *five years* for someone to show up and do something about those cats!" A few minutes later, we had written permission to hunt the place all season and directions through a series of pastures to the ridge we wanted to reach. "And don't forget to come back this spring and kill the bears up there!" she said in parting. Some days it really does pay to get out of bed in the morning.

We planned to run the two–track along the ridge and hope the cat had traveled all the way through the basin. If we didn't cut the track, we'd split up and work our way down through the timber until we found it, and hope we made contact before we ran out of light, snow, or both. But three miles above the ranch house, we spotted a huge, fluffy set of tracks ahead and Rosey had Harley and Joe out of the dog box before the motor stopped running. By the time I had my pack on, we could hear the sound of the dogs barking treed in the timber on the far side of the ridge.

But lion chases seldom turn out to be as simple as they first appear. Despite the dogs' enthusiasm, the first tree looked barren as a telephone pole. False-treeing is an odd phenomenon born of canine frustration. It almost always occurs with more than one dog at the tree, after a long day in the dog box with no track to run. The dogs seem to think that if they all bark hard enough, they can conjure up a lion out of nothing. Unfortunately, this tactic doesn't work no matter how hard the dogs try.

After leashing the hounds, we set out in a series of widening circles until we saw fresh, bounding cat tracks headed back across the ridge. When we released the dogs again, our ears soon lost the sound of the chase to the sigh of the freshening wind, and we set off on foot again through a nasty tangle of thorn brush.

My face and hands were soon scratched and bleeding, but when the sound of dogs at the tree rose to greet us once more, I knew they had the cat. With the promise of the chase's end ahead, I forged ahead through the brush and soon found myself staring up through a canopy of pine boughs at a long, tawny form surrounded by a corona of dappled light.

Years ago I carried my longbow when I hunted cougar, but I found myself in too many situations that required two hands to climb or catch dogs. I then went to a two-piece takedown longbow in my pack, but that tended to snag in heavy brush. For the previous several years, I'd carried a three-piece takedown recurve lion hunting. Buried out of the way in my pack, this option works splendidly on the trail in rough country, but I hadn't had to assemble it quickly in some time.

And nothing makes an argument for simple bow design like a nervous cat in a tree. As I fumbled with the Allen wrench and Mike and Rosey threw together a pair of our takedown wooden arrows, the lion grew increasingly nervous. "He's going to bail!" Rosey shouted as I tightened the last bolt, and then a shower of snow hit me as the tom exploded from the branches overhead. Suddenly, our uncharacteristically easy chase didn't look so easy anymore.

But at this point, the dogs were not to be denied. The cat lead us through another mile of thorn and rocks before he treed again, but this time I reached the towering ponderosa with my bow strung and ready. Making a clean shot on a lion in a tree can be more difficult than it sounds as a lot of our friends have learned the hard way, but when the bottom of the cat's chest appeared through a window in the branches directly overhead, I drew quickly and sent a shaft through it. My second arrow proved totally unnecessary. The big tom was dead before it hit the ground, and not even the work of skinning the hide and boning the meat and getting everything back up the hill before dark could compromise our exhilaration.

I field a lot of questions about hunting cougars with dogs, many from people – including bowhunters I respect – who clearly have reservations, almost always without ever having experienced a lion hunt themselves. Granted, the first week of that season--two days of hunting, two chases, two dead cats--made it look easy. But that's the condensed version of cat hunting. Among other things, I've left out countless miles without a track, long trips down through cliffs in the dark, the way your hands feel when you're skinning a cat at 25-below, high-centered rigs requiring hours of work with a scoop shovel to extract, the heartache of lost hounds, several tons of dog food, and what that dog food turns into when it comes out the other end of a hound. Until you've known all that, you haven't really known lion hunting.

Larry Schweitzer knew all that. He understood the magic of hound music and the odd serenity of the high country in winter. When I finally rolled back into my own driveway at the end of our second long day in the field, I hung the lion's hide and hindquarters in the garage and tended to the dogs. I spent some extra time with Little Joe, scratching his ears a bit longer than necessary and offering him a second piece of jerky, our traditional reward to the hounds at the end of an especially demanding day.

Larry would have understood all that too, and it made me realize how much I missed him.

CHAPTER TWENTY-SEVEN

The Busted Flush
Montana

MY MONTANA BOW SEASON began in classical fashion a few years back. One lovely April morning, I yelped at a pair of gobblers high on a hill above me only to have them throw all caution to the wind and charge. I watched the pair strut their way across half a mile of open meadow while I hastily set up a decoy and dived behind a downed tree for cover. When I finally sent a broadhead crashing into the base of the biggest bird's neck, he promptly collapsed in a heap less than a dozen paces away. Of course that's just how it's supposed to happen, but experienced turkey hunters know how rarely it does, at least when you're hunting with a bow and especially when you're hunting without a blind. I'll admit feeling a bit of pride as I carried the bird out of the woods that morning (you know pride: the stuff that goes before fall.) But by the time I started back to town, I was ready to admit that my success owed more to finding the right bird in the right frame of mind than any particular calling or shooting skill on my part. And I somehow had a nagging feeling that Montana's turkeys weren't done with me for the year.

After shooting well over the summer, I approached the September archery season with considerable confidence. A scheduled trip to Africa to finish some work for my book *The Double Helix* promised to cut my elk season short, so I told myself I'd take the first bull that offered a responsible shot. Early in the season, I mewed in a spike and anchored him with one well-placed arrow. The horns weren't anything but I didn't care, not after the satisfaction of calling in the bull, killing him cleanly, and getting the meat out of the mountains by myself. With a freezer full of elk steaks, I felt content to leave the pursuit of antlers until another year. My only regret about the elk was that I found a nice cinnamon bear on the remains two days after the kill, but since Montana's bear season didn't open until two weeks after the general archery season begins (an unfortunate oversight that has since been remedied) I couldn't make the stalk. At least I got to admire the bear.

After my return from Africa, I filled my antelope tag in the final days of the archery season. I spent the next week looking over a lot of whitetails (and passing up at least one buck I knew I would probably regret.) Then there wasn't much to do but wait for the opening of the firearms season (during which bows are legal in Montana) and the whitetail rut.

Except… Montana's bear regulations were full of peculiarities then, another of which was that the fall season stayed open during the gap between the general archery and firearms seasons. In mid-October, a friend called to report several bear sightings on his ranch, but I couldn't locate the animal. Then I awoke one morning to an unexpected surprise: an early storm had dropped six inches of moist tracking snow on the nearby foothills. Out at my friend's place, it didn't take me long to cut bear tracks and stalk them carefully to their conclusion. The bear wasn't big, but he sported a luxurious auburn coat. Because I've done most of my bear hunting in Alaska where color phase black bears are rare, I'd never killed a cinnamon bear before. After thinking about the bear on the elk carcass earlier in the season and how a pointless quirk in the regulations had prevented me from making the stalk, I decided to take this one, and I did.

During the transition into the second phase of deer season, I suddenly realized that I had already filled a number of fairly difficult tags in my home state. I admit that I've always been a fan of variety in the field. While I admire those with the determination to spend several seasons hunting one individual buck or bull, I prefer to mix it up by hunting as many different species as possible. While this approach to bowhunting has admittedly made me the proverbial jack-of-all-trades (and master of none), it's also been the source of too much fun and adventure to abandon, which is one reason I've chosen to live in Alaska and Montana where opportunities at multiple species of game abound.

Even without hitting the jackpot in any of the high stakes drawings for moose, sheep, or goat, a Montana bowhunter can count on eight big game tags each year: spring and fall turkey, antlerless and either sex deer, elk, antelope, bear, and cougar. Suddenly I realized that I had a chance at a Montana Royal Flush of sorts by filling them all. I'd never done it and I couldn't remember any of my hunting partners doing it either. Since I've never been one for grand slams or record books, I immediately felt a bit uncomfortable with the idea, but I decided that as long as I didn't alter my behavior in the field just to accomplish this goal, it would at least be an interesting ambition.

The easiest of the Flush's remaining legs came next. A non-hunting friend had asked me to contribute a deer to her freezer, and as soon as the season reopened, I killed the first dry doe that passed my stand. Now all I had to do was choose a good whitetail buck, pick off a fall turkey, and wait for lion season.

I usually set some goals for myself at the beginning of every bowhunting year, reflecting the fact that it's never possible to do everything. While I had been quite happy to settle for my elk and antelope on the basis of the quality of the hunt rather than the quality of the horns, I wanted a good whitetail. The deer didn't have to be huge, but I wanted five points on a side, and to complicate matters further, I wanted to shoot him within walking distance of my house. All that may sound a little nuts, but that was the way I wanted to do it, and as the rut got under way in early November, I concentrated my efforts close to home despite a number of promising opportunities elsewhere.

And I enjoyed good whitetail hunting, at least in terms of lots of activity and interesting encounters. The problem was that I just couldn't find a buck I wanted to kill. So I sat and rattled and waited, and with plenty of smaller bucks to distract me I had as much fun as I'd enjoyed in the woods all year.

Somewhat by accident, the next arrow released in my quest for the Montana Flush (or whatever you want to call it) came at a turkey. Our bird numbers fluctuate a lot around the house according to the weather, and I hadn't seen a turkey in some time. And since our fall turkey season runs two weeks past the end of the deer season, I wasn't about to abandon my whitetail program to go look for one until I had killed a buck.

Then one day a blast of serious winter weather hit. As I sat shivering in a stand below the house that afternoon, I heard a turkey yelp off in the distance and managed to get a diaphragm call into my mouth before the flock of several dozen hens (legal during Montana's fall season) appeared over the top of the hill. Most of them looked as if they would pass by just out of range, but when I yelped softly, several of them veered closer to investigate. I've learned two interesting things about fall turkeys over the years: tree stands don't help much when it comes to getting off a shot with a bow, and fresh snow often lets you get away with things that would never happen otherwise. Uncertain how these two conflicting principles would play out, I waited until a mature hen came to a halt 15 yards from the base of my tree. Incredibly, she let me come to full draw without so much as a twitch. Even more incredibly (as at least I like to think), I missed, although the shot was about as calm and controlled as any I can remember at a fall turkey. *C'est la vie*; besides, I was hunting whitetails anyway.

By Thanksgiving afternoon, I still hadn't taken a shot at a buck despite numerous declined opportunities. Since I was scheduled to leave for a Kodiak deer hunt the following day, time was running out quickly. After generous donations of frozen elk to both my parents and our son in college, the freezer looked under-stocked again. I decided that if I still had my tag by late afternoon, I'd take the first buck I saw.

Usually that kind of thinking practically guarantees that you won't see anything, but not this time. Just before dark, a small buck walked up out of the coulee and eventually turned broadside. The arrow passed completely through him and he hit the ground barely 40 yards away.

There followed a week's interlude on the south side of Kodiak Island that, despite excellent companionship and plentiful game, I would in many ways prefer to forget. The problem wasn't the crunchy snow that made the stalking so difficult. The problem was an unexpected and largely inexplicable shooting meltdown on my part. Since I've always complained about writers who never seem to miss anything in print, I am now confessing some world class missing as a matter of principle. Space restrictions (fortunately) prohibit me from describing every detail, but I'll summarize by admitting I had to beg Illinois bowhunter Pat Cebuhar for an arrow or two by the end of the trip.

I finally arrived back home with barely a week's worth of hunting in which to fill my turkey tag. Fortunately, the birds had moved in for the winter and appeared ready to play the game. Clad in whites, I took advantage of fresh snow to close on small flocks several times after work, but I always ran out of light or zigged when I should have zagged, or something like that.

The last weekend of the season, a friend called to tell me he had a large number of turkeys wintering where he was feeding his cattle. I had just started out for his place when a flock of birds crossed the road right in front of me just beyond our barn. The challenge proved too much to resist. I spent the rest of the afternoon stalking turkeys and finally passed up a shot on the wing when the flock flushed right over my head. Before the Kodiak debacle cost me my confidence, I might have loosed an arrow at that bird and in some ways I wish I had, because it seemed as reasonable a shot at a flying turkey as any I've ever seen.

Perhaps the idea of killing game birds on the wing inspired me. The next day, I left my bow behind, rounded up the shotgun and one of our retrievers, and went duck hunting. The truth is I think I needed to prove to myself that I could still hit *something*. A limit of big late season mallards quickly paid the price for this reasoning, much to my old Lab's delight. By the time I came home, shucked off my waders, and started to cook a duck dinner for Lori, I felt perfectly at ease both with myself and my decision to abandon the idea of the Montana Royal Flush forever.

But there was one day left in turkey season. The following morning I was showering in preparation for work when Lori suddenly started banging on the door. "Get dressed and grab your bow!" she exclaimed breathlessly. "The turkeys are crossing the pasture!" No wonder I love my wife the way I do.

After a quick look at the situation from the house, I felt certain where the birds were headed. Dropping downhill to put some terrain between us, I made a wide circle that brought me to a copse of pines I expected the birds to pass through. I set up quickly behind an ancient ponderosa thick enough to hide my outline, and then I listened. Soon I could hear a soft chorus of yelps and purrs approaching from the ridge above, and I eased into a position from which I could shoot with as little motion as possible.

But nothing happened. From the sound of things, the flock seemed to be heading down the field parallel to the ridgeline. Even though I suspected there were still birds in range of the hill's crest, I also knew that I would never get a clean shot at one if I left the cover of the pine tree. So I gave a few lost hen yelps and hoped for the best. This tactic received its reward when a trio of birds headed over the top of the rise in my direction. *This is it!* I told myself as the birds approached. *The whole season is on the line! Pick a spot! Here's your Montana Royal Flush!*

And with that, I sent the arrow whistling over the top of the nearest bird and the idea of the Montana Flush back to the trash heap where it probably belonged all along.

For the record, I did tree a tom cougar not long afterwards, but I didn't really want to kill the cat and I felt glad that the whole crazy idea of the Flush lay dead and buried, busted wide open by a bird with a brain the size of a marble. A friend who had never seen a lion treed before shot the cougar, which was just the way that hunt should have ended. Certainly the look of excitement on his face meant more to me at the end of the day than the achievement of an arbitrary goal on my part.

And therein lies one of several lessons I think that long season taught me: Never let an artificial standard of accomplishment change your behavior in the field or become more important than the things that really matter. And--while we're reviewing those lessons--never grow complacent about your shooting, even when you're on a roll. And finally... *never* think for one minute that any wild turkey is going to be easy with a bow!

The flush-buster in the spring.

September magic in Montana.

CHAPTER TWENTY-EIGHT

This One's for You, Ma
Montana

ONE RECENT SEPTEMBER, the opening day of Montana's elk season broke slowly through low ceilings and leaden skies worthy of Alaska. The front had spit rain all night, turning the prairie into gumbo. As I considered my options over a pot of coffee, I concluded that I'd likely be unable to reach the area I planned to hunt because of poor road conditions between the county road and the mountains. This decision did not come easily, as I knew that area well and felt confident I could locate bugling bulls there. But I couldn't justify tearing up the track running through the rancher's pastures, not after the years of hospitality I'd enjoyed on his place.

Fortunately, I always have a Plan B (and C, D and E, for that matter). An hour later, I eased my way along the edge of the trees on another ranch where I could reach the cover on foot from a gravel road. As shooting light suffused slowly through the cloud cover, I spotted two blocky shapes leaving the alfalfa field ahead. Suddenly, Plan B promised to make me look like a genius.

But my binoculars revealed what I'd suspected as soon as I saw the two forms weaving slowly through the mist: they weren't elk, but mule deer. However, both were large, and one looked as good as I'd seen in my home county in some time. I know plenty of local hunters who'd rather shoot a cow elk than a 30" mulie, but I'm not one of them. In fact, I've argued before that a big mule deer may be the West's toughest bowhunting challenge. With my elk ambitions suspended, I noted a few landmarks and set off along the ridge to circle downwind in front of the deer.

As I entered the woods, the unmistakable crack of antlers striking together filtered toward me above the sigh of the wind. Concentrating on the source of the sound, I picked up my pace. A hundred yards ahead, I noticed a small pine swaying under a determined assault. Broken terrain and steady wind allowed an approach, and I soon peeked over the top of a log to see one of the bucks shredding foliage 15 yards away.

But it wasn't the big one, an observation that triggered a quick mental debate. Although a fine buck, as I began to draw I thought about the consequences of filing my only buck tag so early: no scrape hunting, no tree stands come November, no whitetail season. But as I let off, I realized I was turning down the best mule deer of my life. After a solid minute of back and forth at point blank range, I reminded myself that if you have to think hard about whether or not you really want to kill an animal, you probably don't. Decision made, I quickly lobbed a pinecone toward the deer before I could change my mind.

When the pinecone struck, the buck threw up his head and stared, apparently unable to decide whether to stot off or resume his assault on the tree. Finally, he began to walk away with a nervous, stiff-legged gait. As I eased up to watch his retreat, my smugness dissolved. Two 6-point bull elk were strolling straight down the ridge in my direction. Undisturbed, they almost certainly would have wandered by within bow range of my hiding place, but the nervous deer erased that possibility. I could practically hear the elk thinking as they watched the buck, concluded that his uneasy body language couldn't possibly mean anything good, and reversed direction never to be seen again.

Nice job, genius…

My elk season began in a confused fashion that had nothing to do with weather or mule deer. As described in an earlier chapter, I'd spent the last half of August hiking Alaska's remote North Slope with my friend Doug Borland, which prevented most of my usual pre-season scouting. To complicate matters further, Lori had hit the jackpot in Montana's big game drawing, receiving both sheep and goat tags in prime areas. I'd pretty well accepted the fact that I would be spending most of the season helping her campaign those once-in-a-lifetime projects, and I felt excited for both of us. But there's always been something about bugling bull elk that just won't let me stay away...

Sheep season opened September 15th, and we spent three days in the Missouri River Breaks glassing rams. One excellent stalk fizzled at the last moment. Lori was scheduled to work in the hospital emergency room mid-week (at least *someone* works around here in September) but we left the Breaks delighted by the number of rams we'd seen.

Which brought me to what I call Birthday Week, a personal highlight on my calendar. By some coincidence, the two most important women in my life happened to be born during the peak of archery season for elk and antelope: my mother on September 18 and Lori a day later. In some families, that might have become a source of conflict (What do you mean you're going *hunting*? It's my birthday!), but not in mine. In fact, this year only Lori's professional obligations prevented us from celebrating where we usually do... in the field.

I won't risk embarrassment by revealing the number of candles on my mother's cake, except to note that she was still hunting harder than just about anyone her age I know. On the afternoon of her birthday, I set off to make another attempt to fill my elk tag before we headed for the high country in pursuit of Lori's goat. Trouble was, I still didn't have my usual solid line on the local wapiti. After studying the wind, I finally headed to an area where I'd killed a couple of good bulls in previous seasons.

Lack of cover makes this a difficult place to hunt. Elk often transit through a vast open area, but they often don't reach the property until after shooting light, and lack of cover makes stalking difficult.

I've often watched bulls bugling in the moonlight there, leaving me confounded by lack of daylight and cover. This year, I liked the sign I found in a shallow coulee and decided to set up in a small patch of brush there and hope.

All my earlier success had taken place at last light. This time, I was pleased to hear bulls bugling from the distant trees--and across an unfriendly fence--well before sundown. As the sound of the rut built to a crescendo over the skyline, I realized most of the herd was moving slowly north, a route that would take them nowhere near my position. But then I detected the sound of a single bull distinct from the crowd, heading my way.

Ten minutes later, two cows crossed the horizon a hundred yards away, and I knew the bull would appear shortly. When he did, I felt my spirits sink. I generally avoid shooting any elk smaller than a 6-point during the first two weeks of the season, not because I'm preoccupied with trophy scores, but because I like my elk season to last. Despite plenty of excuses this year I felt stubbornly loyal to this principle, and the bull striding down the draw looked like a 5x5.

But as he angled away from the sun, I noticed a small fork on the end of each main beam that made him a legitimate 6-point, and my concentration shifted from his horns to his heart. Unfortunately, the cows chose a path that took them by just out of range and I expected the bull to follow. But when I mewed softly, he turned in my direction and moments later wound up 15 yards away.

But elk season wasn't over yet. The bull stood quartering slightly toward me with his near foreleg drawn back in front of his chest. At that range he offered a tempting target, and one that I don't doubt some hunters might have taken. But I know my limitations, and determined to wait him out.

Calling again wouldn't have accomplished anything, so I remained frozen and let the bull decide whether to make a mistake or survive. Finally, after one of the longest standoffs in memory, he took a step forward, turned slightly, and bugled. Years ago, Gene Wensel told me that he always makes himself say, "*This one's for you, Ma,*" under his breath before he releases, a simple trick that helps him slow down and pick a spot. Since it was my mother's birthday, his advice couldn't have been more appropriate. My cedar arrow took the bull in the shoulder crease before the last quavering note left his throat. Although I was shooting my #72 recurve, the arrow didn't pass completely through and I felt a bit of anxiety about the penetration as he spun and galloped back up the draw. Without basis, as it turns out; the broadhead had passed through the top of his heart before lodging in the opposite shoulder, and he piled up less than a hundred yards away.

Shortly after sundown, I stopped at the ranch house to call Lori and explain why I'd be late. Since I didn't want to make a long distance call on my friend's phone, I asked her to call my mother, wish her happy birthday and offer my excuses for not calling myself.

I knew she'd understand, and I was right.

Missouri Breaks sheep hunt: the object of the chase.

CHAPTER TWENTY-NINE

Badlands Rams
Montana

IN THE SUMMER OF 2002, my wife Lori received a surprise in the mail to rival a winning lottery ticket: a coveted either-sex sheep tag valid in the Missouri River Breaks north of our Montana home. Since I'd been applying unsuccessfully for the same tag for over 30 years, I could scarcely contain my own excitement.

Those accustomed to hunting wild sheep in alpine habitat may sense something artificial about this herd, but the historical record proves otherwise. On October 1, 1804, William Clark reported "a kind of animal with large, circular horns" along the lower Missouri. The following spring, when the Voyage of Discovery had entered what is now eastern Montana, Meriwether Lewis noted: "On joining Captain Clark, he informed me that he had seen a female and a fawn of the big-horned animal; that they ran for some distance with great apparent ease along the side of the river bluff where it was almost perpendicular. Two of the party fired on them while in motion, without apparent effect." In his usual prescient fashion, Lewis had offered an apt description of the challenges we'd face two centuries later.

Unregulated hunting during the homestead days decimated original populations of the "big-horned animal" and led to the extinction of the Audubon subspecies, but following their successful reintroduction, Montana's carefully managed Breaks bighorn herd rapidly acquired a reputation for quality rams. Thanks to Lori's remarkable stroke of luck, we finally had an opportunity to hunt them.

Few game animals inspire more awe than wild sheep. Once Grancel Fitz coined the notion of the Grand Slam, taking all four species (in fact, two species and two sub-species) became something driven hunters had to do. While neither Lori nor I cared anything about Grand Slams, we did appreciate the significance of the unique opportunity to hunt Breaks bighorns. However, enthusiasm for a big ram never deterred Lori from her commitment to the bow. While her tag didn't limit her to archery tackle, she meant to do it with her recurve or not at all.

Her hunting area included a vast swath of rugged terrain north of the Missouri, intriguing country that hasn't changed much since Lewis and Clark described it. The Clinton administration's controversial creation of the Missouri Breaks National Monument left the area mired in politics we did our best to ignore. We planned to concentrate our efforts in November, when the rams predictably gather near the river to pursue ewes. A borrowed jet boat provided access to huge sections of unpopulated wilderness, and during most of our numerous forays into the area, we never saw another soul.

Not surprisingly, it took several days and a lot of exploring to locate the sheep. The rams we'd located upriver prior to the season had vanished, but the boat provided us mobility independent of the road system, and after a lot of river miles we finally found bighorns concentrated nearly 40 miles downriver from the nearest boat launch. Now all Lori had to do was get within bow range.

Accustomed to long, meticulous stalks on solitary rams during my Alaska sheep hunting days, I beached the boat a mile downstream from the first group of sheep we spotted. We spent an hour analyzing the terrain and wind before beginning our approach. Utilizing the contour, we slowly worked our way into position below the herd, which contained five full-curl rams. Since the sheep were moving slowly in our direction, we decided we'd try to reach a juniper 60 yards away and wait them out. Unfortunately, as we began to crawl a pair of ewes appeared nearby. Although they hadn't seen us, we couldn't continue, so we hunkered down in a clump of sage to await developments.

An hour later, the largest ram in the group stood grazing nonchalantly 10 yards from the juniper as if to remind us how close the hunt had come to ending quickly. Meanwhile, another dozen ewes had drifted into sight, eliminating any possibility of approach. Two more rams broke from the herd and sauntered down to the river, passing just out of bow range. Suddenly, the big ram took offense at another's proximity and assumed a belligerent posture. Moments later, the hills rang with the sound of combat as the two squared off, rose on their hind legs, and cracked their horns together with more force than I could imagine anything surviving. When one of the ewes finally blundered into us and spooked the whole herd, our morning hunt ended without a shot. Even so, I had trouble remembering a more exciting stalk anytime during my long bowhunting career.

Over the course of the next few days, I slowly realized that I needed to forget most of what I'd learned about sheep hunting. In Alaska, winter weather and the season structure prevented me from enjoying an opportunity to hunt sheep during the rut. Once we learned the country Lori and I found the bighorns abundant, spectacular, and sufficiently preoccupied to make them far less wary than expected. The ewes were another matter. Dozens of them always surrounded the rams, and their alert attitude and remarkable eyesight made sneaking into bow range of their boyfriends nearly impossible. That's when we decided to change tactics.

After another bone-chilling boat ride at first light, we encountered sheep again. Instead of crawling through the sage, we simply beached the boat and walked slowly toward the sheep. The results of this admittedly silly-looking approach shocked us. Once we stopped acting like predators, even the wary old ewes seemed to accept our presence...up to a point.

Unfortunately, that point corresponded to a distance of about

50 yards, which is twice Lori's effective bow range. We spent that morning joining the herd, learning the personalities of the individual sheep and what each one would and would not let us do. Exercising admirable restraint, Lori passed up several marginal shot opportunities at a huge ram. At one point, all the mature rams took off in furious pursuit of a hot ewe. We watched in awe as they raced across the cliffs above the river at breakneck speed for over an hour. Unfortunately, the ewe finally bedded down on an absolutely inaccessible ledge while her suitors banged horns in frustration. With nothing but ewes and lambs nearby, we left to look for more sheep... but we'd learned an important lesson.

We'd taken most of the last two weeks of the season off work to hunt. (The patients in our medical practice were used to this sort of thing, and the ones who objected had long since found themselves another doctor.) The weather couldn't have been more cooperative. A serious cold snap could have left the river locked in ice, but fair skies greeted us every morning and we continued to access the remote hunting area by boat. We learned more about our quarry and the fine points of our unusual stalking methods every day. I eventually learned to read the ewes' body language so well I could detect the first signs of discomfort, at which point we'd break off and ignore the sheep until they accepted us again. Finally, after countless hours within what would have been point blank rifle range and a couple of heart-breaking misses, we were down to the last weekend.

We live in a small town full of serious hunters, and they all knew about Lori's sheep tag. As the clock wound down, advice began to pour in, mostly from rifle hunters and switch-hitters who just didn't get it. The most common recommendation was also the simplest. With the season drawing to a close on a once in a lifetime opportunity at a big ram, everyone wanted to know why Lori didn't just take a rifle and kill one.

We'd talked about this issue at length. I'd done my best to assure Lori that this was *her* tag, and she was the one entitled to determine how it should be used. While I felt fully committed to helping her as much as possible, I let her know she didn't have to prove anything to me or the regular hunting partners who often accompanied us. Killing one of those huge rams with a rifle would have been easy and legal, but she never even considered the possibility… as valid a definition of a true bowhunter as I can imagine.

I'd love to report an 11th hour miracle, a bottom-of-the-ninth homer that put one of those majestic rams on the wall, but that never happened. As light faded from the western sky on the last night of the season, Lori was left holding a two by four inch piece of paper from the state rather than a ram's horns. And her stubborn refusal to pick up a rifle caused some grumbling around town from everyone except the handful of real local bowhunters who understood her decision and respected it. Some assumed she hadn't hunted hard enough, implicitly because of her gender. In fact, counting scouting trips, we'd put in over 30 days in remote, rugged terrain, and during November Lori could have legally killed a record book animal with a rifle every day she hunted. On more than one occasion, I had to point out that a special permit is an opportunity to hunt and not a receipt for a set of horns.

The notion that this hunt ended "unsuccessfully" doesn't do justice to that opportunity as we enjoyed it. We spent weeks in wilderness most of our neighbors will never bother to see, much less learn intimately as we did. We enjoyed numerous close range encounters with one of the continent's most spectacular game animals. Best of all, the two of us enjoyed a unique opportunity to spend time together in the wild without distraction, and our marriage will always be stronger as a result. We'll never forget the enduring sense of partnership we forged and the simple pleasure of one another's company at the end of each hard day.

No one has to draw a tag to appreciate such intangibles, and no one will ever be able to take those memories away from us.

Thanksgiving in April: Don with a longbow gobbler.

CHAPTER THIRTY

Thanksgiving in April Montana

THE FIRST REQUISITE for a turkey dinner is a turkey. For most of us nowadays, that means heading to the supermarket for a Butterball. But this is Montana, where hunters still wrest their protein from the woods. So...

I've spent the last hour crouched behind a ponderosa pine felled naturally during a recent windstorm. At first light, a Merriam's gobbler flew down from his perch and landed a hundred yards away across a mountain meadow alive with newly erupted pasque flowers and shooting stars. I probably would have called him into range and killed him by now save for two confounding factors, one of my own choosing, the other not.

The first complication, the one beyond my control, is his company: three hot hens making more noise than a trio of biker babes in a bar at midnight. I've called in my share of turkeys over the years, but I just can't compete with these girls. Spinning like a toy top with a warped axle as he struts, the tom has followed the hens all around the meadow twice, gobbling in response to my every yelp, cluck, and cackle without taking one extra step in my direction. He has come no closer to my pine tree than 30 yards.

That would have been close enough for most turkey hunters. But many seasons have passed since I made the decision to take (or not take) my wild turkeys the same way I kill elk, antelope, and deer: with traditional bows and wooden arrows. This is very hard to do, although most years I fill my spring gobbler tag through a combination of luck and perseverance. But not by shooting at turkeys 30 yards away--half that distance is more like it.

Turkeys are the one and only big game species I hunt that I can still imagine killing with a firearm under anything other than survival circumstances. (And yes, I regard them as big game even though they're covered with feathers rather than hair.) That's because the essence of spring gobbler hunting is calling the bird into close range, and once you've got him there you can certainly argue that you deserve to kill him. More often than not—*far* more often—that just doesn't happen with the bow, especially if you're hunting without a cloth blind.

All henned up, this tom just isn't coming in, and when he finally follows the girls down the mountain and out of my life I'm frankly glad to see him go. Trouble is, I've made a loud boast about providing a traditional wild turkey feast for friends at the end of the week. I'm not ready to concede defeated hubris by reaching for the shotgun and our friends are too shrewd to be fooled by a substitute from the grocery store.

It's time to find a cooperative bird, although I haven't heard another gobbler on the mountain all morning. My run-and-gun turkey hunting style may be anathema to southern turkey hunters accustomed to stealth, thick cover, and high bird densities, but here in the hills you sometimes need to cover some ground. With plenty of terrain ahead I set off around the mountain, pausing every quarter mile to yelp and listen.

Two miles later by my reckoning, I finally hear a reply. One of my cardinal turkey hunting rules forbids calling unless I'm ready for an immediate, aggressive response. To my occasional embarrassment I don't always remember that rule, but I have this time. A boulder nearly my own height lies a few steps away. I've barely settled in behind it when rapidly closing double-gobbles announce birds inbound on the run.

A conveniently located crack in the rock allows me to track their approach undetected. There are two gobblers, and they're both jakes: no trophy toms here, but I have promises to keep. Besides, any turkey is a trophy to a bowhunter.

After all my earlier frustration this almost seems too easy, but I still have to make the shot. Thanks to lucky timing, my recurve is at full draw when the birds round the corner 15 yards away. The broadhead severs the lead gobbler's spine, dropping it in its tracks.

He may not be a longbeard, but he sure looks like turkey dinner.

You'd think the bird would be the hard part, but as someone once noted, it ain't over 'til it's over.

The conic (or black) morel, *Morchella angusticeps*, can be as elusive and highly prized a spring quarry as the wild turkey. The highly prized half of the description should be obvious to anyone who has priced them in specialty markets or upscale restaurants, but *elusive*? We are, after all, discussing mushrooms, simple fungi with no sensory organs or means of locomotion.

But as seasoned morel hunters know, getting them from the woods to the kitchen can be a challenging business. They appear during a narrow window of time during the last few days of April or early May here in the west, with considerable and not always predictable variation according to elevation and weather conditions. On dry years, they never show up at all. Honey holes that produced sacks full of them last year--or last week--may be barren during the next visit. Hunting them successfully turns out to involve wrestling with many of the same imponderables and investing the same kind of legwork as the pursuit of wild turkeys.

Among veteran mushroom gatherers, morels enjoy a unique aura of mystery. The dark, spongiform mushrooms represent the fruiting bodies of a huge subterranean network of mycelia that constitute a single living organism, and enthusiasts guard knowledge of their location like maps to buried treasure. When I lived in Alaska, a close friend knew a prime morel spot 20 miles from his house and a half mile from my own. Every spring, he would feed us morels when we went to his house for dinner and generously give us extras to take home, but he would never tell me the exact location of the spot where he picked them. I understood completely, and like a gentleman I never tried to con the information from him after a few glasses of wine. Much as I love morels, they're not worth the price of a friendship.

Years ago, before anyone in central Montana knew anything about morels (or so I thought), I was fishing a stream that runs through private property owned by a crotchety old rancher I'd known for years. Cutting across a bend in the middle of a blue-winged olive hatch one day, I stumbled into piles of fresh morels beneath the cottonwoods and promptly filled every pocket of my fly vest with mushrooms. When I ran into the rancher back at the truck, we jawed about the fishing and the weather for several minutes. "You wouldn't care if I picked a few of those little black mushrooms down there, would you?" I asked as a belated courtesy.

Although I hadn't anticipated any possible objection, he hesitated ominously before he replied. "If I ever catch you picking any of my morels," he finally snarled, "you're off my property for life." Backing awkwardly into my truck while trying to disguise my vest's bulging pockets, I thanked him and sped away. On return fishing trips during the spring season, I avoided temptation by staying in the water.

My personal relationship with turkeys and morels is symbiotic: I love hunting spring turkeys because that gives me an opportunity to look for morels, and I like finding morels because I love to eat them with wild turkey. Now, with a bird hanging, Lori and I will need to make a dedicated morel excursion. In the wake of a drenching rainstorm the previous week, conditions couldn't be better.

A day later Lori and I are out at bowyer Dick Robertson's place, working our way down through shaded coulees lined with young cottonwoods, the *sine qua non* of Montana morel habitat. Make us 50 years younger and we could be kids on an Easter egg hunt. After an unproductive quarter mile, my attention has started to wander to the usual distractions: cow turds freshly flipped by foraging turkeys (duly noted as intelligence for next year's gobbler season), stumps ripped open by a bear, the remains of a mule deer carcass that demands an autopsy (the CSI conclusion: death by mountain lion). Suddenly Lori emits a whoop appropriate to the discovery of a gold nugget. She's found the year's first morel, and where there's one, there's more.

There sure are. Two hours later, our baskets are full. (Proper etiquette demands collecting mushrooms in porous baskets rather than

[256]

plastic bags, so the spores can disperse as you walk.) Carrying all the mushrooms I feel like processing, we finally have the raw ingredients for our traditional spring feast. It's time to retire to the kitchen.

After all that hunter-gathering the rest should be easy, and it is. But there are still ample opportunities to mishandle the bounty. We spend the following afternoon trying to avoid them.

Most wild mushrooms have a short shelf life if they're not handled properly. Whole morels sautéed in butter are delicious, but they can turn soupy in the pan. Partially dehydrating them makes them store better over time. I address both issues by zapping them in the microwave until their volume is reduced by half. Place the mushrooms on a clean, dry cloth while they're in the oven. Wring out the liquid and save if for a sauce base. Today, the mushrooms we plan to eat for dinner go in the refrigerator, while we vacuum pack the rest in meal-sized aliquots for the freezer.

A remarkable number of people don't like to eat wild turkey, usually for the same reason they don't like wild duck, wild venison, or wild anything else: they overcook it. While it's hard to improve upon classical turkey roasted whole, I've got another plan for tonight, which begins with dressing the bird.

Pluck, don't skin; it's not much extra effort and the retained skin will help keep the meat moist no matter how you cook it. After filleting the breast into two boneless halves, I chop up the legs and place them in a pot on the back burner with a diced onion and celery stalk and start reducing them to stock. No waste there; after a lifetime spent running away from predators, a wild turkey's legs are too tough to eat any other way.

After chilling the breasts in the refrigerator for an hour, I dust them in flour, dip them in beaten egg, and roll them in fresh breadcrumbs and pine nuts that I've ground up in the blender. After browning each breast in a skillet with a teaspoon of butter, I place them in a baking dish skin side up and return them to the refrigerator. They'll take less than an hour to cook, and that can wait until the guests have arrived and someone has opened a bottle of wine.

By the time the doorbell rings, Lori has strained the stock and brought it to a simmer in a covered pot with two cups of wild rice while she works on the salad. Now the turkey breasts go into the preheated medium oven. Since every bird is different, a reliable meat thermometer is the surest way to avoid overcooking, aiming for an internal temperature of 155 degrees. With that work in progress, I start on the morels, sautéing them in butter seasoned with nothing but a dash of salt and pepper, eight or ten mushrooms at a time. As they cook--and they will reduce in size by half again--I remove them to a warmed platter and decant the pan into the container with the liquid reserved earlier.

Next comes a roux, as for any white sauce. When it's starting to turn brown in the bottom of the sauce pan, I blend in the liquid from the mushrooms, beefing up the volume as needed with leftover turkey stock. A third of the sautéed morels go into the sauce, which in turn goes on top of the turkey breasts when they come out of the oven. The remainder we'll serve on the side.

And there you have it: all wild, all natural, with just a little bit more effort than sending out for pizza. All right, a lot more... but the rewards are commensurate, for eating what you shoot and hunting and gathering what you eat are the ultimate expression of our genetics. Beethoven's Fifth and the ceiling of the Sistine Chapel are optional; finding what we eat in the woods is essential to who we are and what we've been since the first prehensile thumb curled around a stick. Doing its preparation justice and sharing the result with friends is as essentially human an impulse as language.

Ours is one of the few cultures that still allows its citizens this opportunity, and for that we should give thanks... at any time of year.

CHAPTER THIRTY-ONE

Nine Nine Ninety-Nine Montana

THINGS SEEMED STRANGE that season, right from the very start. As Lori and I drove over the ridge on the way to our traditional September hunting camp the afternoon before opening day, we saw a vast herd of elk bedded down on a grassy knoll two miles below the cover I expected them to occupy at that time of day. As we stopped to study them, our binoculars revealed the brown heads of over 80 cows lolling in the afternoon sun. Two mature bulls paced about at opposite ends of the herd while a handful of spikes and rag-horns peered anxiously down at the congregation from a stand of nearby timber. "I don't know about this," I mused as we started on toward camp.

"What do you mean?" Lori asked. "I thought you'd be delighted to see so many elk!"

"There are a lot of elk on that hill," I agreed. "But I don't know what they're doing there at this time of day and that makes me nervous."

In fact, I don't appreciate surprises in my elk cover, even surprises that seem favorable at first glance. I know these elk and the terrain they inhabit and I base my hunting strategy on what I've learned during long days of observation in seasons past. Unpredictable elk are hard elk to hunt, and the strange truth is that I would have been happier to see the number of elk I expected—zero--than to blunder into this unanticipated extravaganza.

By the time we had camp set up and the evening meal underway, matters had grown even stranger. Early September in our part of Montana generally means warm, pleasant weather, and we can look forward to sitting around in shirtsleeves while we sharpen broadheads and plan for the excitement of opening day. But this year a dour cold front moved in to dampen our spirits. As we crawled inside the tent and listened to the wind and rain pound against its fabric, it was hard to believe we were in Montana and not Alaska.

The following morning, we awoke in the dark to an eerie silence. The front had passed through during the night leaving dense fog in its wake. By the time we started up the mountain, the slowly breaking dawn confirmed that our visibility didn't extend much beyond bow range. We hadn't heard a single bugle overnight, which was unusual, and the fog made glassing impossible. Rather than risk blundering into elk in the gloom, I elected to hunker down on a strategically situated knoll and call softly. By the time the sun broke through the clouds late that morning, we hadn't seen or heard an elk.

After considering our options, we elected to drop down to a lower elevation and look for antelope. As soon as we broke out onto the rolling country below camp Lori, who has excellent game eyes, alertly spotted a nice mule deer buck bedded down beside a clump of brush with the hillside at his back and the wind in his face. After studying the situation through our glasses and planning an approach, Lori set off on a long, circular stalk.

Half an hour later, I watched her appear over the crest of the rise above the mule deer and begin her final approach. By the time she and the deer were together in the frame of my field glasses, I began to experience a nearly unbearable level of excitement. I was having more fun watching my wife close upon a nice animal than I would have had if I were making the stalk myself. Just then I heard the last sound I expected to hear down in the sagebrush at midday: the high pitched whistle of a bull elk.

Glassing back up toward the base of the mountain, I could see two dozen cows herded along by a splendid 6-point. Never mind that the elk should have been deep in their security cover miles farther up the mountain... there they were, and I had to decide what to do about them. The terrain contained enough cover to offer a chance to intercept them, but the wind would have made any approach tricky. Besides, I had promised to stay put and provide hand signals to Lori in case she lost track of the buck, and after all the work she had put into her stalk it didn't seem right to abandon her. Ignoring the elk, I trained my glasses back in her direction. The deer eventually spooked without offering a shot even though she successfully maneuvered into bow range. The excitement in her voice when we finally rejoined left no doubt that I had made the right decision.

Two nights later, Lori headed back to town leaving me alone on the mountain with the elk. As I sat glassing the base of a long swath of talus where elk often appear at last light, I watched a lone cow emerge from the timber and feed steadily in my direction. I really didn't want to kill her, but I also knew that a scheduled trip to Alaska was going to cut my elk season short at the end of the week. The previous year, operating under similar time constraints, I had shot a spike bull during the first week of the season as described in an earlier chapter. While I never felt any regret, this year I had promised myself I would hold out for something bigger even if that meant eating my elk tag at the end of the season. When the cow finally ambled into bow range, I let her pass undisturbed without a second thought.

By mid-week I was beginning to feel frustrated. I had covered the ground carefully while hunting hard. To the best of my knowledge I had not spooked a single elk, but they seemed to have disappeared from the area. Whatever put the elk in their strange mood had made them leave one of the most productive patches of cover I know. Even the antelope on the plains below camp weren't cooperating. Finally, I decided to call for a new deck of cards. Throwing my sleeping bag and enough food for one night into the truck, I headed for another mountain range altogether.

The date was the ninth of September: 9/9/99. As I drove, the radio offered a host of reports concerning the good fortune this conjunction of numerals allegedly implied. All across the country people were waiting to get married. In Asia, pregnant women were undergoing Cesarean sections in order to provide their offspring with this auspicious birth date.

While my second-choice area has been good to me in the past, it is a difficult location to hunt. The most effective tactic is to set up an ambush at one of a series of springs the elk sometimes visit during their travels. Success requires patience, discipline, and accurate scouting rather than strong legs, but this herd contains some excellent bulls and the rewards can make a lot of quiet time suddenly worthwhile.

After a pleasant visit with the landowners, I set off to scout. I found elk tracks and a few rubs scattered along the coulees containing the springs, although there wasn't much sign of recent wallowing activity. After studying the sign and gauging the wind, I decided to wait out the last two hours of daylight at a spring a mile or so from the place I'd killed a huge bull three years earlier. With no further ado, I set up a ground blind below a steep bank at the downwind edge of the water and settled in for the evening.

After five days of hard hunting, I actually appreciated this relaxing agenda. Normal seasonal weather had returned, and the air felt comfortably invigorating as I checked my shooting lanes and sat down to wait. Because of my position below the edge of the bank I couldn't see anything approaching, but by this point in the season I expected the elk to be quite vocal and anticipated plenty of warning in case a bull came down the draw. Every 30 minutes or so, I offered a single, brief bugle just to suggest the location of the party to any bull in the area.

Half an hour before dark, a four-point whitetail materialized out of the brush. I knew good bucks frequented the area and was quite ready to take a big mule deer, but this specimen didn't arouse anything other than an appreciation of his natural beauty and grace. As he eased by within bow range, I derived a quiet satisfaction from the knowledge that my hiding place had passed muster. If I could fool a cautious whitetail, I ought to be able to fool a rutting bull elk.

The setting sun had painted the western sky a luminous salmon pink by the time I heard a faint rustling in the grass behind me. The high bank prevented me from seeing what had made the disturbance, but the complete absence of bugling all but convinced me that I had heard nothing but another deer. Then as I pivoted slowly about, a suspiciously heavy clop of hoof on rock snapped me to attention. As I watched anxiously, a huge bull climbed up the opposite side of the coulee behind me and stood with the sunset at his back less than 50 yards away. With sweeping main beams and massive sword points silhouetted against the richly colored sky the sight proved riveting, and I found myself longing briefly for my camera.

But not for long. Broadside at that distance, a big elk offers a tempting target, but I'm smart enough to know I'm not that lucky or that good. The bull obviously wanted to continue down the draw in my direction, but he seemed perturbed by something although I never could determine what. To my dismay, he turned slowly and began to retreat in the direction of the setting sun.

Gathering my wits, I licked my diaphragm call into my mouth and chirped as seductively as I knew how. A deep cut in the terrain right behind me could have contained a cow elk, and my job became to convince the bull that was precisely the case. Slowly, he turned and headed down the opposite side of the draw in my direction as I began the mental gymnastics of shifting my attention from his antlers to his vitals. Forty yards out he turned and offered another broadside, but I knew that my effective range hadn't increased by magic. I declined the opportunity once again.

When he turned and started over the hill for the second time I'll admit my spirits began to sink, but he hadn't spooked and I mewed again, doing everything possible to convince him a lonely cow stood awaiting his attentions in the cut just behind me. Once more he turned to investigate. I've been at this long enough to consider myself largely immune to buck fever, but I can't deny my anxiety as the bull marched back in my direction. This time he came to a halt just over 30 yards away. I forced myself to forget entirely about the size of his antlers and the visual drama of their display against the sunset. When he turned and showed me his ribs for the third time, I knew that I had him, and sure enough. The draw felt effortless, as if my friend Dick Robertson had made the bow for this shot and no other. Then I released and my arrow whistled through the elk's chest. Moments later I watched the bull pile up in plain sight at the top of the hill barely 70 yards away. Except for the welcome labor that always follows the successful completion of an elk hunt, that was that.

Lessons? Of course--there are lessons to be learned from every hunt. Adapt the tactics to the terrain--difficult cover demands imaginative means of getting close to game. Trust your interpretation of the sign--animals are always willing to tell you what they've been up to if you look closely enough. Know your limits and stick to them--big horns won't make you a better shot. And above all, persevere. As my father drummed into me years ago, big game hunting isn't like trout fishing or wingshooting. A big elk only has to happen *once*.

The bowhunter's job is to give it him the opportunity to make a mistake when he does.

Don with the 9/9/99 bull.

CHAPTER THIRTY-TWO

The Bentler Buck
Montana

HUNTING STORIES usually convey good news. Even when the big one gets away, wilderness scenery, wildlife encounters, and time afield with friends and family offer plenty of compensation. But my 2006 bow season didn't all work out that way.

I spent the first half of September in Alaska working on writing assignments involving shotguns and fly rods rather than bows and arrows. No regrets, but by the time I returned to Montana I was ready for some face time with the local pronghorns and elk. An unseasonable deluge made antelope country impossible to reach, and then I lost access to my favorite elk cover. Toward the end of archery season I developed a nasty infection that required a week of IV antibiotics to control. By that time, there was nothing left to hunt but deer.

Fortunately I'd drawn an Iowa tag that year, so I could look forward to tackling not one but two whitetail bucks during the November rut. Dick LeBlond, my oldest friend, was a professor of medicine at the University of Iowa at the time, and he and I planned to spend early November with Mike Bentler and his family in the southeastern corner of the state. Mike and I went back a long way. He'd hunted cougars with me in Montana as described in an earlier chapter, come north to Alaska with us for bears, and he and his wife Sandy had joined us on safari in Namibia several years earlier. I'd hunted with him at his place once before, and in my dreams I could still hear the sound of big, corn-fed Iowa bucks approaching through the fallen oak leaves. Only Iowa's non-resident drawing process kept me from visiting every season.

I was scheduled to leave for Iowa on November 3. Mid-October, Mike called to confirm that he'd seen some great bucks on his property. The thought of visiting Mike, Sandy, and their three delightful teenaged daughters Sheena, Shelby and Shayne proved more than enough to rally my spirits after what had been an unusually discouraging bow season.

On the morning of October 15, I arrived home after a morning bird hunt to find Lori with a worried look on her face. "Dick left a message on the answering machine," she explained. "He wants you to call, and he says it's urgent."

Dick doesn't leave such messages casually, and I felt a sense of foreboding as I dialed his number, especially since he'd had a recent cancer scare. He answered on the first ring.

"Sit down," he said, and I did. "Mike Bentler and his whole family were murdered last night," he announced in a shaken voice.

No one knew much at the time, but details of the tragedy emerged on the national news the next day. Mike and Sandra's eldest son had been charged with the crime. According to allegations, he walked into the house early in the morning and shot his mother, father, and three sisters in cold blood. (Shawn Bentler is currently serving five life sentences for the murder of his family.)

Mike had a number of friends here in central Montana, and during the following week we all tried to make sense of this incomprehensible act. We couldn't. I still can't pretend to understand what happened, and I doubt I ever will. Needless to say, all thoughts of Iowa whitetails evaporated. I cancelled my airline ticket and left that anxiously awaited Iowa tag to gather dust in my desk drawer.

All tragedies eventually demand some kind of closure. Rosey and Lisa Roseland eventually joined Lori and me for dinner, and we spent most of the evening reminiscing about the friends we'd lost. Rosey was the one who finally said what needed to be said: "Mike wouldn't want us moping. He'd want us to go hunting."

Fair enough, but the memory of the Bentlers' was on my mind constantly for the rest of the season.

Whitetail deer are an endlessly fascinating species, perhaps more so than any other animal we hunt. While their matting behavior has been analyzed endlessly, I've noticed that the whitetail rut always varies in subtle ways from season to season. That year was no different. One early November morning I took a walk through the coulees around our house and discovered that scrapes had appeared everywhere overnight like mushrooms on a wet lawn. But that burst marked both the beginning and the end of the pre-rut activity that season. Almost none of those scrapes were ever freshened, and I only saw a few new ones. Go figure.

Then a run of unseasonably warm weather seemed to disrupt the usual whitetail feeding patterns and travel routes. Most of the buck movement was still taking place at night long after the imperatives of the rut should have had them traveling during shooting light, and I was seeing remarkably few does on trails I'd studied for years. But I'd seen at least three good bucks among the usual collection of stunted 4x4's and youngsters, and with ample time off during the best two weeks of the season I knew it was only a matter of time.

By the middle of the month I'd filled three doe tags uneventfully. My family lives on wild game, and with no elk in the freezer I couldn't focus on horns to the exclusion of making venison. I'd also let a number of bucks walk by. Every time I rattled an "almost" 4x4 into bow range I found myself asking, "What would Mike do?" As tempting as some of those shot opportunities looked as the season entered its final week, I knew the answer and acted accordingly.

Finally, the temperature dropped. On the first chilly evening of the season, I walked back to the house after dark and found Lori looking like an excited child as she shucked her safety harness and wool coat. Instinct told me that her shaking had nothing to do with the cold. As I kicked off my boots--coincidentally, a pair that Mike had given me the last time I hunted in Iowa--I asked to hear the story.

"I was sitting in the Hot Tub stand," she explained. (The name derives from the stand's proximity to our yard, but it's still a great place to kill a deer.) "About 4 o'clock, I saw deer enter the lower pasture from the north. I'd forgotten my binoculars, but I could tell by its body language that one of them was a rutting buck.

"Nothing was headed in my direction, so I rattled. By this time, I'd lost sight of the buck behind the hill. Next thing I knew, a *gagger* was heading for me on a beeline. He wound up broadside 12 yards away!"

"*And...*" I prompted.

"*And* I was shaking so hard with excitement that I shot right over the top of his back! I haven't had buck fever like that for so long I'd forgotten what it feels like."

I had to commend her attitude. With a clean arrow confirming her miss, there was no wounded deer to anguish over and she was taking events like a trooper. But I had to de-brief her about the deer.

"Big!" was her first response to my request for a description.

"Come on, honey," I replied. "You can do better than that."

"He was just a 4x4," she continued, closing her eyes like a witness trying to recall the details of an accident. "And he wasn't very tall. But he was heavy and wide."

"How wide?"

"*Real* wide!"

"Wider than that?" I asked, pointing to one of the better racks on the wall.

"Much wider," she replied, placing her hands three inches beyond each of the mounted buck's main beams. Lori is a keen observer, and I knew I'd never seen this deer before. Suddenly, we had a mission.

We share the whitetail rut with rifle hunters here in Montana, and I have to admit that I winced a bit harder than usual every time I heard a gunshot on the neighboring property. Selfish? Perhaps. But I would have been delighted if someone else in our bowhunting circle killed that buck, especially Lori. And she made it plain that if I killed "her" deer she'd be delighted too.

By the last day of the season I had yet to spot the buck she'd described. I wondered if he'd fallen to a bullet, or if Lori's description had been fueled by excitement rather than objectivity. But I trusted her enough to take her story at face value, and when a small buck passed by me that final afternoon I felt content to let him walk even if that meant eating my buck tag. With a big buck somewhere in the woods, that's what Mike would have done.

That's the story of the Bentler Buck, as I decided to name him. Deer stories are supposed to end with the description of a successful blood trail and a hero picture, clichés it seemed appropriate to forgo that year. Somehow, *not* shooting a buck helped me balance the emotional ledger, and I still have no regrets.

And I finally did see the buck, five days after the season's close. I was driving back up the hill after an evening duck hunt when I saw deer in our upper pasture silhouetted against the sunset. There he stood, just as Lori had described: four points on a side, heavy, and wide. *Real* wide.

Knowing he was still out there made all the rest a bit easier to accept, just as Mike would have wanted.

Season's end. See you next year.

Lori taking five on a Crazy Mountains goat hunt.

CHAPTER THIRTY-THREE

Crazy Season
Montana

COMPANIONSHIP

"It's a lot easier being the guide," my wife Lori observed as we watched the billy pick his breakfast from the scarp 1500 vertical feet above us. "I've got the fun job this time around."

She knew whereof she spoke. Five seasons previously, she'd drawn a coveted Montana goat tag for these same Crazy Mountains, and we'd spent a week together there in the high country. There was no weapon restriction on the tag, but she'd stuck with her recurve. She didn't kill a goat. The only reason we didn't devote more time to the effort was that she'd also drawn a sheep tag for the Missouri Breaks. (Lori should have headed to Las Vegas that year.) I was proud of her decision. A lot of folks around town didn't understand why she didn't pack in a rifle and kill a billy, but I did.

This year my turn had come round at last, after 30 years of futile application. Now Lori could sit at the bottom of the hill, glass, and critique my stalks while I made the tough final ascents. She was set to enjoy herself, and I didn't blame her.

The smart money was on the goats. At least we knew the terrain after our earlier adventure. The Crazies are a deceptive mountain range.

Located in central Montana 80 miles southwest of our home, you can drive all the way around them in an afternoon, but there are no roads into the goat country and I hope it stays that way. Despite their circumscribed perimeter, the Crazies contain some of the most rugged country in the Lower-48. I had never suffered any illusions that this would be easy.

According to local rumor, the Crazies' name derives from a madwoman who retreated there in search of tortured peace during the pioneer days. She could scarcely have picked a better place to escape the busyness of civilization, such as it was back then. Sheer peaks rise precipitously from tangled valley floors strewn with talus that invites a broken ankle at every step. Bears abound, and the Crazies shelter the largest concentration of wolverines in the contiguous states. Psychically, this was Lear's blasted heath. Now it was up to me to come to terms with it.

We'd made the long, uphill hike to our old campsite the day before, arriving to a welcome sense of neglected familiarity. Less than an hour out of camp that morning, I'd spotted the top of a goat's back disappearing behind a rock just above the creek bottom. Certain that the animal was feeding uphill to bed down for the day, I made a mad scramble to intercept it. Four hundred yards above the creek, I peeked over a boulder to find a goat standing 15 yards away broadside. One glance at its horns told me the animal was a nanny. My tag was valid for either sex, but did I want to shoot a nanny in the first hour of the hunt? I didn't. So there we were the following day, watching a billy feed in terrain that invited technical climbing gear.

Shortly after Lori offered her sunny assessment of her role in the days ahead, the goat vanished in a patch of scrubby juniper. An hour later, it still hadn't emerged. "You *did* come here to hunt goats, didn't you?" Lori finally asked.

"I'll look down at you from time to time," I said as I girded up my loins for the assault. "If the goat reappears you should be able to see him, but I probably won't. You know the hand signals."

Three hours later, I'd clawed and scrambled my way to goat

level. Looking down the mountain toward Lori I saw her staring back at me through her glasses, apparently with no new information to convey. Morning thermal updrafts had developed, and since goats are more alert to danger from below than above I worked my way across the ledges so I could hunt my way downward through the scrub with the wind in my face.

An hour later I emerged at the bottom of the stunted evergreens having found no sign of the billy. Although Lori could see all the way around the trees, when we rejoined at the base of the mountain she told me she'd never seen the goat exit the cover. The mountain seemed to have swallowed the animal, granting me nothing to show for my effort but a few scrapes and bruises. Leave it to goat hunting to redefine one's concept of a good time.

Since the creek tumbling along the valley floor held trout, we'd packed a fly rod and a skeleton fishing kit into camp. By sunrise the following day we were already tired of freeze-dried backpack fare, and Lori carried the fly rod in its aluminum case when we left camp that morning. She said that she just wanted some decent food on our plates that night, but I suspected her real aim was something more exciting to do than give hand signals while I crawled around the cliffs with the goats. Why was I starting to feel as if the lucky member of the party was the one who *hadn't* drawn the goat tag?

Different day, same story... and the same long, fruitless climb up the mountain and back. Lori hadn't abandoned me for her fly rod though. She'd stayed glued to her glasses the whole morning while I scrambled around in the rocks with a billy that just wouldn't let me maneuver into bow range. "Time to go fishing!" she announced cheerily when I rejoined her at the bottom of the rockslide. No argument from me. I wasn't good for more than one honest goat stalk per day.

"Look at the size of that one!" she said once we'd worked our way down to the creek and peered into a beautiful, crystalline pool. The sight below justified her enthusiasm. I knew the creek held some beautiful native cutthroats, but the specimen lying in the current against the far bank looked as if it weighed three or four pounds. Lori spooked

[273]

that one with a cast the breeze drove awry, but she caught several smaller cutts from the same pool, each as gorgeous as any trout I'd ever seen.

That didn't do our dinner aspirations any good though, since cutthroats in Montana streams are appropriately protected. Another pool a mile back toward camp held a pleasant surprise, however: legions of eager, pan-sized rainbows. I hadn't killed a trout in a long time, but these were exceptional circumstances. Introduced rainbows are the biggest environmental threat native cutthroats face, and we were hungry. For once, the laws of man and nature stood in perfect accord. A half-dozen alien rainbows sizzled in the frying pan that night. Trout have never tasted better.

Down to our final night in Round One without having taken a shot, we were trudging back to camp when Lori urgently tugged at my sleeve and whispered, "Goats!" I'd been looking uphill where I was supposed to look, while she had alertly spotted the goats below us, right in the creek. A quick glance as we dropped behind a rock confirmed that at least one of them was big enough to shoot. Unfortunately, a steep ledge separated us from the creek below. "If they go up the other side, we'll never get to them," I whispered. "Our only chance is to hope they come uphill this way toward us. We have to get downwind right now!"

With the goats eclipsed by the steep ledge above the creek and the sound of the current masking my steps, I hustled back down the trail as quickly as possible. Soon the sound of hoofs on rock below confirmed that the goats had done just what we needed them to do. But when I turned back into the breeze to prepare for the slam dunk shot they were about to offer, I saw Lori crouched behind a boulder 60 yards behind me. The goats tried to cross the trail between us, but when they winded Lori they clattered away down the ledge and out of our lives.

Lori immediately realized what had happened. "I was just trying to stay out of your way!" she wailed. "I should have known better!"

"It's okay, honey," I reassured her. And it was. A goat in the trail suddenly seemed too easy, too unlike mountain goat hunting.

A quarter mile down the trail I suddenly realized I was walking alone and stopped. When Lori caught up to me, she was in tears. "After all the effort you put in," she sobbed. "I just can't believe I made such a stupid mistake!"

I leaned my bow against a tree and put my hands on her shoulders. "I wouldn't have traded your company up here for the biggest mountain goat in the world," I told her. And I meant it.

SOLITUDE

After three days of R&R, I was on my way back to the Crazies while Lori fulfilled the definition of a Cajun Trust Fund: a wife with a job. My days as a physician at our local hospital had ended three months earlier--I needed more time to write--but Lori was still gainfully employed part time as a nurse. A mile up the trail, I began to sense how badly I was going to miss her.

But there is a difference between being alone and being lonely, and I thought about the distinction as I downed a macaroni and cheese dinner in the dark that night. Paradoxically, I've always found loneliness a phenomenon of crowded places, while wilderness solitude evokes a different response entirely. I would certainly miss my wife in the days ahead, but the challenge of tackling the goats and the mountains that held them one-on-one felt seductively appealing.

While the bow may not be a particularly efficient means of putting meat on the table, that same inefficiency allows the bowhunter tremendous amounts of time and opportunity to observe and study the object of the chase. No quarry is more worthy of that attention than the mountain goat. *Oreamnos americanus* is a biologically unique species. The only animal I've ever pursued that resembles it in habits is the unrelated Himalayan tahr. Both animals occupy similarly daunting terrain and display the same solid forequarters, the better to pull themselves up cliffs no human should tackle without climbing gear. Since our goat arose in the New World and the tahr in the Old, these similarities represent parallel evolution rather than common genetics. Both species adapted to fill a niche nothing else wanted: high alpine cliffs, where they face no competition for food from other ungulates

[275]

and minimal threat from predators. (Here in North America, eagles nab some kids while falls account for the rest of the high first year mortality rate.) Seldom seen in the wild by most Americans, goats are fascinating animals, and I can watch them all day. Good thing; bowhunting goats involves a lot of watching.

Note to self: solitude allows plenty of silent time for such internal monologues. Are these interludes worth the price of absent human company? Get back to me in a few days.

Those days rolled on, my spirits buoyed by the majesty of the setting and a run of gorgeous weather. But the equinox was approaching, and in Montana that almost always heralds the first real storm of the season. Clouds began to gather as I hiked back down the trail to camp on the last night of summer, and as I muddled my way through dinner (Spam and tortillas, absent Lori's fly rod), rain began to fall along with the temperature.

As I lay in the tent that night and listened to the patter of raindrops swell to a roar, it occurred to me that one function of wilderness is to redefine the notion of comfort. At home, the gathering storm would have been a minor inconvenience at most, with the security of our roof safely masking its implications. Here, the thin fabric of the tent overhead was all that separated me from serous discomfort if not hypothermic disaster. For once, I really knew how good I had it thanks to nothing more than the re-written rules of wild places.

The downpour had stopped by the time I awoke, but gale force winds were howling down the canyon in the wake of the storm front's passage. The new snow line began just a few hundred feet above camp and the goat cliffs lay covered in termination dust--the traditional Alaskan term for the first snow fall at the end of the brief arctic summer, serving notice to seasonal workers to start packing their bags. Lori was expecting me back home that night and the logical course of action would have been to break camp down, hang the gear in a tree, and walk out. But each day I'd learned more about the goats and their habits, and I couldn't resist another morning of hunting.

Back at camp just before noon, I spotted a lone goat at the top of a cliff across the stream and down the valley as I was packing up. Already fatigued, I asked myself a simple question. Was I a man or a mouse? After studying the sheer cliff below the goat, I decided on the latter. However, I left my manhood an option. Because of the terrain, the closest approach to the goat actually began back down the trail toward civilization. I resolved that if I could still see the goat when I drew even with him, I'd shed my heavy pack and make the stalk.

For better or worse, the bedded goat was still visible when I reached the crucial point in the trail. Feeling invigorated, I cached my pack and started to climb. Two hours later, I peeked over a rock to study the lie from a better perspective. After further consideration, I decided that the best approach would be to climb around the back of the mountain and approach the goat from above.

It seemed like a good plan, and it was. After two more hours, I had worked my way into position 60 yards above the goat. With an upslope breeze bathing my face and abundant cover in an old avalanche chute, I felt so confident of my ability to reach bow range that I was already making plans to spend the night on the mountain with the dead goat if I had to. Then the wind faltered. The goat's head shot up, and he disappeared over the edge of the cliff into terrain no mortal man could enter.

My long afternoon of work had unraveled just like that, leaving me to start the long hike out toward Lori and home all over again. I admit that I was talking to myself by the time I started down the last mile of trail in the dark, but at least no one was talking back... yet.

EPILOGUE

By the time mountain goat season ended in November, I'd spent 25 nights in the Crazies, over half of them alone. I lost 25 pounds, one per day of mountain time, but I didn't miss them. My tally read as follows: three blue grouse, three ruffs, six rainbow trout, one deep bruise on my flank, numerous abrasions and lacerations on my hands, one near collapse, and one out of body experience. Credit for the last two goes to a combination of dehydration, extreme exertion, and high altitude. I impart them no deeper meaning.

That list does not include a mountain goat. I had chances. I passed up several more nannies and failed to convert on two good opportunities, which is a euphemistic way of reporting that I blew two shots. Unless I spend enough time back in Alaska to reestablish my residency there, I may well never have a chance to hunt mountain goats again, and that makes me sad. But toward the end of the season I realized that I was pursuing the goat in much the same way Ahab pursued Moby Dick, with a ruthless singularity of purpose that left me immune to all the reflections about life and love I'd experienced in September. I did not enjoy that feeling, and when I recognized it for what it was, I stopped hunting goats.

It's hard to write a hunting story in which no one shoots anything without sounding sappy at some point. Going on about the meaning of the experience eventually begins to start sounding like an excuse. True enough; I wanted to kill a goat and I didn't. But I can honestly report that my month in the Crazies left me feeling wiser and--paradoxically, since wisdom is usually associated with age--younger. I felt wiser because I'd learned new appreciation for my wife and best friend at the same time I was expanding my ability to feel at home with myself. I felt younger because I confirmed the ability to do what I'd done outdoors at age 30, even though it hurt a lot more at 60.

Those insights may not make up for the goat I didn't kill, but they sure come close.

CHAPTER THIRTY-FOUR

Enthusiasm and Restraint
Montana

TWO NIGHTS after my return to Montana after a trip to Alberta, I sat in a stand within sight of my house in the middle of what I call a whitetail rut-a-thon. My actual term for this phenomenon is a little less delicate. I find myself in this position once or twice a season if I'm lucky and there's nothing quite like it: does milling around while multiple bucks circulate through the area, grunting, banging heads, and harassing the ladies. While this represents a great time to kill a deer, it also represents a great time to make a regrettable mental error.

I'd arrived back home to find the whitetail rut in full progress. I'd rattled in seven bucks since my return and passed up other shot opportunities at a dozen more. After studying numerous deer, I finally identified one I wanted to shoot and christened him the King, not because he was the biggest buck in the world, which he certainly wasn't, but because he was the biggest deer on the hill.

And I'd enjoyed my best look at him yet from my stand earlier that afternoon. In fact, for a moment I thought I might have an opportunity to kill him. But then the doe he was chasing inexplicably veered off the trail before she reached me, and the buck veered off right along with her. With darkness falling, I could only hope the commotion below would lure him back into range before I ran out of light.

As sunlight drained from the sky, three different bucks filed past, none the one I wanted. I finally had to acknowledge that it was too late to shoot, but with deer surrounding me I remained still to avoid spooking game. Gradually, bucks became indistinguishable from does. Then I heard a tending grunt right behind me. Using my binoculars to gather the remains of the light, I could barely identify a familiar set of antlers as the 5-point ambled past in the gloom. So near and yet so far... my audience with the King would have to wait for another day.

The source of the activity around that stand wasn't hard to figure out. Ordinarily, water doesn't have any effect on deer movement patterns here by November: the springs are all frozen and snow provides the only source of moisture. But the ground stood bare and brown that season, thanks to unseasonably warm weather. A small spring lay at the bottom of the coulee 50 yards from the stand, and the does were hitting it regularly after feeding in the dry alfalfa between the coulee and the house. And at that time of year, all those does represented buck bait on the hoof.

The following afternoon, I spent some time studying the wind before committing myself. The southwest breeze felt marginal for the stand above the spring, but after due consideration I decided to chance it. While Lori deployed to a favorite stand of her own west of the house, I returned to the scene of all the activity I'd enjoyed the previous night.

After a relaxing hour's wait in the unusually balmy weather, does began to appear in the alfalfa. When they scattered suddenly, I knew a rutting buck had entered the field. Moments later, I was disappointed to see a small 4x4 silhouetted against the skyline. But then another flicker of movement caught my eye, and there stood the King.

Wasting no time asserting himself as the area's dominant buck, he promptly cut a doe from the pack and began to give chase. When she angled in my direction, I pivoted into position to shoot. She chose a trail that took her by just out of shooting range, but the buck peeled off closer to my stand. Suddenly, it seemed that all those long days of patient hunting were about to reach a climax.

I dislike shooting at walking deer, but the buck ground to a stop 20 yards away. He was angling ever so slightly forward, and overhanging limbs provided a bit of distraction. Since he only needed to take one or two more steps to solve both problems for me, I hesitated with tension on the string. Then he suddenly turned and walked off up the hill toward the house without offering a shot.

In the sudden emptiness left behind, I studied the opportunity I'd just passed up. For the second time in a week, I reminded myself that holding back in the face of any hesitation is almost always the responsible choice. But the problem with the shot angle had been minor and ducking a few inches would have eliminated any interference from the branches, assuming I could stay mentally focused. As the tension of the moment passed, I slumped back down in my seat unable to decide whether or not I'd made the right decision.

While the congregation of does I'd seen the night before never materialized, several deer finally filtered down to the spring. As the last mature doe started up the trail in my direction, she hit the brakes. I'm still not sure what made her stop, but she showed absolutely no intention of leaving. The good news: I had a mature doe 15 yards away during the peak of the rut. The bad news: she was on full alert for some reason, obligating me to remain motionless since a snort and flagging tail would spell the end of the evening's hunt.

There we remained for nearly half an hour, with neither of us moving a muscle. Suddenly her head turned and she stared up the hill behind me as I heard the sound of rustling in the grass. With agonizing deliberation, I swiveled my head around to the sight of the King closing from 30 yards.

He was on a trail that would take him by just over 20 yards away. Several large ponderosa pines stood between my stand and the trail, creating a series of narrow shooting lanes. If he stopped broadside in one of them, I'd have a relatively easy shot… assuming I could draw without spooking the doe. If he kept walking, I'd face a considerably more difficult bit of archery. After enduring endless recrimination over the shots I'd passed up, I reached a decision: I was going to kill this deer.

I let him walk through the first two shooting lanes, hoping he'd stop in one of them. When he didn't, I drew as his head disappeared behind the next pine and winced at the sound of movement from the direction of the doe. And when the buck's body filled the final open space, I picked a spot and released.

Over the years, I've developed an accurate ability to know just what my arrow has done when I shoot at an animal. The shaft obviously whistled right through the deer, but my first impression was that I'd hit him a bit far back. The buck tore off at the moment of impact but hesitated briefly on the opposite side of the coulee. There he offered just a glimpse, but I felt certain I could see blood right behind the shoulder. Then the buck walked off into the trees and out of sight, leaving me to wonder which of these contradictory impressions would prove accurate.

Unless I'm absolutely certain that I've made a killing shot or extenuating circumstances like rain, snow, hot weather, or scavengers dictate otherwise, I'll always give a wounded animal's track some time. Despite the warm daytime temperatures, the nights had been cold all week, and there was no precipitation in the forecast. I waited until dark and then climbed down as quietly as possible. When I crossed the trail I made a cursory search for my arrow, which I thought might convey useful information about the hit. When I couldn't locate it in the falling light, I trudged back up the hill to the house and a long, sleepless night.

At first light the following morning, Lori and I returned to the scene. I didn't expect a lot of blood, which turned out to be an accurate prediction. But I did find my arrow a dozen yards down the trail, and the sign all looked favorable: solid lung blood on the fletches, without a trace of paunch. Despite the absence of blood sign, we easily followed a trail of bent and broken grass blades to a welcome sight. The buck lay piled up dead a hundred yards down the coulee, the victim of a perfect double-lung pass through. I still can't explain my pessimistic first impression of the hit, but at that point I frankly didn't care.

And so another season closes, and another book right along with it.

The end of another whitetail season at home.

DESIGNER

Lindsay J. Nyquist
www.ellejaydesign.com

PRESS

Raven's Eye Press

Rediscovering the West
www.ravenseyepress.com

Try our other Raven's Eye Press titles:

A Wilder Life
Ken Wright

Why I'm Against it All
Ken Wright

The Monkey Wrench Dad
Ken Wright

Ghost Grizzlies, 3rd edition
David Petersen

Flies and Lies
Don Oliver

Heartsblood
David Petersen

Racks
David Petersen